DICKENS AND TRAVEL

The Start of Modern Travel Writing

This book is dedicated to the memory of Anna Knee, my dear friend and much-loved travelling companion. You are missed every day.

Putting on a backpack will never feel the same again.

DICKENS
AND TRAVEL
The Start of Modern Travel Writing

LUCINDA HAWKSLEY

PEN & SWORD
HISTORY

AN IMPRINT OF PEN & SWORD BOOKS LTD.
YORKSHIRE - PHILADELPHIA

First published in Great Britain in 2022 by
PEN AND SWORD HISTORY
An imprint of
Pen & Sword Books Ltd
Yorkshire – Philadelphia

Copyright © Lucinda Hawksley, 2022

ISBN 978 1 52673 563 8

The right of Lucinda Hawksley to be identified as Author of this work has been asserted by her in accordance with the Copyright, Designs and Patents Act 1988.

A CIP catalogue record for this book is available from the British Library.

All rights reserved. No part of this book may be reproduced or transmitted in any form or by any means, electronic or mechanical including photocopying, recording or by any information storage and retrieval system, without permission from the Publisher in writing.

Typeset in Times New Roman 11.5/14 by
SJmagic DESIGN SERVICES, India.
Printed and bound in the UK by CPI Group (UK) Ltd.

Pen & Sword Books Limited incorporates the imprints of Atlas, Archaeology, Aviation, Discovery, Family History, Fiction, History, Maritime, Military, Military Classics, Politics, Select, Transport, True Crime, Air World, Frontline Publishing, Leo Cooper, Remember When, Seaforth Publishing, The Praetorian Press, Wharncliffe Local History, Wharncliffe Transport, Wharncliffe True Crime and White Owl.

For a complete list of Pen & Sword titles please contact
PEN & SWORD BOOKS LIMITED
47 Church Street, Barnsley, South Yorkshire, S70 2AS, England
E-mail: enquiries@pen-and-sword.co.uk
Website: www.pen-and-sword.co.uk

Or
PEN AND SWORD BOOKS
1950 Lawrence Rd, Havertown, PA 19083, USA
E-mail: Uspen-and-sword@casematepublishers.com
Website: www.penandswordbooks.com

Contents

Acknowledgements vii

Introduction viii

Exhausted Horses and Drunken Post-boys 1

To Yorkshire with Phiz 9

Our English Watering Places 15

'Perfectly Terrible ... An Awful Place': Travels Around Scotland 23

The Search for Drowned Corpses in Wales 30

'A Very Picturesque and Various Country': Reading Tours in Ireland 33

Killed with Kindness: A Grand Tour to North America 40

New York City: Dazzling Dresses and Wretched Poverty 60

Philadelphia: Not Quite the Land of the Free 68

To Washington and Beyond: Magnificent Intentions 75

The Journey to Italy 104

A New Life in Genoa 113

Pictures from Italy 140

The Ghosts of Rome 147

The Continuing Influence of Italy 165

Dickens and Travel: The Start of Modern Travel Writing

'My Hat Shall Ever Be Ready to Be Thrown Up For ... Switzerland' 177

Dickens the Francophile 193

Paris – 'Bright ... Wicked ... and Wanton' 198

Boulogne: The Best Wine and Delicious Views 210

Condette: La Maison Dickens 221

A Study in Idleness 223

The Uncommercial Traveller 228

Ruminating on the Railways 234

Returning to America 239

'Revolving Restlessly, Australia in My Head' 253

Travelling with Dickens 260

Dickens and Travel Bibliography 262

Index 264

Acknowledgements

I would like to thank my agent Broo Doherty from DHH and my publisher Jon Wright. My thanks also to everyone from Pen and Sword who has worked on this book, including Laura Hirst and Kate Bohdanowicz. This book was also made possible by the brilliance of the Charles Dickens Museum staff, including the director Cindy Sughrue, curators Louisa Price and Frankie Kubicki, Adam Kalinowski and Jaanuja Sriskantha.

Introduction

Even though Charles Dickens is usually described as a 'London author', he had a love-hate relationship with the city. London was not the place of his birth, nor the place of his death, and, although he lived in London for many years, he often sought to escape both it and the British Isles. In his childhood, he travelled in his imagination, falling in love with the *Arabian Nights* and *Tales of the Genii* – a fascination which inspired him to compose his first play, at the age of nine: *Misnar, the Sultan of India* (the play does not survive). As an adult he took joy in heading off, often for months at a time, to experience life in different countries.

Dickens was prone to depression and, when he was feeling at his lowest, the British climate would make him feel even lower. The nineteenth century was a time of extraordinarily rapid change, as the Industrial Revolution transformed suburbs into cities and countryside into suburbs; a time when Britain's cities were covered with a stultifying, often fatal, smog. Factories belched smoke and chemicals into the atmosphere and every household, that could afford to, used coal or wood fires for heating and cooking. This smog hung above London and other industrial cities constantly. Even on the hottest, and what should have been the brightest, of summer days, Britain's cities would be covered by a thick grey cloud of man-made smog, through which the sun could seldom penetrate. In *Our Mutual Friend*, Dickens described London with the harsh words, 'Such a black shrill city ... such a gritty city; such a hopeless city, with no rent in the leaden canopy of its sky; such a beleaguered city.' It was at times like these, when the greyness made Dickens depressed, that he sought to leave Britain and find adventure.

It is not surprising that London could evoke bad memories for Dickens. It was after they had moved to the city, that the 12-year-old Charles had been condemned to work long hours in a factory, while his father, mother and younger siblings were incarcerated in a debtors'

Introduction

prison. Yet there was something about London that would always draw the adult Dickens back, from all over the world. In his lifetime, London was the world's largest city and when he was away from it, Dickens often missed the excitement and thrill of the place he so often sought to escape. No matter how picturesque or exotic his surroundings, when seeking inspiration for his writing, he often hankered after the bustle, throng and rich characters of the capital – even whilst finding it frustrating to live there.

He described London to his friend John Forster as a 'magic lantern', a description redolent with mystery and adventure. In 1844, he wrote to Forster from Genoa that he had never 'staggered' with his writing so much, as he did when working on *The Chimes*, his second Christmas book. This he attributed to having moved away from London to live in Italy: 'I seem as if I had plucked myself out of my proper soil ... and could take root no more until I return to it.'

In 1863, in an article for his series *The Uncommercial Traveller*, Dickens wrote:

> The shabbiness of our English capital, as compared with Paris, Bordeaux, Frankfort [*sic*], Milan, Geneva – almost any important town on the continent of Europe – I find very striking after an absence of any duration in foreign parts. London is shabby in contrast with Edinburgh, with Aberdeen, with Exeter, with Liverpool, with a bright little town like Bury St. Edmunds. London is shabby in contrast with New York, with Boston, with Philadelphia. In detail, one would say it can rarely fail to be a disappointing piece of shabbiness, to a stranger from any of those places. There is nothing shabbier than Drury-lane, in Rome itself. The meanness of Regent-street, set against the great line of Boulevards in Paris, is as striking as the abortive ugliness of Trafalgar-square, set against the gallant beauty of the Place de la Concorde. London is shabby by daylight, and shabbier by gaslight. No Englishman knows what gaslight is, until he sees the Rue de Rivoli and the Palais Royal after dark.[1]

---

1. 'The Boiled Beef of New England', 15 August 1863

Many of the travels which Dickens undertook can be viewed in the light of a Grand Tour: the journey wealthy and privileged young men of the eighteenth and nineteenth centuries took as the final stage of their education. This was something the Dickens family could never have afforded, but to which the author had long aspired. When he became financially secure through his writing, Dickens took himself and his family on his own versions of mini Grand Tours.

Dickens travelled to alleviate his depression, his boredom and his exhaustion, yet he would return home when he needed to be inspired. The travelling Dickens and the domestic Dickens often rivalled one another, and almost as soon as he arrived home, even when he had been longing to do so, the author would grow bored and start planning his next adventure.

Surprisingly, Dickens is little known today as a travel writer, yet his journeys spawned two travelogues, several chapters in his novels and multiple travel articles. His desire to see the world never abated and, at the end of his life, he was trying to decide whether to take up the offer of a tour of Australia. It was a plan which never came to fruition, as Dickens died very unexpectedly at the age of just 58.

Exhausted Horses and Drunken Post-boys

'There never was anybody connected with newspapers who, in the same space of time, had so much express and post-chaise experience as I....'
from *The Life of Charles Dickens*
by John Forster

In around 1830 or 1831, Charles Dickens began working as a freelance journalist – although his overriding ambition was to be on the stage. He didn't dream of becoming a novelist; what he really wanted was to be another Shakespeare, writing plays and performing in them. This desire had been thwarted early, when he was forced to leave school at the age of 11 because his parents could not afford the fees. This dream had another, even more serious, kick when, just after his twelfth birthday, he was found a job, at Warren's Blacking Factory on the Strand, in a desperate bid to save the family's finances. His time as a child labourer endured through the miserable months when his father, John Dickens, was arrested and imprisoned for debt, followed by his mother and younger siblings having to move into John's cell at the Marshalsea Debtors' Prison in South London, because they couldn't afford to pay rent.

When John Dickens's mother died, and left both her sons a small legacy, John was able to pay his debts, leave prison and go back to work. This meant the young Charles Dickens went back to school for a couple of years, until his father got into debt yet again. At the age of 15, Charles had to leave school and find work. This first adult job was as a clerk in a solicitor's office. The adolescent Dickens became bored very quickly, and he soon moved on to another solicitors' office, which he found equally unsatisfying. He was determined to continue the education he had missed through his interrupted schooling and yearned to 'better' himself and be something – and someone – unusual. As soon as he was old enough to do so, he joined the British Museum Library, where he spent much of his rare spare time in the round Reading Room, inside the British Museum. Desperate to move away from his life as a solicitor's clerk, Charles decided to teach himself a very employable new skill: shorthand. His mother's brother, Thomas Barrow, had founded a radical newspaper, *The Mirror of Parliament* and Charles's father, who had been pensioned off from his clerking job with the Navy, had recently started working for his brother-in-law as a freelance journalist. The young Charles Dickens soon began his literary career at *The Mirror of Parliament*.

Charles worked diligently with his fellow journalists, taking notes at law courts and parliamentary sessions and proving his worth, both as a writer and an observer. He became renowned for the accuracy of his reporting and for his remarkable energy. It was during this early stage in his career that his desire to see more of the world first began to be fed. He travelled around the country, chasing stories or performing errands for his uncle or his father. In the very first biography of Dickens, his friend John Forster recalled the author writing to him in 1845 – by which time he was famous – and reminiscing about these early work journeys:

> I have had to charge for half a dozen break-downs in half a dozen times as many miles. I have had to charge for the damage of a great-coat from the drippings of a blazing wax candle, in writing through the smallest hours of the night in a swift-flying carriage-and-pair. I have had to charge for all sorts of breakages fifty times in a journey.... I have charged for broken hats, broken luggage, broken chaises, broken harness – everything but a broken head, which is the only thing they would have grumbled to pay for.[2]

The excitement of these journeys comes across in Forster's biography: the quickening pulse of a young man setting his career in motion and being determined to rise as high as he could. These adrenaline-fuelled travels are full of excitement and interest, and are markedly different from the earliest stagecoach journey about which Dickens wrote: that of his solitary journey to London, as a boy, when his schooling had come

---

2. John Forster, *The Life of Charles Dickens*, 1872–1874

to an abrupt end. This sad journey later inspired the chapter in *David Copperfield* (1850) in which young David travels to London by himself, and in which Dickens includes wry observations about fellow travellers:

> ... being put between two gentlemen (the rough-faced one and another) to prevent my tumbling off the coach, I was nearly smothered by their falling asleep, and completely blocking me up. They squeezed me so hard sometimes, that I could not help crying out, 'Oh! If you please!' – which they didn't like at all, because it woke them. Opposite me was an elderly lady in a great fur cloak, who looked in the dark more like a haystack than a lady, she was wrapped up to such a degree. This lady had a basket with her, and she hadn't known what to do with it, for a long time, until she found that on account of my legs being short, it could go underneath me. It cramped and hurt me so, that it made me perfectly miserable; but if I moved in the least, and made a glass that was in the basket rattle against something else (as it was sure to do), she gave me the cruellest poke with her foot, and said, 'Come, don't YOU fidget. YOUR bones are young enough, I'm sure!'
>
> ... As the sun got higher, their sleep became lighter, and so they gradually one by one awoke. I recollect being very much surprised by the feint everybody made, then, of not having been to sleep at all, and by the uncommon indignation with which everyone repelled the charge. I labour under the same kind of astonishment to this day, having invariably observed that of all human weaknesses, the one to which our common nature is the least disposed to confess (I cannot imagine why) is the weakness of having gone to sleep in a coach.

A decade later, Dickens returned to this early travelling memory in a series of essays known as *The Uncommercial Traveller*. These were written throughout the 1860s and published in his magazine, *All The Year Round*. In one of the essays, the traveller reminisces about his childhood:

> I call my boyhood's home ... Dullborough. Most of us come from Dullborough who come from a country town. As I left

> Dullborough in the days when there were no railroads in the land, I left it in a stage-coach. Through all the years that have since passed, have I ever lost the smell of the damp straw in which I was packed – like game – and forwarded, carriage paid, to the Cross Keys, Wood-street, Cheapside, London?

The forlorn little travelling boy, who was remembered with pity by the ageing Dickens, was a world away from the energetic young man in his twenties, haring around the country on speeding stagecoaches and about to propel himself to the front of the literary world.

In 1865, the year in which Dickens turned 53, he recalled these early years of journalistic travels. In a speech to the Newspaper Press Fund he said:

> Returning home from exciting political meetings in the country to the waiting press in London, I do verily believe I have been upset in almost every description of vehicle known in this country. I have been, in my time, belated on miry by-roads, towards the small hours, forty or fifty miles from London, in a wheelless carriage, with exhausted horses and drunken post-boys, and have got back in time for publication.

Dickens stated in his speech that the speed at which horse-drawn carriages travelled in the 1830s was around fifteen miles an hour. This makes his trips from London to such far-flung places as Exeter and Bath all the more remarkable, because he and his colleagues had to be back in London on time to file their copy with the printers.

As a writer with the soul of a traveller, Dickens focused on the journey itself, not just the destination. When writing *A Tale of Two Cities*, a novel set in the eighteenth century, he researched what it would have been like to travel by mail coach, always fearing the attack of a highwayman. He evokes the journey at the start of the novel, drawing his reader into a world of nervous travellers, journeying from England to France by the mail coach, a coach so unsuited for passengers that at steep hills they had to get out and walk:

> He walked up hill in the mire by the side of the mail, as the rest of the passengers did; not because they had the least relish

for walking exercise, under the circumstances, but because the hill, and the harness, and the mud, and the mail, were all so heavy, that the horses had three times already come to a stop, besides once drawing the coach across the road, with the mutinous intent of taking it back to Blackheath.... In those days, travellers were very shy of being confidential on a short notice, for anybody on the road might be a robber or in league with robbers.... So the guard of the Dover mail thought to himself ... as he stood on his own particular perch behind the mail, beating his feet, and keeping an eye and a hand on the arm-chest before him, where a loaded blunderbuss lay at the top of six or eight loaded horse-pistols, deposited on a substratum of cutlass.... When the mail got successfully to Dover, in the course of the forenoon, the head drawer at the Royal George Hotel opened the coach-door as his custom was. He did it with some flourish of ceremony, for a mail journey from London in winter was an achievement to congratulate an adventurous traveller upon.

Dickens never forgot the exhilaration of these journalistic journeys, of urging the driver to go at ever greater speeds, of willing the horses to go faster, and of being jolted all through the night inside a carriage, often bound for somewhere previously unknown. Despite the lack of comfort, which he wrote about with mock horror, for years to come he yearned to recapture that intensity of his youth and he never stopped longing to experience the excitement of discovering new places.

These 1830s coach journeys also aided Dickens when it came to the naming of one of his most famous characters. Travel between London and Bath, when Dickens was a young journalist, was made possible by a fleet of stagecoaches, owned by Eleazer Pickwick and his nephew Moses Pickwick. Emblazoned across the sides of the coaches was the name 'Pickwick'. Dickens knew the coaches and their timetables intimately. Eventually the name Pickwick would grow in the young writer's mind to have a very distinctive human character.

Dickens's first published work of fiction was a short story, published anonymously in the *Monthly Magazine* in December 1833. 'A Dinner at Poplar Walk' (later changed to 'Mr Minns and his Cousin') was the first of a series of stories. His subsequent stories were published under the pseudonym of 'Boz', the family nickname of his youngest brother, Augustus. Boz's stories were a huge success, mostly because the writing style was so fresh and funny. They were about everyday events and ordinary people, which meant that readers found it easy to relate to them. They could understand the characters, and they could empathise with the often ridiculous, but very human, situations that 'Boz' captured so well. These short stories were later collated into the book *Sketches by Boz*.

Some years later, a fellow journalist, Charles Mackay, was interviewed about his recollections of Dickens:

> I was then in my twenty-second year, and Mr. Dickens was two years my senior. We were both of us comparatively unknown in literature, but Dickens had acquired some reputation as the author of some lively sketches which he contributed to the *Evening Chronicle* ... under the celebrated signature of 'Boz'. He was one of the twelve parliamentary reporters of the *Chronicle*, and had the reputation of being the most rapid, the most accurate, and the most trustworthy reporter then engaged on the London press.... He earned a salary of five guineas a week in that capacity, supplemented by an extra salary of two guineas a week for his brilliant sketches of London life and manners.... My remembrance of Charles Dickens at that time is of a fresh, handsome, genial young man, with a profusion of brown hair, a bright eye, and a hearty manner – rather inclined to what was once called 'dandyism' in his attire, and to a rather exuberant display of jewellery on his vest and on his fingers...[3]

Using a pen name turned out to be an excellent marketing idea. All around the country, readers speculated about the identity of the mysterious Boz. This led to Dickens being approached by the publishing company Chapman and Hall. They wanted him to write about a group called the Nimrod Club. It was Dickens who decided to change the group's name to the Pickwick Club. The club was led by the character he had dreamt up, a Mr Samuel Pickwick. Dickens could envisage his character in his mind, but the project's chosen illustrator, Robert Seymour, had already

---

3. Collins, Philip, ed., *Dickens Interviews and Recollections*, Macmillan, 1981

made a number of drawings for the leader of the club. Seymour had also envisaged the character in his imagination and his drawings depicted a tall, lean fellow. After much discussion and argument, Dickens got his way, and Seymour was prevailed upon to make Mr Pickwick a short, fat gentleman, who wore a straining waistcoat and distinctive round glasses.

Within weeks of the first instalment appearing in print, in March 1836, the whole country was talking about Mr Pickwick and his friends. Because the name of Pickwick coaches would have been known to every Victorian traveller in the south of England, Dickens paid a tongue-in-cheek homage to the stagecoach proprietor who had enabled so many of his early travels. When Mr Pickwick's servant, Sam Weller, first sees a Pickwick coach he is struck by the impertinence of his master's name being emblazoned across the coach door:

'Here's rayther a rum go, sir,' replied Sam.

'What?' inquired Mr. Pickwick.

'This here, Sir,' rejoined Sam. 'I'm wery much afeerd, sir, that the properiator o' this here coach is a playin' some imperence vith us.'

'How is that, Sam?' said Mr. Pickwick; 'aren't the names down on the way-bill?'

'The names is not only down on the vay-bill, Sir,' replied Sam, 'but they've painted vun on 'em up, on the door o' the coach.' As Sam spoke, he pointed to that part of the coach door on which the proprietor's name usually appears; and there, sure enough, in gilt letters of a goodly size, was the magic name of Pickwick!

'Dear me,' exclaimed Mr. Pickwick, quite staggered by the coincidence; 'what a very extraordinary thing!'

Within *The Posthumous Papers of the Pickwick Club* (to give the book its full title), Dickens gave a cleverly observed view of what travelling was like, for men of financial means, at that time. He wrote about the coaching inns, the journeys and the fellow travellers encountered by the Pickwickians. The book gives a fascinating glimpse of what it would have been like to be a passenger on the road in England in the first decades of the nineteenth century. Perhaps when Dickens described Mr Jingle as 'a traveller in many countries and a close observer of men and things', he was describing what he would like to be.

In 1891, Percy Fitzgerald, who had been a friend of Dickens and a contributor to his magazine *Household Words*, published a book entitled *The History of Pickwick*. Over two decades after Dickens's death, Fitzgerald paid tribute to his evocation of this period of British travel:

> One of the most attractive sides of 'Pickwick' is the complete picture it offers of an old English state of manners which has now disappeared or faded out. These characters and incidents belong to the state of society that then existed – nay, are its product. Thus the slow and deliberate mode of travelling by coach, the putting up at inns, enforced a sort of fellowship and contact, and led to ready acquaintanceship and to a display of peculiarities. The same conditions of travel, too, promoted a species of adventure, often not without its farce.

John Forster, who first met Dickens when they were both in their twenties, recalled the way in which Charles and his wife Catherine travelled in the early years of their marriage. They had their own carriage: 'a small chaise with a smaller pair of ponies, which, having a habit of making sudden rushes up by-streets in the day and peremptory standstills in ditches by night, were changed in the following year for a more suitable equipage.' A chaise was a small horse-drawn carriage, described as being for 'pleasure', and used mostly for short journeys – it was the fashionable man's choice of vehicle, perhaps akin to the sports car of today. For Charles, it was another step further away from what he considered the shame of his impoverished childhood.

By the time Percy Fitzgerald's book was published British travel had changed almost beyond recognition. It evolved rapidly during Dickens's lifetime, with the advent of the railways and inventions using steam power, yet after his death the changes became even more remarkable. In 1892, a year after Fitzgerald's book was published, Frederick Bremer began working on the very first British automobile (which he built in Walthamstow, East London). This early motor car made its first appearance on a public highway in December 1894. The modes of transport used by Samuel Pickwick and his friends had become ancient history within a few decades.

To Yorkshire with Phiz

> *'We have had for breakfast, toast, cakes, a Yorkshire pie, piece of beef about the size and much the shape of my portmanteau, tea, coffee, ham and eggs – and are now going to look about us.'*
> Letter from Charles Dickens to his wife Catherine, 1838

On the morning of 30 January 1838, 'Boz' met his illustrator 'Phiz' (aka Hablot Knight Browne) outside the Saracen's Head, an old coaching inn at Snow Hill, in the heart of London. Snow Hill was an aptly named starting point, as the morning was bitterly cold. References to the inn, which was destroyed in 1868 to make way for the new Holborn Viaduct, can be found as far back as the 1500s. Over the centuries, generations of travellers left London from the Saracen's Head, in a variety of travelling contraptions. Dickens and Phiz were beginning not only a journey, but an investigation: an undercover trip to England's largest county, to discover the fate of unwanted children sent to 'Yorkshire schools'.

Dickens was posing as the concerned friend of a widow with children, seeking to find a school for her fatherless sons. In reality, he was researching a story that had haunted him since his early days of court reporting, and was intending to use it in latest novel *The Life and Adventures of Nicholas Nickleby*. He had, by now, become very well known, and realised his social campaigning could be more effective through fiction than journalism.

In his novel, Nicholas, newly impoverished following the death of his father, needs to find a job. He also begins his journey to Yorkshire from the Saracen's Head. In the descriptions in the novel, Dickens gives a wonderful insight into the practicalities of travelling. He writes of Nicholas stepping outside the house in which he has been staying, onto a London street, and seeking 'a man to carry his box' (his travelling trunk). Nicholas, followed by the man with his luggage, walks to the Saracen's Head, pays the man and sees his trunk 'safely deposited in the coach-office' before finding the 'coffee-room'.

Nicholas is going to Yorkshire to start a new job, as an assistant schoolmaster. He is travelling with the school's headmaster, Wackford Squeers, and five unfortunate new pupils:

> ...the coachman and guard were comparing notes for the last time before starting ... porters were screwing out the last reluctant sixpences, itinerant newsmen making the last offer of a morning paper, and the horses giving the last impatient rattle to their harness.... A minute's bustle, a banging of the coach doors, a swaying of the vehicle to one side, as the heavy coachman, and still heavier guard, climbed into their seats; a cry of all right, a few notes from the horn ... and the coach was gone too, and rattling over the stones of Smithfield.
>
> The little boys' legs being too short to admit of their feet resting upon anything as they sat, and the little boys' bodies being consequently in imminent hazard of being jerked off the coach, Nicholas had enough to do over the stones to hold them on. Between the manual exertion and the mental anxiety attendant upon this task, he was not a little relieved when the coach stopped at the Peacock at Islington.

Perhaps Dickens was recalling his and Phiz's own journey when he described the coach's snuff-taking guard, 'a stout old Yorkshireman', and how cold it was on the coach: 'The weather was intensely and bitterly cold; a great deal of snow fell from time to time; and the wind was intolerably keen.'

Yorkshire Schools were a scandal of cruelty, and Dickens wanted everyone to know about them. In his preface to *Nicholas Nickleby*, Dickens recalled how he had met a pupil of one of the schools during his early childhood in Kent:

> I cannot call to mind, now, how I came to hear about Yorkshire schools when I was a not very robust child ... but I know that my first impressions of them were picked up at

that time, and that they were somehow or other connected with a suppurated abscess that some boy had come home with, in consequence of his Yorkshire guide, philosopher, and friend, having ripped it open with an inky pen-knife. The impression made upon me, however made, never left me. I was always curious about Yorkshire schools – fell, long afterwards and at sundry times, into the way of hearing more about them – at last, having an audience, resolved to write about them.

At around the same time that the young Charles Dickens met that injured schoolboy, William Shaw, the headmaster of Bowes Academy in Yorkshire, was on trial for alleged abuse of children in his care. In 1823, Shaw had placed the following advertisement in the newspapers:

EDUCATION, by Mr. SHAW, and able ASSISTANTS, at BOWES ACADEMY, near Greta-bridge, Yorkshire. Youth are carefully instructed in the English, Latin, and Greek languages, writing, common and decimal arithmetic, bookkeeping, mensuration, &c., and are provided with board, clothes, and every necessary, at 20 guineas per annum each. No extra charges whatever. No vacations. N.B. The French language 2 guineas per annum extra. Further particulars may be known on application…

Those reading between the lines would have worked out what 'no extra charges' and 'no vacations' would have meant: that parents, step-parents or guardians could send their children to Bowes Academy and forget about them. If they didn't want to see them again, they didn't need to. Not everyone read between the lines, however, and many people were duped into believing this was just an affordably cheap boarding school.

On 30 October 1823, a case was brought against Shaw by a Mr Jones, a publican from London and the father of two boys sent to Shaw's school. The *Leeds Intelligencer* published the story under the heading of 'Cheap Schools!!!' writing that Jones's sons were so ill-treated and 'greatly injured in their health' that both developed a dangerous eye condition, resulting in one of the boys becoming permanently blind. The reporter wrote of regular beatings, rotten food and insanitary conditions. There was a horse trough, without running water, in which all 300 boys had to wash – and only two towels for all the boys to share. There weren't enough clothes, so some boys had to spend days without a jacket or even trousers – instructed to hide under tables if any visitors came to call. Many of the 'beds' were simply made from hay or straw, 'four or five boys slept in each bed' with only one sheet to cover them, lice and fleas were rife and the food was so full of maggots that one boy boasted of having been able to catch 'a pot full'.

On 10 November 1823, a rather extraordinary letter was sent to newspaper editors, allegedly signed by dozens of boys who had been educated at Shaw's Academy, refuting the claims, and stating they had been 'respectfully educated' by Mr Shaw, and were 'desirous of assuring the Parents and Friends of the Young Gentlemen now resident there, as well as of performing an act of gratitude and justice towards Mr Shaw, [we] do hereby unanimously declare, that we ... are perfectly satisfied with the treatment and education we received.'

Despite these protestations, another parent, a Mr Okaby, also took Shaw to court for ill treatment of his son. The headmaster was found guilty in both cases, and ordered to pay £300 damages to both fathers – yet he was not banned from keeping a school. Over a decade later, Dickens discovered that many abusive boarding schools still operated in Yorkshire. He wanted to use *Nicholas Nickleby* to expose them.

Dickens and Phiz broke their long journey at Grantham, where they stayed at the George Inn. There they were warmed by the fire and plied with plentiful food and drink, the perfect way to blot out the misery of the journey. Dickens lauded The George in *Nicholas Nickleby* as 'one of the best inns in England' (remembered today in a blue plaque). Nicholas and his travelling companions were not so fortunate as the author and illustrator. Dickens gave himself and Phiz a little cameo in Nicholas's journey, as the two wise 'outside passengers':

> The night and the snow came on together, and dismal enough they were. There was no sound to be heard but the howling of the wind; for the noise of the wheels, and the tread of the horses' feet, were rendered inaudible by the thick coating of snow which covered the ground, and was fast increasing every moment.... . Twenty miles further on, two of the front

outside passengers, wisely availing themselves of their arrival at one of the best inns in England, turned in, for the night, at the George at Grantham. The remainder wrapped themselves more closely in their coats and cloaks...

Boz and Phiz were up early in the morning to take the Royal Glasgow Mail to Greta Bridge, with the horses battling through snow and ice. Coaches on this route were usually able to travel at around eight or nine miles per hour. Dickens wrote to Catherine that he was impressed by how cheap their coach tickets were, just £6 4s for the two of them to travel 'inside' – the most coveted part of the coach in winter.

They arrived at Greta Bridge at 11.00pm on a bitterly cold night and were nervous as they clambered down from the stagecoach. They were intending to stay at The George and New Inn, yet it seemed to be deserted. The following morning Dickens described their arrival to his wife:

> I was in a perfect agony of apprehension, for it was fearfully cold and there were no outward signs of anybody being up in the house. But to our great joy we discovered a comfortable room with drawn curtains and a most blazing fire. In half an hour they gave us a smoking supper and a bottle of mulled port (in which we drank your health) and then we retired to a couple of capital bedrooms in each of which was a rousing fire half way up the chimney.

Following an enormous breakfast, the two men hired a post-chaise and, while the accompanying horses were being prepared, wandered around in the snow. When the carriage was ready, they set out to explore the Yorkshire schools – including Bowes Academy – armed with fictitious names, their fictitious story and a mendacious letter of recommendation, written by a solicitor friend. Unfortunately, even in these early days of his career, Dickens was already too famous to carry out undercover work. Their meeting with William Shaw was extremely brief as Dickens's identity had been discovered.

In the nearby village of Barnard Castle[4], they wandered around the graveyard. Phiz sketched, Dickens made notes, and both men were

---

4. Barnard Castle is in County Durham now, but in 1838 it was in the county of Yorkshire.

deeply saddened by how many of the graves were of schoolboys. The two men stayed at the Kings Head, which Dickens recommends in *Nicholas Nickleby*, having his character Newman Noggs write to Nicholas: 'P.S. If you should go near Barnard Castle, there is a good ale at the Kings Head.'

This journey to Yorkshire was just one of hundreds that Dickens would make all over the British Isles. The way he wrote about the journey, adding his own factual experience to the fictional characters' travels, presaged the two travelogues he was to write in the future. As with all of Dickens's travels, he recounted the journey in letters to his wife and friends, for future use in books and articles.

Our English Watering Places

'Old gentlemen and ancient ladies, flirt, after their own manner, in two readings rooms.... Other old gentlemen look all day through telescopes and never see anything....'
Letter from Charles Dickens to
Cornelius Felton, 1843

By the time of his journey to Yorkshire, the young Charles Dickens had been married for two years and had become a father. His wife was Catherine Hogarth, the daughter of newspaper editor George Hogarth (the man who had commissioned the short stories now known as *Sketches by Boz*). Their wedding was on 2 April 1836, at St Luke's Church in Chelsea, London. Throughout their early marriage and the beginning of their family life, the county of Kent played a significant role. This was where Dickens had spent the happiest years of his childhood, and he wanted his wife to experience it. They took their honeymoon in the pretty Kent village of Chalk and returned a year after their wedding, with their new baby Charley. It was not long, however, before another part of Kent became their favoured family holiday spot. The seaside town of Broadstairs, with its golden sand beach, was not far from Chatham, where the Dickens family had lived happily, before John Dickens's job was relocated to London. For Charles, Chatham and its environs represented an innocent and happy time.

From the early 1840s, the ever-growing family travelled to Broadstairs regularly. Occasionally Dickens would arrive alone and stay at the Albion Hotel, from where he would seek a family home to rent, with easy access to the beach. By this date, the name of Charles Dickens was growing increasingly famous, and the town grew proud of its close associations with the author. Because the author visited so frequently, a number of buildings display plaques stating that Dickens stayed there. These are so ubiquitous that one householder has put up a plaque specifically to state Charles Dickens didn't ever stay there. All through the years of holidaying in Broadstairs, while the Dickens children built sandcastles on the beach, their father worked on some of his most famous books. Not only did he write large swathes of *David Copperfield* in the town, but he even based one of its most memorable characters, Betsey Trotwood, on a local woman, Mary Pearson Strong, who lived in the house that would later become the town's Dickens House Museum. Today, the town also holds an annual Dickens Festival in memory of one of its most famous – albeit temporary – residents.

One of the reasons Dickens fell in love with Broadstairs was because it was so tranquil and unspoilt. He wanted a place where his family could have fun, but which was also quiet enough for him to work in peace. In July 1841, Dickens wrote to his friend Miss Allan extolling the beauties of the town: 'A good sea – fresh breezes – fine sands – and pleasant walks – with all manner of fishing-boats, light houses, piers, bathing machines and so forth are its only attractions, but it's one of the freshest and free-est little places in the world.'

After a few years, however, Dickens grew frustrated that his once-peaceful haven had become so busy and noisy. Something that plagued his working day was the sound of German bands, which had become increasingly prevalent in Britain since the marriage of Queen Victoria to Prince Albert of Saxe-Coburg-Gotha, in 1840. The bands were popular with many British holidaymakers, but Dickens really disliked their music.

He was bemused by how the quiet seaside town had suddenly become so busy. The streets and beach were now filled with visiting families and day trippers. It seems he was unaware that the reason for Broadstairs' sudden surge in popularity was because it was known the famous author took his family on holiday there. Unwittingly, Dickens had become an integral part of the town's tourist attractions.

In the early 1840s, Dickens decided to journey to the farthest point of south-west England. He wrote to his friend Dr Thomas Southwood Smith that he wanted to visit 'the very dreariest and desolate portion of the sea-coast of Cornwall… . Can you tell me … what is the next best bleak and barren part?'

Southwood Smith's reply suggested 'The coast about Land's End' and gave him an introduction to a friend of his in Cornwall, a Dr Charles

Barham. He also advised 'the place above all others for dreariness is Tintagel (King Arthur's) castle, near Camelford. There shall you see nothing but bleak looking rocks and an everlastingly boisterous sea, both in much the same state as when good King Arthur reigned.'

On 27 October 1842, Dickens travelled to Cornwall in the company of fellow writer John Forster and the artists Daniel Maclise and Clarkson Stanfield. They travelled from London to Exeter, where Dickens's parents were living, then to Plymouth and on to Cornwall. Forster recalled:

> Railways helped us then not much; but where the roads were inaccessible to post-horses, we walked. Tintagel was visited, and no part of mountain or sea consecrated by the legends of Arthur was left unexplored. We ascended to the cradle of the highest tower of Mount St. Michael, and descended into several mines. Land and sea yielded each its marvels to us; but of all the impressions brought away ... I doubt if any were the source of such deep emotion to us all as a sunset we saw at Lands-end.

The four men were a well-matched group of friends, and all of them looked back on the holiday with great affection. For Dickens, temporarily released from the responsibilities of father and householder, the effect was intoxicating. On New Year's Eve he wrote a nostalgic letter to his American friend Cornelius Felton:

> Such a trip as we had into Cornwall.... . Sometimes we travelled all night, sometimes all day, sometimes both.... . Heavens! If you could have seen the necks of bottles, distracting in their immense varieties of shape, peering out of the carriage pockets! If you could have witnessed the deep devotion of the post-boys, the wild attachment of the hostlers, the maniac glee of the waiters! If you could have followed us into the earthy old churches we visited, and into the strange caverns on the gloomy sea-shore, and down into the depths of mines, and up to the tops of giddy heights where the unspeakable green water was roaring, I don't know how many hundred feet below! If you could have seen but one gleam of the bright fires by which we sat

in the big rooms of ancient inns at night, until long after the small hours had come and gone.... I never laughed in my life as I did on this journey.... Seriously, I do believe there never was such a trip. And they made such sketches, those two men, in the most romantic of our halting-places, that you would have sworn we had the Spirit of Beauty with us, as well as the Spirit of Fun.

After several family holidays in Kent, in 1849 Charles and Catherine decided to take their children to the Isle of Wight, a place they had visited early in their marriage. This island, which lies off the south coast of England, became a very popular destination in the mid-nineteenth-century after Queen Victoria and Prince Albert built a holiday home there. Construction on the monarch's beautiful Osborne House began in 1845 and placed the small island firmly onto the tourist map. This influx of visitors soon became a Bohemian artistic crowd. Among the famous Victorians who lived on the island, or had second homes there, were the photographer Julia Margaret Cameron, the scandalous poet Algernon Charles Swinburne, and the Poet Laureate, Alfred, Lord Tennyson.

Catherine and Charles had visited the island for the first time in September 1839. They stayed in Alum Bay, where Dickens had worked on his final chapters of *Oliver Twist*. In June 1849, in preparation for their family holiday, Dickens travelled to the island with his friend John Leech. Both wanted to find homes to rent for the summer. Dickens wrote to Catherine on 16 June to tell her he had rented a house belonging to one of their acquaintances, Reverend James White:

> I have taken a most delightful and beautiful house, belonging to White, at Bonchurch; cool, airy, private bathing, everything delicious. I think it is the prettiest place I ever saw in my life, at home or abroad.... I have arranged for carriages, luggage, and everything.... P.S. – A waterfall on the grounds, which I have arranged with a carpenter to convert into a perpetual shower-bath.

In July, the Dickens family arrived for a long summer holiday. Their holiday home in Bonchurch was a short distance from the Leeches in Ventnor and the two families spent much of their time together. John

Leech had gained fame as the illustrator of *A Christmas Carol* and went on to become a renowned cartoonist for *Punch* magazine. On the Isle of Wight, he sketched Dickens's 'waterfall' shower – Dickens was punctilious about good hygiene and sanitation – which obviously caused great merriment amongst the author's friends. Sadly the sketch no longer survives. That holiday also sealed the friendship between Leech and Dickens in a dramatic manner. While John Leech was swimming, he was caught up by a rough wave and dashed against the rocks. He suffered a head injury and was knocked unconscious. The local doctor, who ironically prescribed a course of leeches, was considered useless. Instead, the Leech family attributed the artist's recovery to Dickens's practising of a new skill, the art of mesmerism (a method of healing by hypnotic trance). After Leech recovered from his injury, he remained convinced that Dickens had saved his life.

Another of Dickens's friends on the Isle of Wight that summer was fellow author William Makepeace Thackeray. He wrote to his friend Jane Brookfield that he had seen Dickens at Ryde Pier, accompanied by Catherine, her sister Georgina Hogarth and the children 'all looking abominably coarse vulgar and happy'.

The Isle of Wight did not supersede Broadstairs, however, and the family continued to spend time there, albeit with less frequency. In 1850, Dickens wrote to the poet Richard Henry Horne from the home they had rented for the summer, Fort House: 'I hope you and Mrs. Horne will come down and see us at Broadstairs this year, where I have a good bold house on the top of a cliff, with the sea winds blowing through it, and the gulls occasionally falling down the chimneys by mistake.'

Between 1837 and 1851 the Dickens family visited Broadstairs twelve times. Initially, they travelled by boat from London to nearby Margate and, after 1846, they had the option to take the train to neighbouring Ramsgate. In the year of their final family holiday to Broadstairs, Dickens, who was now an expert traveller, wrote a nostalgic article. 'Our English Watering Place' was published in his magazine *Household Words* in August 1852. The seaside town that had given his children so many happy memories was described:

> Sky, sea, beach, and village, lie as still before us as if they were sitting for the pictures. It is dead low-water. A ripple plays among the ripening corn upon the cliff, as if it were

faintly trying from recollection to imitate the sea; and the world of butterflies hovering over the crop of radish-seed are as restless in their little way as the gulls are in their larger manner when the wind blows. But the ocean lies winking in the sunlight like a drowsy lion... . In truth, our watering-place itself has been left somewhat high and dry by the tide of years. Concerned as we are for its honour, we must reluctantly admit that the time when this pretty little semicircular sweep of houses, tapering off at the end of the wooden pier into a point in the sea, was a gay place, and when the lighthouse overlooking it shone at daybreak on company dispersing from public balls, is but dimly traditional now.

So many children are brought down to our watering-place that, when they are not out of doors, as they usually are in fine weather, it is wonderful where they are put: the whole village seeming much too small to hold them under cover. In the afternoons, you see no end of salt and sandy little boots drying on upper window-sills. At bathing-time in the morning, the little bay re-echoes with every shrill variety of shriek and splash – after which, if the weather be at all fresh, the sands teem with small blue mottled legs. The sands are the children's great resort. They cluster there, like ants: so busy burying their particular friends, and making castles with infinite labour which the next tide overthrows... . It is curious, too, to observe a natural ease of approach that there seems to be between the children and the boatmen. They mutually make acquaintance, and take individual likings, without any help. You will come upon one of those slow heavy fellows sitting down patiently mending a little ship for a mite of a boy, whom he could crush to death by throwing his lightest pair of trousers on him. You will be sensible of the oddest contrast between the smooth little creature, and the rough man who seems to be carved out of hard-grained wood – between the delicate hand expectantly held out, and the immense thumb and finger that can hardly feel the rigging of thread they mend – between the small voice and the gruff growl.

Another seaside destination Dickens returned to repeatedly was the Sussex town of Brighton; which was, at the time of Dickens's birth, recently connected with the Prince Regent (who became King George IV). Charles and Catherine visited Brighton for the first time in the autumn of 1837 and the visit was recorded in the *Sussex Express*: 'The talented author of the "Pickwick" Magazines has been staying at the Old Ship Hotel, Brighton; he returned to town on Tuesday. He is a young man, but he does not exhibit in his person any appearance denoting such a lively imagination as his writings would seem to justify.'

Dickens returned to Brighton in 1845, with John Forster, and used it as a location in *Dombey and Son*. When little Paul Dombey is sent away to school, it is to Miss Pipchin's establishment in Brighton:

> This celebrated Mrs Pipchin was a marvellous ill-favoured, ill-conditioned old lady, of a stooping figure, with a mottled face, like bad marble, a hook nose, and a hard grey eye, that looked as if it might have been hammered at on an anvil without sustaining any injury… . She was generally spoken of as 'a great manager' of children; and the secret of her management was, to give them everything they didn't like, and nothing that they did… . The Castle … was in a steep by-street at Brighton, where the soil was more than unusually chalky, flinty, and sterile, and the houses were more than usually brittle and thin; where the small front-gardens had the unaccountable property of producing nothing but marigolds, whatever was sown in them; and where snails were constantly discovered holding on to the street doors…. In the winter time the air couldn't be got out of the Castle, and in the summer time it couldn't be got in.

The Dickens family visited Brighton several times, including in February 1849, when they visited with the Leech family. Their stay in a lodging house took a dramatic turn one night by both the landlord and his daughter 'going mad'. The families left for the sanctuary of the nearby Bedford Hotel, from which Dickens wrote to Forster:

> If you could have heard the cursing and crying of the two; could have seen the physician and nurse quoited out into the

passage by the madman at the hazard of their lives; could have seen Leech and me flying to the doctor's rescue; could have seen our wives pulling us back; could have seen the M.D. faint with fear; could have seen three other M.D.s come to his aid; with an atmosphere of Mrs Gamps, strait-waistcoats, struggling friends and servants surrounding the whole; you would have said it was quite worthy of me, and quite in keeping with my usual proceedings.

Undaunted by the experience, the Dickens family returned in the early spring of 1850 and again in 1852, and Charles returned several times towards the end of his life, on his reading tours. On 18 November 1858, the *Brighton Gazette* reported:

The popular novelist, Mr Charles Dickens, in the course of his peregrinations, reached Brighton on Friday last, and entertained numerous and fashionable assemblages at the Town Hall, with readings from some of his popular works. The great attraction was, of course, the reader himself.

'Perfectly Terrible ... An Awful Place': Travels Around Scotland

> *'We are now in a bare white house on the banks of Loch Leven, but in a comfortably-furnished room ... with the rain pattering against the window as though it were December, the wind howling dismally, a cold damp mist on everything without, a blazing fire within half way up the chimney, and a most infernal Piper practicing under the window.'*
> Letter from Charles Dickens to
> John Forster, 1841

Dickens first travelled to Edinburgh as a journalist, in 1834. He was sent to write a story for *The Morning Chronicle* about a banquet in honour of Lord Grey (the prime minister whose government had introduced the Reform Bill of 1832). This first experience of the city inspired an episode in *The Pickwick Papers*, 'The Story of the Bagman's Uncle'. It is a wildly melodramatic ghost story, in which Dickens provides carefully observed descriptions of Edinburgh. In the story, the bagman explains that his uncle

> collected debts, and took orders, in the north; going from London to Edinburgh, from Edinburgh to Glasgow, from Glasgow back to Edinburgh, and thence to London... .
> I don't know whether any of you, gentlemen, ever partook of a real substantial hospitable Scotch breakfast, and then went out to a slight lunch of a bushel of oysters, a dozen or so of bottled ale, and a noggin or two of whiskey to close up with. If you ever did, you will agree with me that it

requires a pretty strong head to go out to dinner and supper afterwards... . One night ... my uncle supped at the house of a very old friend of his, a Bailie Mac something and four syllables after it, who lived in the old town of Edinburgh... . It was a wild, gusty night when my uncle closed the bailie's door... . The bailie's house was in the Canongate, and my uncle was going to the other end of Leith Walk, rather better than a mile's journey. On either side of him, there shot up against the dark sky, tall, gaunt, straggling houses, with time-stained fronts, and windows that seemed to have shared the lot of eyes in mortals, and to have grown dim and sunken with age. Six, seven, eight storey high, were the houses; storey piled upon storey, as children build with cards – throwing their dark shadows over the roughly paved road, and making the dark night darker. A few oil lamps were scattered at long distances, but they only served to mark the dirty entrance to some narrow close, or to show where a common stair communicated, by steep and intricate windings, with the various flats above....

Catherine had grown up in Scotland, so when, on 19 June 1841, she and her husband set off on a journey to Edinburgh, Dickens was eager to explore the country of his wife's childhood. He was proud of her nationality, always telling people his children were half Scottish[5]. On this trip to Edinburgh, he was no longer an unknown journalist. This time a grand banquet was being held for them, and Dickens was awarded the Freedom of the City. When Charles and Catherine visited the Adelphi Theatre, the orchestra played *Charlie is My Darling* in his honour.

It has been alleged that Dickens wrote in his diary about taking an evening walk around Canongate churchyard, where he saw the grave of one Ebenezer Lennox Scroggie – some journalists have even claimed Scroggie as a relative of the economist Adam Smith. Despite persistent articles insisting upon Dickens's momentous discovery, Edinburgh, cannot claim to be the birthplace of Ebenezer Scrooge. Sadly, the story

---

5. Charles and Catherine would eventually have ten children, seven sons and three daughters (one of whom died in infancy in 1852). I am descended from Henry Fielding Dickens, the eighth child.

has no credence. Although Dickens did keep appointment diaries, he would destroy them at the end of each year and his diary for 1841 has not survived. The archives in Edinburgh have no records for burials at Canongate churchyard prior to the time Charles and Catherine Dickens visited the city, so the burial and grave of an Ebenezer Scroggie cannot be verified or disputed, but the minutes of council meetings from the 1930s do survive. It has been claimed the gravestone was destroyed during building works at some point during the decade. However, the minutes of council meetings record all the renovations carried out around the city, and there is no record of the alleged work at Canongate churchyard which are said to have destroyed the grave. The story persists in being resurrected, however, in a type of journalistic game of Chinese Whispers, and its tenacity proves the popularity of Dickens's writing, almost two centuries after the publication of *A Christmas Carol*.

Catherine and Charles spent a month travelling around Scotland. After Edinburgh, they went north with a Scottish friend, the artist Angus Fletcher, who had sculpted a bust of Dickens in 1839. Dickens found him amusingly eccentric and wrote letters to John Forster about their friend's quirks. Forster and Dickens had often talked of visiting Glencoe and Dickens wrote to him on 9 July 1841 with his impressions of the site of the notorious massacre:

> We left Loch Earn Head last night, and went to a place called Killin, eight miles from it, where we slept. I walked some six miles with Fletcher after we got there, to see a waterfall; and truly it was a magnificent sight, foaming and crashing down three great steeps of riven rock... . To-day we have had a journey of between 50 and 60 miles, through the bleakest and most desolate part of Scotland, where the hill-tops are still covered with great patches of snow, and the road winds over steep mountain-passes, and on the brink of deep brooks and precipices. The cold all day has been intense, and the rain sometimes most violent. It has been impossible to keep warm, by any means; even whiskey failed; the wind was too piercing even for that. One stage of ten miles, over a place called the Black Mount, took us two hours and a half to do; and when we came to a lone public called the King's House, at the

entrance to Glencoe, – this was about three o'clock, – we were wellnigh frozen. We got a fire directly, and in twenty minutes they served us up some famous kippered salmon, broiled; a broiled fowl; hot mutton ham and poached eggs; pancakes; oat-cake; wheaten bread; butter; bottled porter; hot water, lump sugar, and whiskey; of which we made a very hearty meal. All the way, the road had been among moors and mountains.... Now and then we passed a hut or two, with neither window nor chimney, and the smoke of the peat fire rolling out at the door. But there were not six of these dwellings in a dozen miles; and anything so bleak and wild, and mighty in its loneliness, as the whole country, it is impossible to conceive. Glencoe itself is perfectly terrible. The pass is an awful place. It is shut in on each side by enormous rocks from which great torrents come rushing down in all directions. In amongst these rocks on one side of the pass (the left as we came) there are scores of glens, high up, which form such haunts as you might imagine yourself wandering in, in the very height and madness of a fever. They will live in my dreams for years – I was going to say as long as I live, and I seriously think so. The very recollection of them makes me shudder...

He continued with a description of the postal service and of Angus Fletcher – who seemed to be related to everyone in the Highlands – imperiously ordering the postman to wait until the letter was finished. Dickens added in a postscript, 'They speak Gaelic here, of course, and many of the common people understand very little English.'

His descriptions, which Forster used in the biography of his friend, are memorable early examples of Dickens's travel writing, a style of literature he was finding increasingly appealing, although it was never to prove as popular as his fiction. In January 1867, the author Joseph Leyland sent Dickens a copy of his book *Adventures in the Far Interior of South Africa; including a journey to Lake Ngami, and Rambles in Honduras*. Dickens thanked him saying, 'I have a passion for books of travel.'

On 11 July 1841, Dickens wrote to Forster again, relating their terrifying journey to Dalmally:

As there was no place of this name in our route, you will be surprised to see it ... our being here is a part of such moving accidents by flood and field as will astonish you.... . To get from Ballyhoolish (as I am obliged to spell it when Fletcher is not in the way; and he is out at this moment) to Oban, it is necessary to cross two ferries, one of which is an arm of the sea, eight or ten miles broad. Into this ferry-boat, passengers, carriages, horses, and all, get bodily, and are got across by hook or by crook if the weather be reasonably fine. Yesterday morning, however, it blew such a strong gale that the landlord of the inn, where we had paid for horses all the way to Oban (thirty miles), honestly came up-stairs just as we were starting, with the money in his hand, and told us it would be impossible to cross. There was nothing to be done but to come back five-and-thirty miles, through Glencoe and Inverouran, to a place called Tyndrum, whence a road twelve miles long crosses to Dalmally, which is sixteen miles from Inverary. Accordingly we turned back, and in a great storm of wind and rain began to retrace the dreary road we had come the day before.... . It had rained all night, and was raining then, as it only does in these parts. Through the whole glen, which is ten miles long, torrents were boiling and foaming, and sending up in every direction spray like the smoke of great fires. They were rushing down every hill and mountain side, and tearing like devils across the path, and down into the depths of the rocks. Some of the hills looked as if they were full of silver, and had cracked in a hundred places ... one great torrent came roaring down with a deafening noise, and a rushing of water that was quite appalling. Such a spaet, in short (that's the country word), has not been known for many years ... and the horses were very much frightened (as well they might be) ... we were obliged to go on as we best could ... getting out every now and then, and hanging on at the back of the carriage to prevent its rolling down too fast, and going Heaven knows where. Well, in this pleasant state of things we came to King's House again, having been four hours doing the sixteen miles...

The account of their journey continued for several pages. Dickens and Fletcher had got out of the carriage to walk, but Catherine stayed inside until her husband persuaded her it would be safer to be outside with him, as the rushing water was becoming increasingly swollen. After reaching a high bank and feeling they were in safety, they witnessed the dramatic arrival on horseback of

> a wild Highlander, in a great plaid, whom we recognized as the landlord of the inn, and who, without taking the least notice of us, went dashing on, – with the plaid he was wrapped in, streaming in the wind, – screeching in Gaelic to the post-boy on the opposite bank and making the most frantic gestures you ever saw, in which he was joined by some other wild man on foot, who had come across by a short cut, knee-deep in mire and water.

They were trying to prevent the boy driver from taking the carriage and horses into the water, but he was already caught up in the flood. For a terrifying moment, they thought that all would be drowned, and Dickens felt sick at the knowledge that Catherine could have been trapped inside. At last the carriage emerged, with the driver and horses miraculously safe.

The group was taken back to the inn, seated by the fire and brought 'eggs and bacon, oat-cake, and whiskey'. Dickens was disconcerted by the sight of fifty drunk Highlanders, 'They were lying about in all directions: on forms, on the ground, about a loft overhead, round the turf-fire wrapped in plaids, on the tables, and under them.'

They left the inn as soon as they were dry and travelled to Dalmally, where Dickens wrote of being 'overjoyed' to find an 'English inn, with good beds (those we have slept on, yet, have always been of straw), and every possible comfort.' They stayed the night and ate a hearty breakfast at Dalmally, before travelling on to Inveraray and Melrose. The rest of their travels were far less dramatic and they returned to England full of stories about their Scottish holiday.

Dickens retained his love of Scotland and returned many times, performing on stage in amateur theatricals in Edinburgh and Glasgow. He was, however, unimpressed by Edinburgh's memorial to Sir Walter Scott, one of his heroes. In a letter to Forster, he wrote, 'the Scott

Monument is a failure. It is like the spire of a Gothic church taken off and stuck in the ground.'

He also returned to Scotland on his reading tours, which began in 1858 (after the end of his marriage), performing public readings in Edinburgh, Glasgow, Dundee, Perth and Aberdeen. After what was considered an experimental reading of *Dr Marigold* in April 1866, Dickens wrote to his eldest daughter Mary, known as Mamie, 'We had a tremendous house again last night at Glasgow. Not only that, but they were a most brilliant and delicate audience, and took "Marigold" with a fine sense and quickness not to be surpassed... . The thundering of applause last night was quite staggering.' From Edinburgh the following day, Dickens wrote to his sister-in- law Georgina, 'They were, as usual, here, remarkably intelligent, and the reading went brilliantly. I have not sent up any newspapers, as they are generally so poorly written.'

The following year, Dickens was back in Glasgow but wanted to spend a couple days away from the city, which George Dolby (his reading tour manager) described as having a 'gloomy atmosphere'. So Dickens and Dolby travelled to the Bridge of Allan and Dolby wrote in his memoirs,

> Being fortunate in our weather, we passed a most enjoyable time, especially in the long walks so dear to Mr Dickens. In one of those rambles, we made our way into Stirling and thoroughly explored the Castle, finishing up the afternoon with an inspection of the gaol. At the inhospitable-looking door a warder answered our knock, and Mr. Dickens sent in his card to the governor, who, with true politeness, came to the gate to receive us.

The two men were taken around the prison, where Dickens spoke to many of the prisoners; this included being taken into the side of the building where debtors were incarcerated. As Dolby related, 'One of the debtors recognized Mr. Dickens, who was very soon surrounded by this queer company.' Neither the governor nor Dolby could have known how poignant this visit was to Dickens.

In 1868, a reviewer for *The Scotsman*, one Scottish newspaper which Dickens had praised for its journalism, wrote: 'Hear Dickens, and die; you will never live to hear anything of its kind so good.'

The Search for Drowned Corpses in Wales

'I had come bowling down, and struggling up, hill-country roads; looking back at snowy summits; meeting courteous peasants well to do, driving fat pigs and cattle to market: noting the neat and thrifty dwellings, with their unusual quantity of clean white linen, drying on the bushes; having windy weather suggested by every cotter's little rick, with its thatch straw-ridged and extra straw-ridged into overlapping compartments like the back of a rhinoceros.'
Charles Dickens, 'The Shipwreck' from
The Uncommercial Traveller, January 1860

In 1839, Dickens visited Wales, but was thwarted in his plans of travelling around the country when he became ill. He did not return for two decades, when he travelled to Anglesey (Ynys Mon) to write an article.

On the night of 25 October 1859, a hurricane hit Britain causing the sinking of dozens of ships with many hundreds of lives. The biggest loss of life happened when the *Royal Charter*, a steam clipper, was wrecked off the Welsh coastline in the early hours of 26 October. There had been around 490 people on board, but only forty survived. The story of the tragedy appeared in newspapers around the world, because the clipper had sailed all the way from Melbourne, Australia, en route to Liverpool. Many of the passengers had struck lucky in the Australian gold rush, and were returning home triumphantly wealthy. There was so much gold on board that the ship's cargo had been given a police guard at the docks in Melbourne. Most of the news articles focused on this now-sunken treasure.

Dickens travelled to Anglesey at the very end of 1859. He was not interested in the treasure, he wanted to write about the people. The local vicar, Reverend Stephen Hughes, had been part of the rescue effort. After helping any survivors, the next heartbreaking task was to identify and then bury the numerous corpses. Reverend Hughes's brother was also a clergyman, in a neighbouring parish, and the two men mourned for all those who had perished and gave them burials in their churchyards. The brothers then wrote letters of condolence to the bereaved families, telling them their deceased loved ones had been treated with kindness and respect.

As he stood looking out to sea trying to imagine what it must have been like on that stormy October night, Dickens found it hard to conjure up an image of the devastation, because, at the end of December, the sea was calm and peaceful, glinting in the 'bright light of the sun.... So orderly, so quiet, so regular.' The gruesome reality was, however, brought home to him by the sight of divers searching for pieces of the ship and its treasure. Then, when Dickens was interviewing the Reverend Hughes, a diver came to report that no bodies had been found that day. Even though Dickens visited two months after the tragedy, the locals were anticipating that corpses would keep being found for several months to come.

Dickens wrote in 'The Shipwreck' of travelling 200 miles to meet Reverend Hughes:

> the kind and wholesome face.... I had heard of that clergyman, as having buried many scores of the shipwrecked people; of his having opened his house and heart to their agonised friends; of his having used a most sweet and patient diligence for weeks and weeks, in the performance of the forlornest offices that Man can render to his kind; of his having most tenderly and thoroughly devoted himself to the dead, and to those who were sorrowing for the dead. I had said to myself, 'In the Christmas season of the year, I should like to see that man!'

He found this visit to Anglesey very emotional, and the most affecting moment was when he was taken inside the church and realised that marks on its stone floor were stains from sodden corpses that had lain there awaiting burial. He felt those stains would never be erased. This was a sentiment often expressed in his writing, that the marks of violence and the atmosphere of sadness never leave a place. He noted solemnly, 'Some faded traces of the wreck of the Australian ship may be discernible on the stone pavement of this little church, hundreds of years hence, when the digging for gold in Australia shall have long and long ceased out of the land.' 'The Shipwreck' was published in his magazine *All The Year Round* on 28 January 1860.

Dickens was, however, less kind to another Anglesey institution, in a later article for *The Uncommercial Traveller*. In 'Refreshments for Travellers' (24 March 1860), Dickens wrote about the varied discomforts of the travelling life, venting his spleen about Ye Olde Bull's Head pub in Beaumaris:

> Count up your injuries, in its side-dishes of ailing sweetbreads in white poultices, of apothecaries' powders in rice for curry, of pale stewed bits of calf ineffectually relying for an adventitious interest on forcemeat balls. You have had experience of the old-established Bull's Head stringy fowls, with lower extremities like wooden legs, sticking up out of the dish; of its cannibalic boiled mutton, gushing horribly among its capers, when carved; of its little dishes of pastry – roofs of spermaceti ointment, erected over half an apple or four gooseberries.

The author's only other recorded journeys to Wales were on those occasions when he travelled to the port of Holyhead to catch a boat to Ireland. These always seemed to be treacherous crossings, written about with a shudder at the memories of his seasick companions.

Dickens suffered from seasickness with regularity. His eldest child, Charley, wrote in *Reminiscences of My Father*, about a Channel crossing in the 1850s, which Charley remembered as 'perfectly calm and smooth', yet on which his father lay down 'on the deck enveloped in all the coats and rugs he could get hold of ... complexion a damaged orange; and delivering himself, an absolutely unresisting prey, to sea-sickness.'

'A Very Picturesque and Various Country': Reading Tours in Ireland

'a very picturesque and various country; and the amazing thing is, that it is all particularly neat and orderly, and that the houses (outside at all events) are all brightly whitewashed and remarkably clean.'
Letter from Charles Dickens
to his daughter, Mamie, 1858

By the time Dickens toured Ireland, in 1858, he had been thinking about visiting the country for a long time. When he was working on *Master Humphrey's Clock*, a weekly magazine he wrote and edited in the late 1830s, he considered writing a series of travel articles which involved travelling around either Ireland or America. His plans for America came to fruition within a few years, but it took almost two decades for him to travel to Ireland.

The year 1858 was one of turmoil and unwanted scrutiny for the Dickens family. Unsurprisingly, the ending of Charles and Catherine's marriage became headline news and the author needed to do something to distract both his own guilty conscience and the newspapers. So he began a new phase in his career: public readings of his works. These enabled him to go back to his childhood dream of performing on stage, gave him a lucrative new income stream and gave him the chance to go on the road, escaping the demons that beset him at home, and the disapproval of so many of his friends.

He had often longed to be back on the road, albeit in much greater comfort than in his days as a young journalist, and he wanted to connect with his public and boost his popularity. On the eve of Dickens's first visit to Ireland, his tour manager, Arthur Smith, and his assistants were celebrating their exhausting but very successful tour so far. On the night before they sailed, Dickens wrote to Georgina Hogarth from the Adelphi

Hotel in Liverpool, saying: 'They turned away hundreds, sold all the books, rolled on the ground of my room knee-deep in checks [sic], and made a perfect pantomime of the whole thing.'

On Saturday 21 August, an ebullient Dickens and his entourage travelled to Holyhead for the ferry to Dublin. They suffered through very rough seas, although Dickens reported triumphantly to Mamie that 'Arthur was incessantly sick the whole way. I was not sick at all.' In Dublin, they stayed at the exclusive Morrison's, which Dickens described to Mamie as 'a beautiful hotel.... Our bedrooms too are excellent, and there are baths and all sorts of comforts.'

Dickens spent a couple of days preparing, sightseeing and making notes about his observations of the city. Dublin was bigger, prettier, and far less poverty-ridden than he had expected and the countryside outside the city was 'picturesque and various'. He described the city as 'no shabbier than London', remarking that its people seemed to enjoy themselves more than Londoners did. He was fascinated by the Irish accent and wrote to his family that he had perfected the Irish accent and was keen to 'play an Irish part some day'.

On 23 August, Dickens began his four nights of public readings at the Rotunda Rooms on Parnell Square. The Dublin press and public welcomed him, although he was alarmed on his first night to see so many empty seats. In Dublin, people took their seats just before the curtain was about to rise – and some of the audience came in after Dickens had already started speaking. Overall, he was very pleased with the way the Irish press covered his performances and appearance – except for one letter to a Cork newspaper, which expressed surprise at Dickens being only 46 because the letter writer thought he looked 'like an old man'.

After his performance on 25 August, Dickens wrote to Georgina:

> Everybody was at 'Little Dombey' to-day, and ... the effect was unmistakable and profound. The crying was universal, and they were extraordinarily affected. There is no doubt we could stay here a week with that one reading, and fill the place every night.... It was a most decided and complete success.
>
> Arthur has been imploring me to stop here on the Friday after Limerick, and read 'Little Dombey' again. But I have positively said 'No.' The work is too hard. It is not like

> doing it in one easy room, and always the same room. With
> a different place every night, and a different audience with
> its own peculiarities every night, it is a tremendous strain.

After the difficulties of the preceding months, Dickens was cheered to be treated as such an honoured guest. He wrote to his family that people smiled at him on the street and wanted to shake his hand, and that every night the buttonhole flower in his coat was given to an adoring fan. During his reading from *Dombey and Son* he would scatter geranium leaves on the stage as one of his props – and he was gratified to hear that, after he left the stage, members of the audience climbed onto it and picked up the leaves to keep as mementoes.

When they moved on to Belfast, a city renowned for its carriage makers, both Dickens and Arthur Smith commissioned new vehicles, to be sent to their homes in England. Dickens described his to Georgina as 'a trim, sparkling, slap-up Irish jaunting car!' with which he hoped to 'astonish' the people of Kent.

By this date, Dickens had moved out of London to live at Gad's Hill Place, in Kent. In later years (after the death of Arthur Smith), Dickens's new tour manager, George Dolby, mentioned the Belfast carriage in his memoirs:

> A drive through the pleasantest of the Kentish country, either on an 'outside' Irish jaunting car; or, in fine weather, in a basket carriage, with the nattiest of ponies, driven by Mr Dickens; or, in wet weather, with a brougham drawn by the most knowing and best trained of cobs with a 'hogmain'; always escorted by three or four enormous dogs of the Mount St Bernard, mastiff, or Newfoundland species, brought the visitor to the house.

Dolby was in charge of Dickens's second tour to Ireland in 1867. This took place after much discussion about safety because of the dangerous political situation. Dolby recalled in his memoirs: 'we had the additional excitement of visiting Dublin at a time when that city was in a state of semi-siege, owing to an anticipated Fenian rising on St Patrick's Day.' The journey was not an easy one, plagued by a heavy storm and a snowdrift blocking the railway line as they attempted to make their way to catch the boat in Holyhead, where a 'furious gale' postponed the crossing. When they arrived at what was then called Kingstown (now Dún Laoghaire) the customs officers were convinced they were carrying dangerous explosives. Dolby had to explain that the gas piping was part of Dickens's stage set, for lighting up his reading desk.

As Dickens wrote to Mamie from Dublin, on 16 March 1867:

> There is considerable alarm here beyond all question, and great depression in all kinds of trade and commerce. To-morrow being St Patrick's Day, there are apprehensions of some disturbance, and croakers predict that it will come off between to-night and Monday night. Of course there are preparations on all sides, and large musters of soldiers and police, though they are kept carefully out of sight. One would not suppose, walking about the streets, that any disturbance was impending; and yet there is no doubt that the materials of one lie smouldering up and down the city and all over the country... . If any riot were to break out, I should immediately stop the readings here.

Dickens and Dolby enjoyed themselves in Dublin, where they were invited to a St Patrick's Day party, but the tension was palpable, and when Dickens wanted to take a walk around the city at night, he was only allowed to go in a carriage, with a police escort. Dolby wrote in his memoirs, 'we did not see more than about half a dozen persons in the streets, with the exception of the ordinary policemen on their beats.' He also gave an account of what it was like to travel home from Ireland in 1867.

> As the mail boat leaves Kingstown for England[6] at an inconveniently early hour in the morning, we decided on sleeping on board the steamer... . The intention was good, but the execution was a failure, for at about two o'clock in the morning we were awakened by the tramping of soldiers on the deck overhead, and as the sound was a disconcerting one in such a place and at such a time, we went up to see what

---

6. They were actually heading for Holyhead, which is in Wales, not England.

'A Very Picturesque and Various Country': Reading Tours in Ireland

was the matter. There we found a strong escort of marines in charge of some of the arrested Fenians.... These persons having been carefully stowed away in the lower part of the vessel, the marines and police were free to roam about the ship at their will, and they created such a disturbance as to prevent anything like sleeping in comfort; so Mr. Dickens and myself spent the three or four hours before daybreak in the saloon, playing cribbage, after which we started off for a walk around the harbour until the time for the sailing of the mail boat.

Arrived at Holyhead, all the passengers were detained on the steamer until the Fenians were disposed of in the train, and at every stopping place on the road from Holyhead to London there were strong escorts of police.

At Euston Square we were all locked in our carriages until the cavalcade of mounted police with the vans containing the prisoners had left the station, and then we were allowed to go our several ways, and glad we were allowed to do so after ten days full of adventure, and many fears and anxieties as to the result of our visit to Ireland in troublesome times.

The Fenian dislike of the English was growing in Irish communities all over the world. On 12 March 1868 (a year after Dickens had returned to Ireland), their cause made global headlines when Prince Alfred, Duke of Edinburgh[7] was shot on a beach at Clontarf, a suburb of Sydney, while travelling in Australia. The gunman claimed to be a Fenian (although other Fenians disputed this). Miraculously, the prince survived the bullet wound, but Henry O'Farrell, his would-be assassin, was arrested and hanged. The attack caused a great deal of racist violence against the Irish all over the English-speaking world, which, in turn, led to increased anti-English feeling in Ireland.

Despite all this political tension, Dickens returned to Ireland in 1869, as part of his final reading tour. A letter sent a few months before his visit gives an insight into his travelling arrangements and his preference for the independence of a hotel, rather than accepting invitations to stay

---

7. Prince Alfred was the fourth child of Queen Victoria and Prince Albert.

in people's homes. It was written to the Marquis of Dufferin and Ava, who had invited him to stay in Belfast:

> ... the work on such occasions is so very hard, that I long ago found any private enjoyment to be quite incompatible with it. I travel with a staff of whom the greatest exactness in business is required, and I never leave them. I invariably live at an hotel with my Secretary.

For Dickens, the ability to be by himself in his hotel room, instead of singing for his supper as the honoured guest, was vital after the rigours of his speaking engagements. The performances were exhausting, especially at this stage of his life.

On this third and final visit to Ireland, Dickens gave readings in Belfast at the Ulster Hall and at The Rotunda Rooms in Dublin. The schedule was punishing. On 5 January, he wrote to the Lord Chief Justice of Ireland, excusing himself from being able to undertake any other engagements:

> It is a most miserable fact that I have not one single free day in Dublin! I read there on three consecutive nights, and on the following day start back for Belfast where I shall already have read once. At Belfast I have engaged to dine out once, after reading; and then I shall have to come to London with the greatest precipitation, being announced to read there on Tuesday the 18th.

In Dublin, Dickens continued with his gruelling writing schedule, in addition to his three performances, on 11, 12 and 13 January 1869. He wrote home gleefully of scenes of chaos because his readings were sold out: the glass at the box office had been smashed and people were offering to pay as much as £5 (a huge amount) for a ticket. To his friend and solicitor, Fred Ouvry, Dickens wrote from Dublin of 'Enormous Houses [audiences] here, and unbounded enthusiasm'. In his memoirs, George Dolby recalled that 200 extra chairs were needed for Dickens's final reading, and that 'a strong body of police – mounted and on foot' was required for crowd control and to manage the traffic.

Dickens began and ended his final Irish reading tour in Belfast and left the city exhausted and very stressed. His letters show that he found the Belfast audiences harder to please than those in Dublin, but as he was struggling emotionally and physically he was possibly too harsh in his assessment of how successful his Belfast readings had been. On 18 January 1869, *The Belfast Morning News* included a glowing account of his performance:

> …the rich literary treat will not soon be forgotten by those who were privileged to hear it … his delivery and action were easy and effective, and manifested the ability of the author not less than the art of the reader. The entertainment altogether was highly appreciated, and those present will have only one regret, that the 'final farewell' cannot be repeated.

The advertising pamphlet for his Dublin readings had proclaimed dramatically:

> Messrs. Chappell & Co. beg to announce that
> they have made arrangements with
> Mr. Charles Dickens for three
> FAREWELL READINGS,
> THE LAST THAT WILL EVER TAKE PLACE IN DUBLIN

The flyer went on to state that 'any announcement made in connexion with these FAREWELL READINGS will be strictly adhered to and considered final; and that on no consideration whatever will Mr. Dickens be induced to appear an extra night in any place in which he shall have been once announced to read for the last time.' The wording was correct. These really were his last public readings in Ireland. Within eighteen months, Charles Dickens was dead.

Killed with Kindness: A Grand Tour to North America

'America and England ... may they never have any division but the Atlantic between them!'
From a speech given by Charles Dickens
in Boston in 1842

Ever since childhood, Dickens had longed to visit faraway places and, as a young man, had listened with envy to tales of wealthy men's travels. It was during the family holiday to Broadstairs in 1841 that he began to plan a grand overseas adventure.

Four years earlier, Dickens had discovered that *Sketches by Boz* was being published in America by a company in Philadelphia. Because there was no international copyright law, British authors had no control over what happened to their works overseas. As his reputation increased, the company contacted him and offered a one-off payment – although their letter was addressed to a Samuel Dickens, confusing the author with his characters.

Dickens frequently received fan letters from across the Atlantic and realised just how many pirated copies of his works were being sold there, for which he was receiving no royalties. The latest instalment of his book would be taken by ship to America, transcribed en route and printed on arrival. Perhaps the catalyst for travelling to the USA was when he learnt of the reception in New York of *The Old Curiosity Shop*. People had thronged the city's harbour, calling to passengers on arriving ships to ask about the fate of Little Nell. As Dickens sat at his desk in Broadstairs, he began to plan a journey to North America, poring over maps and reading stories of American travels.

For many years, he had been a fan of the American author Washington Irving. The two men began a correspondence and Dickens asked Irving's advice about his idea for a tour. Irving responded that a tour 'would be such a triumph from one end of the States to the other'.

Catherine, now the mother of four young children, including a new baby, was devastated at the thought of travelling so far from her family, but Dickens was adamant. He arranged for his brother Fred to live with the children and for their friends, William and Catherine Macready, to act as stand-in parents while they were away. Catherine's sister Georgina also promised to visit the children every day.

The travellers arrived in Liverpool on 3 January 1842 and checked into their cabin on the *SS Britannia*, one of the Cunard Line's fleet of ships. They were underwhelmed by the size of what, he had been assured when booking, was their 'state room'. As he wrote wryly, in his ensuing travelogue *American Notes*, he and Catherine had entertained grand imaginary pictures of their onboard state room:

> That this state-room had been specially engaged for 'Charles Dickens, Esquire, and Lady,' was rendered sufficiently clear even to my scared intellect by a very small manuscript, announcing the fact ... this was the state-room concerning which Charles Dickens, Esquire, and Lady, had held daily and nightly conferences for at least four months preceding ... that small snug chamber of the imagination, which Charles Dickens, Esquire, with the spirit of prophecy strong upon him, had always foretold would contain at least one little sofa, and which his lady, with a modest yet most magnificent sense of its limited dimensions, had from the first opined would not hold more than two enormous portmanteaus in some odd corner out of sight (portmanteaus which could now no more be got in at the door, not to say stowed away, than a giraffe could be persuaded or forced into a flower-pot) ... I sat down ... and looked, without any expression of countenance whatever, at some friends who had come on board with us ... by very nearly closing the door, and twining in and out like serpents, and by counting the little washing slab as standing-room, – we could manage to insinuate four people into it, all at one time; and entreating each other to observe how very airy it was (in dock), and how there was a beautiful port-hole which

could be kept open all day (weather permitting), and how there was quite a large bull's-eye just over the looking-glass which would render shaving a perfectly easy and delightful process (when the ship didn't roll too much); we arrived, at last, at the unanimous conclusion that it was rather spacious than otherwise.

After bidding farewell to their friends and relatives, Charles, Catherine, and Catherine's maid, Anne Brown, were mildly cheered by the discovery that their state room adjoined a 'ladies' cabin', a public sitting room which they hoped they could use as an extra living space. They were amazed by the artistry of the ship's design and Dickens marvelled at the

> stewardess ... actively engaged in producing clean sheets and table-cloths from the very entrails of the sofas, and from unexpected lockers, of such artful mechanism, that it made one's head ache to see them opened one after another, and rendered it quite a distracting circumstance to follow her proceedings, and to find that every nook and corner and individual piece of furniture was something else besides what it pretended to be, and was a mere trap and deception and place of secret stowage.

With their luggage safely stowed, they went to watch the bustle of activity that preceded the sailing. A group of workers were bringing a cow on board, to provide milk throughout the journey, while others loaded meat, vegetables and fruit, packed in ice. Sailors were doing unknowable things with ropes, porters were overseeing the hoisting of heavy luggage, and the travellers had the sensation that nothing else in the world could be happening, as everyone on earth seemed so intent on readying their ship for the voyage.

They sailed for Boston the following morning. The Scottish stewardess assured them – in a kindly mendacious fashion – that previous January voyages had all seen smooth seas, with 'dancing from morning to night' and nobody suffering seasickness. Catherine was soothed by the accent of her childhood and by the stewardess's comment that mothers separated from their children by the Atlantic Ocean, were really not too far away, it would take just a short voyage to be back with them. These cheerful expectations were, however, soon to be rudely disproved, as seasickness descended on the party and they found themselves in a storm so brutal that, as Catherine wrote to Charles's sister, Fanny, the waves 'broke ... the life-boat to pieces'.

Their experiences on the *Britannia* determined Dickens to book a different type of vessel for their return journey and, within a few days of disembarking, he wrote to Forster,

> I never will trust myself upon the wide ocean, if it please Heaven, in a steamer again. When I tell you all that I observed on board that *Britannia*, I shall astonish you. Meanwhile, consider two of their dangers. First, that if the funnel were blown overboard the vessel must instantly be on fire, from stem to stern; to comprehend which consequence, you have only to understand that the funnel is more than 40 feet high, and that at night you see the solid fire two or three feet above its top. Imagine this swept down by a strong wind, and picture to yourself the amount of flame on deck; and that a strong wind is likely to sweep it down you soon learn, from the precautions taken to keep it up in a storm, when it is the first thing thought of. Secondly, each of these boats consumes between London and Halifax 700 tons of coals; and it is pretty clear, from this enormous difference of weight in a ship of only 1200 tons burden in all, that she must either be too heavy when she comes out of port, or too light when she goes in. The daily difference in her rolling, as she burns the coals out, is something absolutely fearful.

The *Britannia* arrived in Boston on 22 January, docking at 5.00pm. Catherine was extremely relieved to be off the boat and away from 'all the horrors of a storm at Sea'. Dickens wrote to Forster of his astonishment at his reception:

> I was standing in full fig on the paddle-box beside the captain, staring about me, when suddenly, long before we were moored to the wharf, a dozen men came leaping on board at the peril of their lives... . What do you think of their tearing violently up at me and beginning to shake

hands like mad men?.... A Mr Alexander, to whom I had written from England promising to sit for a portrait, was on board directly we reached the land.

Amongst the group watching Dickens's arrival was a young James T. Fields. Some years later, Fields would become Dickens's authorised American publisher. He and his wife Annie would be instrumental in persuading Dickens to return to America in the 1860s.

According to the writer Henry Dana (grandson of the poet Henry Wadsworth Longfellow),

> This portrait painter, Francis Alexander, continued to dance attendance on Dickens, escorting him through the crowds at the dock in Boston, driving him in a carriage up State Street and along Tremont Row to the Tremont House, where another crowd was waiting.... From the very day he landed in America ... Dickens ... was besieged by every sort of invitation and attention. On the Saturday night of his arrival, as soon as he had got settled into his room, he set out in high spirits to make his first tour of Boston streets and shops, accompanied by a group of enthusiastic young men.

The Tremont House in downtown Boston was a grand hotel at the intersection of Tremont Street and Beacon Street. At the hotel, and everywhere he went, Dickens felt like a celebrity. He and Catherine were dazzled by finding themselves not only in a new country, but in a new continent, and overwhelmed at how much excitement their visit had created. Catherine wrote home, 'We are constantly out two or three times in the evening. The people are most hospitable, and we shall both be killed with kindness.'

Shortly after his arrival, Dickens made the acquaintance of a young man with the fabulous name of George Washington Putnam, who was one of Francis Alexander's pupils. When Alexander heard Dickens talk about his wish for a secretary to travel with him, he suggested Putnam. The two men liked each other at once, and Dickens asked him to start work the following morning. For the next few months, Putnam travelled with Charles and Catherine and greatly enjoyed his job. He wrote in his memoirs that 'The people flocked to the Tremont day by day' in an attempt to see the English author. He also left a fascinating account of what daily life was like for the young couple at the start of their American adventure:

> On Friday morning I was there at nine o'clock, the time appointed. Mr. and Mrs. Dickens had their meals in their own rooms, and the table was spread for breakfast. Soon they came in, and, after a cheerful greeting, I took my place at a side-table and wrote as he ate his breakfast, and meanwhile conversed with Mrs. Dickens, opened his letters, and dictated the answers to me.
>
> In one corner of the room, Dexter the sculptor was earnestly at work modelling a bust of Mr. Dickens. Several others of the most eminent artists of our country had urgently requested Mr. Dickens to sit to them for his picture and bust, but, having consented to do so to Alexander and Dexter, he was obliged to refuse all others for want of time.
>
> While Mr. Dickens ate his breakfast, read his letters and dictated the answers, Dexter was watching with the utmost earnestness the play of every feature, and comparing his model with the original. Often during the meal he would come to Dickens with a solemn, business-like air, stoop down and look at him sideways, pass round and take a look at the other side of his face, and then go back to his model and work away for a few minutes; then come again and take another look and go back to his model; soon he would come again with his callipers and measure Dickens's nose, and go and try it on the nose of the model; then come again with the callipers and try the width of the temples, or the distance from the nose to the chin, and back again to his work, eagerly shaping and correcting his model. The whole soul of the artist was engaged in his task, and the result was a splendid bust of the great author. Mr. Dickens was highly pleased with it, and repeatedly alluded to it, during his stay, as a very successful work of art.

A Bostonian named Sarah Preston Everett Hale, sister of the US Ambassador to Britain, Edward Everett, wrote to her brother in London: 'The town has been thrown into great commotion by the arrival of

Dickens. His books have been universally read here ... and admired by all classes of people.' She claimed there was such fervour that cab drivers 'called out for the privilege of taking "Boz" for nothing' and wrote of the author being 'very much liked here. The young folks think he is a perfect beauty.' After meeting Dickens, she pronounced him 'very simple and unaffected' and 'really touched at the interest people manifested in his works'.

Two nights after their arrival, the 'perfect beauty' and his wife went to the Tremont Theatre to watch a play called *Boz! A Masque Phrenologic*, described on the poster as having been 'Written for the occasion'. The role of Boz was played by a Mr. J. M. Field. Other characters in the play were named Skyblue (a neglected genius), Ideality, Mirth, Self-Esteem, Firmness, Wonder, Time and Tune. Queen Victoria also appeared, as did characters from *The Pickwick Papers, Oliver Twist, Nicholas Nickleby, Barnaby Rudge* and *The Old Curiosity Shop*. Several tableaux of his works were also performed. Tableaux were very popular Victorian entertainments, where a scene was recreated in one frozen moment by actors striking a pose and holding it as if in a painting.

Two days after the Tremont Theatre performance, Dickens met some of the young men who had been instrumental in creating such a buzz around his visit. These were three professors from Harvard: Henry Wadsworth Longfellow, Cornelius Felton and Jared Sparks (who would become President of Harvard in 1849). Dickens wrote to Forster, 'The Professors at the Cambridge University ... are noble fellows'. Longfellow wrote to his father,

> Dickens is a glorious fellow ... [he] has not a moment's rest; – calls innumerable – invitations innumerable; – and is engaged three deep for the remainder of his stay, in the way of dinners and parties. He is a gay, free and easy character; – fine bright face; blue eyes, long black hair...

Their first meeting on 26 January 1842 was the beginning of a lifelong friendship, with regular letters exchanged and Longfellow visiting Dickens in England twice. Dickens and Felton also kept up a regular correspondence.

Not everyone was as laudatory of Boz as Longfellow and Sarah Preston Everett Hale, however. Many Americans were bemused, and often disconcerted, by Dickens. In Britain, as well as in America, Dickens's love of brightly coloured waistcoats and high 'dandified' fashion caused some to deride him as vulgar or showy. Dickens never stopped loving the brightly coloured fashions of his youth: he had been born in the Georgian age, growing up surrounded by the flamboyancy of the Regency period, and he had been 25 before Queen Victoria came to the throne. Bored by the dull, sober style of clothing that Victorian men were expected to wear, Dickens eschewed a palette of dull dark browns, greys and black, for vivid colours and beautiful patterns.

In Boston, Dickens met the author and lawyer Richard Henry Dana, a prominent member of Boston society. Dana's recollections of Dickens are interesting, because they begin with a rather snobby disappointment but grow into adulation. After meeting him for the first time, on 26 January 1842, Dana wrote:

> Disappointed in D.'s appearance. We have heard him called 'the handsomest man in London' &c. He is of the middle height (under if anything) with a large expressive eye, regular nose, matted, curling, wet-looking black hair, a dissipated looking mouth with a vulgar draw to it, a muddy olive complexion, stubby fingers & a hand by no means patrician, a hearty, off-hand manner, far from well bred, & a rapid, dashing way of talking. He looks 'wide awake', 'up to anything', full of cleverness, with quick feelings & great ardour. You admire him, and there is a fascination about him which keeps your eyes on him, yet you cannot get over the impression that he is a low bred man.... . He has what I suppose to be the true Cockney cut...

The following day, Dana met Dickens again and already his opinion was changing:

> Like Dickens here very much. The gentlemen are talking their best, but Dickens is perfectly natural & unpretending. He could not have behaved better. He did not say a single thing for display. I should think he had resolved to talk as he would at home, & let his reputation take care of itself.

Dickens and Travel: The Start of Modern Travel Writing

After their next meeting, Dana wrote, 'Dickens spoke excellently. I never heard a speech wh. went off better. He speaks naturally, with a good voice, beautiful intonations, & an ardent, generous manner', and by the time Dickens was about to bid farewell to Boston, Dana was enthusing, 'He is the cleverest man I ever met. I mean he impresses you with the alertness of his various powers...'.

Many years later, another recollection of Dickens's first days in America was published by Mrs Elizabeth Wormeley Latimer, who had been present at a dinner party given by Judge and Mrs Prescott. In 1893, Wormeley Latimer wrote 'A Girl's Recollection of Dickens' for *Lippincott's Magazine*. She recalled:

> [Dickens] had brought with him two velvet waistcoats, one of vivid green, the other of brilliant crimson; these were further ornamented by a profusion of gold watch-chain ... a black satin waistcoat was almost the national costume of gentlemen in America: so that Mr. Dickens's vivid tints were very conspicuous. Mrs Dickens ... showed signs of having been born and bred her husband's social superior.

Despite half a century having elapsed, she was still offended that Dickens had scandalised the party with what she considered a lewd comment and continued, 'I do not think the personality of Mr Dickens was altogether pleasing to the very refined and cultivated literary men and women of Boston at that period, but they did their best to entertain him with consideration and hospitality. They were not sorry, however, to pass him on to New York.'

The scandal at the dinner party became legend, handed down through generations of Dickensians, and related by Edward F. Payne, President of the Boston Dickens Fellowship, in his 1927 book *Dickens Days in Boston: A Record of Daily Events*:

> Elizabeth Wormeley (afterward Mrs. Latimer) was present on this evening and thus describes the affair: '...So far as I can remember after so many years, we were eighteen at table.... In the course of the entertainment a discussion arose among the gentlemen as to which was the more beautiful

woman, the Duchess of Sutherland or Mrs. Caroline Norton. "Well, I don't know," said Dickens, expanding himself in his green velvet waistcoat, "Mrs. Norton perhaps is the more beautiful, but the Duchess, to my mind, is the more kissable person." Had a bombshell dropped upon Judge Prescott's dinner table it could hardly have startled the company more than this remark.'

Although Dickens did not impress the snobby elite of Boston society, who expected that a visiting Briton should be aristocratic and stuffy, in other circles he was very much welcomed. The sculptor William Wetmore Story wrote admiringly:

> Dickens himself is frank and hearty ... his eyes are fine, and the whole muscular action of the mouth and lower part of his face beautifully free and vibratory. People eat him here! ... But he is too strong and healthy a mind to be spoiled even by the excessive adulation and flattery that he receives.

In 1870, following Dickens's death, George Washington Putnam published a book entitled *Four Months with Charles Dickens*. He wrote of how many Bostonians wanted to meet Dickens:

> Statesmen, authors, poets, scholars, merchants, judges, lawyers, editors, came, many of them accompanied by their wives and daughters, and his rooms were filled with smiling faces and resounded with cheerful voices.
>
> Meanwhile the press was active in describing his looks and manners, and all things connected with the arrival of the distinguished strangers. Go where you would in the city, – in the hotels, stores, counting-rooms, in the streets, in the cars, in the country as well as the city, – the all-absorbing topic was the 'arrival of Dickens!' The New York and Philadelphia papers repeated all that was published by the Boston press, and delegations from societies, and committees of citizens from distant cities, came to see the great author and arrange for meetings and receptions in other places.

Putnam also left his recollections of Catherine:

> Mrs. Dickens was a lady of moderate height; with a full, well-developed form, a beautiful face and good figure. I call to mind the high, full forehead, the brown hair gracefully arranged, the look of English healthfulness in the warm glow of color in her cheeks, the blue eyes with a tinge of violet, well-arched brows, a well-shaped nose, and a mouth small and of uncommon beauty. She was decidedly a handsome woman, and would have attracted notice as such in any gathering of ladies anywhere. She had a quiet dignity mingled with great sweetness of manner; her calm quietness differing much from the quick, earnest, always cheerful, but keen and nervous temperament of her husband, – a temperament belonging to the existence, and absolutely necessary to the development, of a great genius like that of Charles Dickens.

On the Dickenses' second weekend in Boston, Henry Wadsworth Longfellow took his fellow author on a ten-mile walk around the city. They walked along the waterfront and Longfellow showed him where the Boston Tea Party had happened. They walked past the docks and into the sailors' haunts, where a sermon was being preached to the mariners – and where the two authors were singled out as iniquitous sinners. Longfellow wrote to his friend Sam Ward that after the sermon they 'made a pilgrimage through North End, over Copp's Hill to Bunker's.' At Copp's Hill they visited a graveyard and Longfellow told him tales of Civil War battles and grievances.

For weeks, Boston had been abuzz with the prospect of the Dickens Dinner, at which Charles and Catherine were honoured guests. It was held at Papanti's Hall – made famous by the resident dancing teacher Lorenzo Papanti – on 1 February. The tickets were expensive, costing each guest $15. Henry Dana later wrote about what his grandfather had told him: 'There were no less than ten courses, each course offering a wide variety of choices, including oysters in three different forms and veal in four forms. Countless toasts were drunk in innumerable wines and tributes were paid to Dickens by some thirty different orators.'

Dickens also paid tribute to his hosts with a speech about friendship between Britain and America including the much-appreciated words, 'May they never have any division but the Atlantic between them!'

Catherine was also receiving media attention. A New York paper commented, 'Mrs Dickens is a fine-looking Englishwoman' (a description guaranteed to annoy a Scottish woman), and when an illustration purportedly of Catherine appeared in a newspaper, she posted it home with glee, surrounded by multiple exclamation marks, because it looked so astoundingly nothing like her. Once she was beyond the memories of her seasickness and the toothache that had plagued her during their first days in America, Catherine enjoyed the wonderful adventure, although she missed her children, Charley, Mamie, Katey and Walter, constantly. Charles was also taken by surprise by just how much he craved their company. Before their departure, their artist friend Daniel Maclise had presented Catherine with a drawing of the four children, and Grip, the pet raven. Putnam recalled how the couple would look longingly at the portrait and how they 'talked constantly of their children and seemed to derive great comfort from the pictured presence of their little ones.'

For the last day of their time in Boston, Longfellow arranged a special breakfast at the house he was living in. This was the Craigie House, a beautiful Italianate mansion, famous as the place where George Washington created his headquarters during the Siege of Boston in the 1770s (today, it is known as the Longfellow House). All the guests were male, so Dickens went without Catherine, walking through Boston to Cambridge, where he was met by several Harvard professors. After the breakfast, Dickens was taken on a tour of the Harvard Library.

Dickens never forgot the kindness and hospitality shown to him by Longfellow. On 23 February, knowing Longfellow was already planning a trip to Europe, Dickens wrote to him from New York:

> Write to me from the continent, and tell me when to expect you. We live quietly – not uncomfortably – and among people whom I am sure you would like to know; as much as they would like to know you. Have no home but mine ... and let me be your London host and cicerone. Is this a bargain?
> Always Faithfully, Your Friend, Charles Dickens

Dickens had been longing to try American railways and in *American Notes* he recorded his first journey:

> Before leaving Boston, I devoted one day to an excursion to Lowell.... . I made acquaintance with an American railroad, on this occasion, for the first time.... . There are no first and second class carriages as with us; but there is a gentleman's car and a ladies' car: the main distinction between which is that in the first, everybody smokes; and in the second, nobody does. As a black man never travels with a white one, there is also a negro car; which is a great, blundering, clumsy chest, such as Gulliver put to sea in, from the kingdom of Brobdingnag. There is a great deal of jolting, a great deal of noise, a great deal of wall, not much window, a locomotive engine, a shriek, and a bell.
>
> The cars are like shabby omnibuses, but larger: holding thirty, forty, fifty, people... . In the centre of the carriage there is usually a stove, fed with charcoal or anthracite coal; which is for the most part red-hot. It is insufferably close; and you see the hot air fluttering between yourself and any other object you may happen to look at, like the ghost of smoke.
>
> In the ladies' car, there are a great many gentlemen who have ladies with them. There are also a great many ladies who have nobody with them: for any lady may travel alone, from one end of the United States to the other, and be certain of the most courteous and considerate treatment everywhere.... . Politics are much discussed, so are banks, so is cotton. Quiet people avoid the question of the Presidency, for there will be a new election in three years and a half, and party feeling runs very high: the great constitutional feature of this institution being, that directly the acrimony of the last election is over, the acrimony of the next one begins...

In Lowell, Dickens visited factories, where he made notes about the working conditions, compared them to those of mills and factories he had visited in Britain, and found the American factories better for the workers than those at home. He wrote about how well-dressed and clean the working women looked. Always a champion for hygiene, he was very pleased to see that there were good washing facilities for the workers inside the factories. Dickens wanted to check how the employees were housed, so he visited the women's boarding houses and was very impressed to see pianos for the workers to play, to discover that 'nearly all these young ladies subscribe to circulating libraries' and to be shown the publication they had set up. They gave him a copy of it: 'four hundred good solid pages, which I have read from beginning to end.' He was particularly impressed by the social healthcare programme created for the workers: 'The weekly charge in this establishment for each female patient is three dollars, or twelve shillings English; but no girl employed by any of the corporations is ever excluded for want of the means of payment.'

On his return train journey to Boston, Dickens pretended to be asleep after an over-zealous fellow passenger decided to tell him how he should write his next book, but the lure of the railway was too great and he peeped out of his feigned slumber:

> ...from the corners of my eyes, I found abundance of entertainment for the rest of the ride in watching the effects of the wood fire, which had been invisible in the morning but were now brought out in full relief by the darkness: for we were travelling in a whirlwind of bright sparks, which showered about us like a storm of fiery snow.

A rather weary Dickens wrote his impressions of Boston to Forster, and admitted that he and Catherine were so exhausted by the constant social invitations they had pretended to be ill to get out of a party they had been invited to. Of Boston itself, Dickens commented,

> I will only say, now, that we have never yet been required to dine at a table-d'hôte; that, thus far, our rooms are as much our own here as they would be at the Clarendon; that but for an odd phrase now and then – such as *Snap of cold weather*; *a tongue-y man* for a talkative fellow; *Possible?* as a solitary interrogation; and *Yes?* for indeed – I should have marked, so far, no difference whatever between the parties here and those I have left behind. The women are

very beautiful, but they soon fade; the general breeding is neither stiff nor forward; the good nature, universal. If you ask the way to a place – of some common waterside man, who don't know you from Adam – he turns and goes with you. Universal deference is paid to ladies; and they walk about at all seasons, wholly unprotected.... This hotel is a trifle smaller than Finsbury Square; and is made so infernally hot (I use the expression advisedly) by means of a furnace with pipes running through the passages, that we can hardly bear it. There are no curtains to the beds, or to the bedroom windows. I am told there never are, hardly, all through America. The bedrooms are indeed very bare of furniture.

At this early stage of their journey, Dickens was filled with the enthusiasm of the adventurous and overly optimistic traveller, eager to see all the places the normal tourists didn't get to see. He wrote home of his desire to travel around the southern United States and then travel all the way up to Canada. When local people warned him the journey was too difficult, especially for the women of the party, with many areas having no proper roads, just 'a track known only to travelling merchants', Dickens, wrote that he was 'staggered, but not deterred.... If I find it possible to be done ... I mean to do it; being quite satisfied that without some such dash I can never be a free agent, or see anything worth the telling.' Although his many advisors were keen to claim that Catherine would find travelling too arduous, she proved herself perfect capable and tirelessly good humoured throughout their travels. In April, Charles wrote proudly to Forster that his wife had 'made a most admirable traveller in every respect. She has never screamed or express[ed] alarm under circumstances that would have fully justified her in doing so, even in my eyes; has never given way to despondency or fatigue, though we have now been travelling incessantly.'

Today, when people talk about the Dickenses' marriage, it is always with the knowledge that, in 1858, it would come to a bitter end, and unfortunately that has now overshadowed all their earlier years together. Yet they were married for twenty-two years before separating, and for many years it was a very happy marriage. In Boston, Catherine was befriended by a local woman named Elizabeth Latimer, who later wrote:

'There was no sign then of any disagreement or incompatibility … it struck me with the greatest surprise when several years afterwards I learned that conjugal difficulties in the Dickens household had led to estrangement and separation.' George Washington Putnam, who spent so many months travelling with them, admired how Catherine's mild temperament helped to smooth over much of the stress that her husband felt while travelling: 'She had a quiet dignity mingled with great sweetness of manner; her calm quietness differing much from the quick, earnest, always cheerful, but keen and nervous temperament of her husband.'

Catherine and Charles Dickens left Boston on the afternoon of 5 February 1842, for Hartford, Connecticut. They had been advised to stop on the way at Worcester, Massachusetts. As they travelled through New England, Charles was impressed by the 'delicate slopes of land, gently-swelling hills, wooded valleys, and slender streams'. Everything they saw was an exciting new adventure in a land so very different from the places they had grown up:

> Every little colony of houses has its church and school-house peeping from among the white roofs and shady trees; every house is the whitest of the white; every Venetian blind the greenest of the green; every fine day's sky the bluest of the blue. A sharp dry wind and a slight frost had so hardened the roads when we alighted at Worcester, that their furrowed tracks were like ridges of granite. There was the usual aspect of newness on every object, of course. All the buildings looked as if they had been built and painted that morning, and could be taken down on Monday with very little trouble.

In Worcester they attended church – although Dickens bemoaned the newness of the church and felt a homesick longing to see an old building with an ancient graveyard. One local churchgoer, a teacher named John Park, became furious at the large number of people in the congregation – people who had attended the service solely to see the English author. The people of Worcester flocked to get a glimpse of Dickens and, once again, he and Catherine were treated as celebrities. The governor of Massachusetts invited them to a grand and exclusive dinner at his home.

John Park was also invited to the dinner, but he and his wife declined, thinking it would be far too showy – then regretted their decision.

When Charles and Catherine were waiting to board their train to leave Worcester, Park was also at the station and he talked to the author. This brief chat changed Parks's opinion and he wrote, '[Dickens] appeared to me a frank, unassuming animated character – much at his ease, but far from supercilious.'

It was in Worcester that one of the early descriptions of Dickens by an American journalist appeared in print. It was published in the *Worcester Aegis* and described the author critically, with a damning final line:

> ...a middle sized person, in a brown frock coat, a red figured vest, somewhat of the flash order, and a fancy scarf cravat, that concealed the dickey, and was fastened to the bosom in rather voluminous folds by a double pin and chain.... His hair, which was long and dark, grew low upon the brow ... naturally or artificially corkscrewed as it fell on either side of his face.... His features, taken together, were well-proportioned, of glowing and cordial aspect, with more animation than grace and more intelligence than beauty.

Dickens wrote glowingly to Forster, 'The village of Worcester is one of the prettiest in New England.' When they left this 'prettiest' of villages, he and Catherine continued their journey by train, to Springfield. The plan had been to travel the final twenty-five miles to Hartford by road, but as it was winter the roads were impassable, so they travelled by boat, a journey which had been specially arranged for them, as Dickens recorded in *American Notes*:

> Fortunately, however, the winter having been unusually mild, the Connecticut River was 'open,' or, in other words, not frozen. The captain of a small steamboat was going to make his first trip for the season.... It certainly was not called a small steamboat without reason. I omitted to ask the question, but I should think it must have been of about half a pony power.... I am afraid to tell how many feet short this vessel was, or how many feet narrow: to apply

the words length and width to such measurement would be a contradiction in terms. But I may state that we all kept the middle of the deck, lest the boat should unexpectedly tip over; and that the machinery, by some surprising process of condensation, worked between it and the keel: the whole forming a warm sandwich, about three feet thick.

It rained all day as I once thought it never did rain anywhere, but in the Highlands of Scotland. The river was full of floating blocks of ice, which were constantly crunching and cracking under us… . Nevertheless, we moved onward, dexterously; and being well wrapped up, bade defiance to the weather, and enjoyed the journey. The Connecticut River is a fine stream; and the banks in summer-time are, I have no doubt, beautiful… .

After two hours and a half of this odd travelling (including a stoppage at a small town, where we were saluted by a gun considerably bigger than our own chimney), we reached Hartford, and straightway repaired to an extremely comfortable hotel: except, as usual, in the article of bedrooms, which, in almost every place we visited, were very conducive to early rising.

Dickens arrived in Hartford on his thirtieth birthday. That evening, 7 February 1842, he and Catherine attended a public banquet in their honour. Dickens had been invited to give a speech. Unlike his speech in Boston, in which he had called so movingly for eternal friendship between America and England, he used his birthday speech to call for an international copyright law.

He berated America and Americans for making money out of British writers without paying them royalties. He recalled the 1841 trip he and Catherine had taken to Scotland, when they had visited Abbotsford, the former home of Sir Walter Scott. Catherine had a personal connection to the author: her father, George Hogarth, had worked as his legal advisor, and Catherine's aunt was married to one of Scott's friends. Dickens had been very upset at discovering that Scott had worked himself into an early grave. In his speech, he claimed that Sir Walter Scott's death could be partially attributed to the author having been cheated by pirated American sales.

The American media reacted furiously. *The Hartford Times* reported pompously, 'It happens that we want no advice on this matter.' *The Boston Morning Post* admonished, 'You must drop that, Charlie, or you will be dished.'

In *American Notes*, Dickens made no comment about his controversial speech, writing simply: 'I shall always entertain a very pleasant and grateful recollection of Hartford. It is a lovely place, and I had many friends there, whom I can never remember with indifference.'

As Catherine had been feeling unwell, and was exhausted, they decided to change their plans and rest for a few days in Hartford, which Dickens described as 'beautifully situated in a basin of green hills'. His idea of a quiet time perhaps differed from that which Catherine had hoped for. In his *Life of Charles Dickens* John Forster recalled that Dickens wrote to him that in Hartford they held 'a formal levée every day for two hours, and receiving on each from two hundred to three hundred people.'

He also busied himself visiting as many local institutions as possible. He wrote in *American Notes*, 'I found the courts of law here, just the same as at Boston; the public institutions almost as good. The Insane Asylum is admirably conducted, and so is the Institution for the Deaf and Dumb.'

They left Hartford on the evening of Friday, 11 February 1842, travelling by train to New Haven. The journey took three hours, including an unexpected stop at Wallingford, where Dickens believed 'the whole town had turned out to see me.' They arrived in New Haven, 'a fine town ... with rows of grand old elm-trees', at around 8.00pm, and spent the night at its 'best inn'. As they were staying only one night, the townspeople were desperate to meet them. Dickens told Forster that he believed he and Catherine had shaken hands 'with considerably more than 500 people', including a cohort of students from Yale, between finishing eating dinner and being able to go to bed. Having finally managed to escape to their room, they were astounded to hear the sound of the college choir singing to them underneath their window.

Early the next morning, they boarded a steam packet to New York. Another reception committee was waiting to meet them on the deck of the boat. Dickens wrote in *American Notes*:

This was the first American steamboat of any size that I had seen; and certainly to an English eye it was infinitely less like a steamboat than a huge floating bath. I could hardly persuade myself, indeed, but that the bathing establishment off Westminster Bridge, which I left a baby, had suddenly grown to an enormous size; run away from home; and set up in foreign parts as a steamer.

They were very pleased to discover that one of their fellow passengers was Cornelius Felton. Dickens wrote, 'We drank all the porter on board, ate all the cold pork and cheese, and were very merry indeed.' Catherine and Charles marvelled over the names of places they passed – such as Hell Gate, the Hog's Back, and the Frying Pan – and they started to relax, as they awaited their first sight of New York City.

New York City: Dazzling Dresses and Wretched Poverty

*"'All men are alike in the U-nited States, an't they? It makes no odds whether a man has a thousand pound, or nothing, there. Particular in New York, I'm told, where Ned landed."
"New York, was it?" asked Martin, thoughtfully.
"Yes," said Bill. "New York. I know that, because he sent word home that it brought Old York to his mind, quite vivid, in consequence of being so exactly unlike it in every respect."'*

From *Martin Chuzzlewit*
(serialised 1842–1844)

'We ... emerged into a noble bay, whose waters sparkled in the now cloudless sunshine.... Then there lay stretched out before us, to the right, confused heaps of buildings, with here and there a spire or steeple, looking down upon the herd below; and here and there, again, a cloud of lazy smoke; and in the foreground a forest of ships' masts, cheery with flapping sails and waving flags. Crossing from among them to the opposite shore, were steam ferry-boats laden with people, coaches, horses, waggons, baskets, boxes: crossed and recrossed by other ferry-boats: all travelling to and fro: and never idle.... Beyond, were shining heights, and islands in the glancing river, and a distance scarcely less blue and bright than the sky it seemed to meet. The city's hum and buzz, the clinking of capstans, the ringing of bells, the barking of dogs, the clattering of wheels, tingled in the listening ear.'

New York City: Dazzling Dresses and Wretched Poverty

This was how Dickens described their entry into New York City in *American Notes*. Although he wrote that the city was 'beautiful', he went on immediately to compare New York unfavourably to Boston: it was not as clean as Boston, the houses weren't so freshly painted, the 'bricks not quite so red', the painted signs weren't painted as well nor as brightly, the brass nameplates and door knockers weren't so well polished, and he compared the less salubrious quarter, the Five Points, to the slums of central London.

Charles and Catherine stayed at the Carlton House Hotel on Broadway, from which they walked around the city. Although it was only February, it was unusually warm and Dickens was astounded by the heat of the sun. He was also impressed by the large number of omnibuses, compared to the main streets of London: 'Half-a-dozen have gone by within as many minutes. Plenty of hackney cabs and coaches too.' They were shocked at seeing so many black servants in livery, aware this was a sign of slavery, something neither Charles nor Catherine were fully prepared for before their visit. In *American Notes*, Dickens wrote angrily of 'Some southern republican that, who puts his blacks in uniform, and swells with Sultan pomp and power.'

In a letter to Forster written from Boston at the start of his time in America, Dickens had listed their proposed itinerary and included the words:

> When we reach Baltimore, we are in the regions of slavery. It exists there, in its least shocking and most mitigated form; but there it is. They whisper, here (they dare only whisper, you know, and that below their breaths), that on that place, and all through the South, there is a dull gloomy cloud on which the very word seems written. I shall be able to say, one of these days, that I accepted no public mark of respect in any place where slavery was; – and that's something.

In New York City, Putnam recorded that Dickens

> was constantly invited to visit the schools, the benevolent asylums, and the prisons in and around the metropolis; and he and Mrs. Dickens often had three or four engagements of an evening to social gatherings at the homes of the elite

of the city. Professor Felton was often with him, and some quiet evening walks about the metropolis were taken by the two, in which they doubtless visited some of the fashionable restaurants of the city;... . Washington Irving came very often ... [and] a great ball was given in honor of Mr. Dickens and lady, a full account of which was given in the paper.

While Dickens's fashion sense and love of colour had caused a stir in Boston, in New York City Dickens himself was dazzled by the colour and variety of clothing:

Heaven save the ladies, how they dress! We have seen more colours in these ten minutes, than we should have seen elsewhere, in as many days. What various parasols! what rainbow silks and satins! what pinking of thin stockings, and pinching of thin shoes, and fluttering of ribbons and silk tassels, and display of rich cloaks with gaudy hoods and linings!

Fashion and clothing always interested, and often amused, Dickens. From Switzerland, in 1846, he wrote to Daniel Maclise, 'The women, in their immense straw hats and gay dresses looked like parti-colored Mushrooms.'

The sensory attractions of New York were both inspirational and shocking. Charles and Catherine were surprised by the sight of pigs wandering along Broadway, and impressed by the variety of carriages: 'gigs, phaetons, large-wheeled tilburies, and private carriages – rather of a clumsy make ... but built for the heavy roads beyond the city pavement.' He observed the people with great interest, writing with affection about 'a child with laughing eyes' peeping out of a window to watch a dog on the street below, and perhaps a young Jacob Marley can be discerned in the Wall Street traders he observed:

Many a rapid fortune has been made in this street, and many a no less rapid ruin. Some of these very merchants whom you see hanging about here now, have locked up money in their strong-boxes, like the man in the Arabian Nights, and opening them again, have found but withered leaves.

New York City: Dazzling Dresses and Wretched Poverty

Hot, thirsty and back on Broadway, they were cheered by the sight of blocks of ice being carried into bars and by fresh pineapple and watermelon 'profusely displayed for sale' on the street; exotic fruits that were rare and expensive in England.

Passing into the Bowery, they noted that the people looked drabber, the shops looked poorer and the brightly coloured carriages had been exchanged for sturdy workhorses and carts. Here, Dickens wrote of seeing 'ready made' clothes and 'ready cooked' meat and of stalls selling 'Oysters in every style'. Having returned in the evening, he wrote nostalgically, 'They tempt the hungry most at night, for then dull candles glimmering inside, illuminate these dainty words, and make the mouths of idlers water, as they read and linger.' New York at night reminded him of London in many ways, but he missed the street performers of his home city, and wondered what New Yorkers did for entertainment.

One night he was escorted by police officers to be guided through the notoriously dangerously area known as Five Points:

> Poverty, wretchedness, and vice, are rife enough where we are going now… . Such lives as are led here, bear the same fruits here as elsewhere. The coarse and bloated faces at the doors, have counterparts at home, and all the wide world over. Debauchery has made the very houses prematurely old. See how the rotten beams are tumbling down, and how the patched and broken windows seem to scowl dimly, like eyes that have been hurt in drunken frays… . So far, nearly every house is a low tavern; and on the bar-room walls, are coloured prints of Washington, and Queen Victoria of England, and the American Eagle… . What place is this, to which the squalid street conducts us? A kind of square of leprous houses, some of which are attainable only by crazy wooden stairs without. What lies beyond this tottering flight of steps, that creak beneath our tread?—a miserable room, lighted by one dim candle, and destitute of all comfort, save that which may be hidden in a wretched bed … hideous tenements which take their name from robbery and murder: all that is loathsome, drooping, and decayed is here.

Dickens's scathing description of the living conditions in Five Points and the general neglect of the city's poorest people haunted New York for decades. It inspired other writers and artists to 'slum it' and visit the area, just as wealthy men in London liked to venture into the poorest, most dangerous parts of the East End, in an attempt to prove their manliness.

He also visited Five Points in the daytime, to visit its infamous prison, known as 'The Tombs'. It had been built just a few years earlier and the authorities were proud of its Egyptian Revival architecture, but Dickens wrote disparagingly of it as 'this dismal-fronted pile of bastard Egyptian, like an enchanter's palace in a melodrama!' He interviewed the 'man with keys' who showed him around. Dickens was appalled by the sight of the cells and by hearing how seldom the prisoners were allowed to exercise – if at all. When he commented that the cells at the bottom must be 'unwholeseome', the man's shocking response was, 'We *do* only put coloured people in 'em. That's the truth.'

Seeing the women's prison, in which children were also incarcerated, made Dickens even more sad. He reported in *American Notes* a transcript of his conversation with the prison guard, which begins with the author describing him as 'civil and obliging' and ends with the reader firmly convinced the man has no compassion at all. Dickens asks why the prisoners' clothes are scattered around the floors of their cells, surprised that they're not given hooks to hang them on to keep the cells tidy. The guard points to marks on the walls where hooks used to hang and states, 'When they had hooks they *would* hang themselves.'

Dickens wrote about the prison with fury in *American Notes*:

> What! do you thrust your common offenders against the police discipline of the town, into such holes as these? Do men and women, against whom no crime is proved, lie here all night in perfect darkness, surrounded by the noisome vapours which encircle that flagging lamp you light us with, and breathing this filthy and offensive stench! Why, such indecent and disgusting dungeons as these cells, would bring disgrace upon the most despotic empire in the world!

His words seem to weep as he writes about the high number of suicides and the prisoners who never glimpse nor smell fresh air for their entire incarceration. Dickens's readers had no knowledge of how intimately the author had known the inside of a prison, but every prison he visited was a heartbreaking reminder of his own family's incarceration – and, grim as their cell had been, they had lived in conditions kinder than those he was witnessing at The Tombs.

The journalist was always prevalent in Dickens, and whenever and wherever he travelled, he tried to visit institutions such as schools, hospitals, orphanages, baby farms, almshouses and workhouses, as well as prisons, making a note of the conditions and either praising or condemning them – most often the latter. He wrote in *American Notes* about his visit to 'Long Island, or Rhode Island: I forget which'. This was actually Blackwell's Island (now renamed Roosevelt Island) off Manhattan, where he visited a newly built asylum, known as the Octagon. Dickens wrote:

> The building is handsome; and is remarkable for a spacious and elegant staircase. The whole structure is not yet finished, but it is already one of considerable size and extent, and is capable of accommodating a very large number of patients.
>
> I cannot say that I derived much comfort from the inspection of this charity. The different wards might have been cleaner and better ordered; I saw nothing of that salutary system which had impressed me so favourably elsewhere; and everything had a lounging, listless, madhouse air, which was very painful.

There is an unwittingly poignant sentence in *American Notes*, the significance of which Dickens could not have known, but which, with hindsight, is very moving: 'In the suburbs there is a spacious cemetery: unfinished yet, but every day improving. The saddest tomb I saw there was "The Strangers" Grave. Dedicated to the different hotels in this city".' Seventy years after Charles and Catherine visited New York, their son Alfred, who was not yet born in 1842, would die in a New York hotel, a visiting stranger, with none of his family around him. He was visiting New York as part of a long lecture tour, at the age of 66. Alfred had migrated to Australia as a young man. By the time he arrived in New York, he was a widower, with two daughters who lived with him in Melbourne, and was currently serving as the president of the

Dickens and Travel: The Start of Modern Travel Writing

International Dickens Fellowship. In 1910, he had returned to Britain for the first time in forty-five years and at the end of the following year was in New York on his way back to Australia. He died at the Astor Hotel, on the afternoon of 2 January 1912.

His father's celebrity ensured that Alfred's coffin was not placed in the Strangers' Grave. His siblings in England were hastily contacted and they gave permission for him to be buried in the city. The funeral and burial of Alfred D'Orsay Tennyson Dickens (1845–1912) was kindly paid for by New Yorkers. Today, his grave can be visited in the Wall Street section of the Trinity Church Cemetery.

Although in *American Notes* Charles Dickens wrote scathingly about much that he saw in New York, he was an admirer of the city and he also wrote that allowances should be made for the fact that, as a big city, New York necessarily had a much higher number of people living in poverty than a smaller town would have done. It is apparent that he was trying to even the balance between his criticism and praise by writing lavishly, using adjectives such as 'meritous' and 'admirable' – even about places he hadn't visited but had heard good things about.

He heaped praise upon the city's three theatres, but was disappointed by how little they were attended. He thought New York's architecture 'elegant' and 'handsome' and the women 'singularly beautiful'. He also praised the countryside around the city as 'surpassingly and exquisitely picturesque' and wrote about the 'beautiful Bay'. His initial impressions of New York may have been less favourable than of Boston, but by the end of their visit he and Catherine were enjoying the differences in New York society from that in Boston, particularly the fact that the people of New York held 'later and more rakish hours'. He was less impressed, however, with the cost of his hotel in New York. The bill for two weeks, during which they had only eaten in the hotel once and consumed four bottles of wine, came to the equivalent of £70.

New Yorkers were very excited about Dickens travelling to their city and he was greeted with great hospitality. According to contemporary reports, Charles Tiffany commissioned a 'Dickens bust' for sale, which was displayed in the shop window on Broadway (although sadly neither the records nor a description survive in Tiffany & Co's archives).

New York City: Dazzling Dresses and Wretched Poverty

In common with all travellers, Catherine and Charles looked forward to receiving news from home. The late or occasionally non-arrival of post by ship was a regular fear of the nineteenth-century traveller. In the 1850s, the Paris correspondent for a number of British papers ranted about stormy weather preventing the arrival of the post:

> English residents to-day are excessively annoyed, – the English mail has, from bad weather in the Channel, not arrived, and they are consequently without letter or newspaper, or tidings whatever from England, and what is worse, the Post Office in answer to enquiries says that no mail will come in all day long! ... Ought not some alteration to be made in this respect? We are not at that season of the year in which the weather is often bad in the Channel; and really it is no slight thing for those of us who dwell in a foreign land to be an entire day without news from home.

In late February, Dickens wrote a despairing letter to Forster about the delay caused to the post from England, because of the late arrival of the Cunard ship. He was even tempted to return 'to Boston, alone, to be nearer news'. After a violent storm at sea, the ship had been badly damaged, and had 'returned disabled to Cork'. The passengers – and Dickens's much-longed-for post – were transferred to another ship to make the journey belatedly. It would arrive when the Dickenses had travelled on to Washington.

Philadelphia: Not Quite the Land of the Free

'We reached the city, late that night. Looking out of my chamber-window, before going to bed, I saw, on the opposite side of the way, a handsome building of white marble, which had a mournful ghost-like aspect, dreary to behold. I attributed this to the sombre influence of the night, and on rising in the morning looked out again, expecting to see its steps and portico thronged with groups of people passing in and out. The door was still tight shut, however; the same cold cheerless air prevailed: and the building looked as if the marble statue of Don Guzman could alone have any business to transact within its gloomy walls. I hastened to inquire its name and purpose, and then my surprise vanished. It was the Tomb of many fortunes; the Great Catacomb of investment; the memorable United States Bank.'

From *American Notes* (1842)

On 5 March 1842, Charles and Catherine took a train and two ferries from New York City to Philadelphia, a journey that 'usually occupies between five and six hours'. Their train carriage was next to 'the gentlemen's carriage', and they were bemused by the sight of what they took to be feathers being scattered to the winds by the carriage's occupants. Eventually they came to a more prosaic realisation: what they had thought were feathers were elongated globules of spit being projected at great speed through the open window.

Dickens's letters and travelogues are filled with witty observations about the people he met travelling: from those with whom he shared interesting conversations to those he feigned sleep to avoid. On this journey they met

> a mild and modest young quaker, who opened the discourse by informing me, in a grave whisper, that his grandfather was the inventor of cold-drawn castor oil. I ... [think] it probable that this is the first occasion on which the valuable medicine in question was ever used as a conversational aperient.

Catherine and Charles arrived in Philadelphia late at night and went straight to their hotel. As always, Charles wanted to walk around and discover everything the city had to show him, noting afterwards: 'It is a handsome city, but distractingly regular. After walking about it for an hour or two, I felt that I would have given the world for a crooked street.'

Putnam recorded with astonishment:

> A day or two after his arrival in Philadelphia an individual somewhat prominent in city politics came with others and obtained an introduction. On taking his leave, he asked Mr. Dickens if he would grant him the favor to receive a few personal friends the next day; and Mr. Dickens assented. The next morning it was announced through the papers that Mr. Dickens would 'receive the public' at a certain hour! At the time specified the street in front was crowded with people, and the offices and halls of the hotel filled. Mr. Dickens asked the cause of the assembling, and was astonished and indignant when he learned that all this came of his permission to the individual above mentioned to 'bring a few personal friends for an introduction,' and he positively refused to hold a 'levee'. But the landlord of the house and others came and represented to him that his refusal would doubtless create a riot, and that great injury would be done to the house by the enraged populace; and so at last Mr. Dickens consented, and, taking his place in one of the large parlors up stairs, prepared himself for the ordeal. Up the people came, and soon the humorous smiles played over his face, for, tedious and annoying as it was, the thing

had its comic side, and, while he shook hands incessantly, he as usual studied human character. For two mortal hours or more the crowd poured in, and he shook hands and exchanged words with all, while the dapper little author of the scene stood smiling by, giving hundreds and thousands of introductions, and making, no doubt, much social and political capital out of his supposed intimacy with the great English author. This scene is substantially repeated in *Martin Chuzzlewit*, when his new-made American friends insisted upon Martin's 'holding a levee'.

Charles and Catherine spent four days in Philadelphia, and of the many people they met, perhaps the most memorable, to a modern reader, was a young author who wrote to Dickens, enclosing several of his own stories and his review of *Barnaby Rudge*, asking if they could meet. On 6 March, Dickens replied 'I shall be very glad to see you.... I have glanced over the books you have been so kind as to send to me; and more particularly at the papers to which you called my attention.' They met at Dickens's hotel, the United States Hotel on Chestnut Street. There, the two men talked of writing, about the difficulties of finding a good publisher and of Dickens's pet raven, Grip, who had been immortalised in *Barnaby Rudge*, and by whom the American writer was fascinated.

Dickens explained that Grip had died as a consequence of pilfering: he had used his beak to prise off the lids of tins of lead paint, and then drank the paint. Dickens had been distraught at his raven's death, paying several vets to try and save him and faithfully writing down all the talking bird's 'last words'. After his death, Dickens paid a taxidermist to preserve him. Grip was then placed in a glass case and hung over the author's desk, so he could keep an eye on him as he wrote. (Dickens owned two subsequent ravens, both named Grip.) The American writer's name was Edgar Allan Poe. Three years after meeting Dickens, Poe published his narrative poem *The Raven*.

Poe died just a few years later, at the age of 40. Twenty-one years later, following Dickens's death, a fan of Poe purchased Grip in his glass case, at an auction of Dickens's household effects. Grip was then transported to Poe's native Philadelphia. Today, Grip can be visited in the Rare Books section of the Philadelphia Free Library.

Philadelphia: Not Quite the Land of the Free

Dickens summed up his impressions of Philadelphia in *American Notes*:

> My stay in Philadelphia was very short, but what I saw of its society, I greatly liked. Treating of its general characteristics, I should be disposed to say that it is more provincial than Boston or New York, and that there is afloat in the fair city, an assumption of taste and criticism.

He was, however, appalled by one of the institutions of which Philadelphia was most proud, its new, state-of-the-art prison, the Eastern Penitentiary. The name derives from the contemporary belief that a prison should be a place where prisoners became penitent. When it opened, in 1829, it was proud to call itself the most expensive prison in the world. It was also the first to come up with the system of solitary confinement. If his Philadelphian hosts had known about Dickens's own history, they might have realised he was not likely to be impressed. He was not. In *American Notes* he wrote forcefully:

> The system here, is rigid, strict, and hopeless solitary confinement. I believe it, in its effects, to be cruel and wrong.
>
> In its intention, I am well convinced that it is kind, humane, and meant for reformation; but I am persuaded that those who devised this system of Prison Discipline, and those benevolent gentlemen who carry it into execution, do not know what it is that they are doing. I believe that very few men are capable of estimating the immense amount of torture and agony which this dreadful punishment, prolonged for years, inflicts upon the sufferers.... I hold this slow and daily tampering with the mysteries of the brain, to be immeasurably worse than any torture of the body.... Standing at the central point, and looking down these dreary passages, the dull repose and quiet that prevails, is awful. Occasionally, there is a drowsy sound from some lone weaver's shuttle, or shoemaker's last, but it is stifled by the thick walls and heavy dungeon-door, and only serves to make the general stillness more profound. Over

the head and face of every prisoner who comes into this melancholy house, a black hood is drawn; and in this dark shroud, an emblem of the curtain dropped between him and the living world, he is led to the cell from which he never again comes forth, until his whole term of imprisonment has expired. He never hears of wife and children; home or friends; the life or death of any single creature. He sees the prison-officers, but with that exception he never looks upon a human countenance, or hears a human voice. He is a man buried alive; to be dug out in the slow round of years; and in the mean time dead to everything but torturing anxieties and horrible despair.

...In another cell, there was a German, sentenced to five years' imprisonment for larceny, two of which had just expired. ... a more dejected, heart-broken, wretched creature, it would be difficult to imagine. I never saw such a picture of forlorn affliction and distress of mind. My heart bled for him; and when the tears ran down his cheeks, and he took one of the visitors aside, to ask, with his trembling hands nervously clutching at his coat to detain him, whether there was no hope of his dismal sentence being commuted, the spectacle was really too painful to witness. I never saw or heard of any kind of misery that impressed me more than the wretchedness of this man... . Sitting upon the stairs, engaged in some slight work, was a pretty coloured boy. 'Is there no refuge for young criminals in Philadelphia, then?' said I. 'Yes, but only for white children.' Noble aristocracy in crime!

Amongst the many inmates Dickens met was a man working as a shoemaker. Seventeen years later, in *A Tale of Two Cities*, when Doctor Manette is released from his cell in the Bastille, he has been trained as a shoemaker.

Another aspect of American life which disgusted Dickens was spitting. He wrote to Forster:

spitting is universal. In the courts of law, the judge has his spittoon on the bench, the counsel have theirs, the witness has his, the prisoner his, and the crier his.... There are spit-boxes in every steamboat, bar-room, public dining-room, house of office, and place of general resort, no matter what it be. In the hospitals, the students are requested, by placard, to use the boxes provided for them, and not to spit upon the stairs. I have twice seen gentlemen, at evening parties in New York ... spit upon the drawing-room carpet. And in every bar-room and hotel passage the stone floor looks as if it were paved with open oysters – from the quantity of this kind of deposit which tessellates it all over...

Charles and Catherine Dickens left Philadelphia by steamboat – after an argument about their hotel bill, having been charged for food and drink on days they had been absent from the hotel. Dickens felt he had no choice but to pay, as otherwise the hotel landlord would write to the newspapers, accusing the English author of trying to cheat him. He was well aware that the American media was turning against him, and he knew from friends' letters that the controversy about his trip was in British newspapers too. Dickens vented his thoughts about the American press in *Martin Chuzzlewit*. When Martin arrives in New York City, his ears are assailed by the cries of newspaper sellers:

'Here's this morning's New York Sewer!' cried one. 'Here's this morning's New York Stabber! Here's the New York Family Spy! Here's the New York Private Listener! Here's the New York Peeper! Here's the New York Plunderer! Here's the New York Keyhole Reporter! Here's the New York Rowdy Journal! Here's all the New York papers!'

It was not only the newspapers about which Dickens was angry. Every day, he was seething about slavery and he and Catherine were becoming increasingly concerned about what they would witness during their travels in the 'land of the free'. Slavery had been outlawed in British territories for several years, but even before it had been outlawed, it had not usually been apparent. The majority of British-owned slaves had been held captive in far-off lands, so most British people – untravelled and carelessly ignorant of the realities of slavery – had enjoyed products produced by slave labour, while being sheltered from the brutalities of slavery in action. It had been removed from everyday life, something all too easy to ignore. In 1840s America, Charles and Catherine Dickens experienced its horrifying realities for the first time.

While they were travelling to Washington, DC, Dickens wrote to Forster, 'The scenes that are passing in Congress now, all tending to the separation of the States, fill one with such a deep disgust that I dislike the very name of Washington (meaning the place, not the man), and am repelled by the mere thought of approaching it.'

To Washington and Beyond: Magnificent Intentions

'One day it is hot summer, without a breath of air, the next, twenty degrees below freezing, with a wind blowing that cuts your skin like steel.'
Charles Dickens on
Washington, DC in 1842

On Charles and Catherine's journey to Washington, the train stopped in Baltimore, where people swarmed to find their carriage and pressed their faces against its windows. Putnam wrote that they could hear people discussing them quite openly, whilst staring at them, as though they were exotic animals in a cage. Dickens's chief memory of the occasion, however, was more depressing. He wrote with shame,

> We stopped to dine at Baltimore, and being now in Maryland, were waited on, for the first time, by slaves. The sensation of exacting any service from human creatures who are bought and sold, and being, for the time, a party as it were to their condition, is not an enviable one. The institution exists, perhaps, in its least repulsive and most mitigated form in such a town as this; but it is slavery; and though I was, with respect to it, an innocent man, its presence filled me with a sense of shame and self-reproach.

When they reached Washington, DC, they stayed in a small hotel, later to attain fame as the much grander Willard's Hotel, as patronised by Abraham Lincoln. Here, spitting was everywhere and Dickens nicknamed Washington 'the head-quarters of tobacco-tinctured saliva'.

He was disappointed with the city about which he had heard so much, calling it 'the City of Magnificent Intentions' – intentions which were not being fulfilled. He couldn't understand why anyone would live there unless they were obliged to:

> Take the worst parts of the City Road and Pentonville, or the straggling outskirts of Paris, where the houses are smallest... . Burn the whole down; build it up again in wood and plaster; widen it a little; throw in part of St. John's Wood; put green blinds outside all the private houses, with a red curtain and a white one in every window; plough up all the roads; plant a great deal of coarse turf in every place where it ought not to be; erect three handsome buildings in stone and marble, anywhere, but the more entirely out of everybody's way the better; call one the Post Office; one the Patent Office, and one the Treasury; make it scorching hot in the morning, and freezing cold in the afternoon, with an occasional tornado of wind and dust; leave a brick-field without the bricks, in all central places where a street may naturally be expected: and that's Washington.

The dignitaries in Washington, however, Dickens liked. On 10 March he was taken to the House of Representatives, where he met former president and elder statesman John Quincy Adams, who invited them to dinner two days later. On 15 March, Dickens was invited to the White House to meet John Tyler, the tenth US president; Washington Irving was also on the guest list. Dickens wrote to a friend in England, the journalist Albany Fonblanque, that Tyler told him he was 'astonished to see so young a man'. Dickens admitted he had been unable to pay him the same compliment in return as he was struck by how 'worn and anxious' the president looked, adding 'and well he might; being at war with everybody – but the expression of his face was mild and pleasant.'

Dickens wrote to Forster:

> I have the privilege of appearing on the floor of both Houses here, and go to them every day. They are very handsome and commodious. There is a great deal of bad speaking, but there are a great many very remarkable men, in the

> legislature: such as John Quincy Adams.... Adams is a fine old fellow – seventy-six years old, but with most surprising vigor, memory, readiness, and pluck...

On Dickens's frequent visits to the Senate and the House of Representatives he was infuriated both by political corruption and the plague of spat-out tobacco juice: 'I strongly recommend all strangers not to look at the floor; and if they happen to drop anything, though it be their purse, not to pick it up with an ungloved hand on any account.'

Catherine and Charles's initial plan had been to travel from Washington to Charleston, but a friend dissuaded them because 'The country, all the way from here, is nothing but a dismal swamp.... The weather is intensely hot there; the spring fever is coming on; and there is very little to see.' So from Washington, they left for Virginia. It was a brief foray into the slavery-ridden South, a journey which left them heartsick and miserable.

One reason that Putnam was so liked by his employers was because he was a fervent abolitionist. In *Four Months with Charles Dickens*, he wrote his own impressions of this journey to Virginia:

> At Fredericksburg we took the cars for Richmond. After travelling awhile we came to a very lonely and dismal-looking country. We passed plantations long ago deserted, the houses and barns rotting down, and the ground as barren of soil as a New England street. A gentleman told me that the vast pine barrens, stretching miles away, through which we were occasionally passing, were, years ago, the same as these barren fields; for only pines of the most meagre growth could grow on this slavery-cursed soil. I called the attention of Mr. Dickens to the sterility and ruin all around us, and he seemed astounded at the fact that this land was once fertile, the very 'garden of America!' Turning to his wife, he exclaimed 'Great God! Kate, just hear what Mr. P. says! These lands were once cultivated! And have been abandoned because worn out by slave labor!' At sight of this widespread desolation his already deep detestation of slavery became intensified.

In Richmond, they stayed at the newly built Exchange Hotel, a grand building in the fashionable Gothic Revival style. Charles and Catherine were invited to a dinner given in honour of 'Boz' and Dickens was taken on a tour of a tobacco factory where, wryly noted by Putnam, he was shown 'the happy slaves singing at their work'. Despite having previously praised the American people and their courteous manners, Dickens and Catherine were astounded by the rudeness they encountered from many people in Richmond. In a town where people were accustomed to forcing slaves to do whatever they ordered, perhaps it was not surprising that the visitors were also expected to do their bidding. After an exhausting few days of strangers calling constantly at the Dickenses' hotel, expecting to be received with great enthusiasm, Charles was told that he had greatly angered a group of uninvited guests. They had arrived unannounced, and were informed that he was unavailable. This, he was curtly informed, had offended 'three people of great fashion'. On the same night, Charles and Catherine went to bed early, knowing they had to be up at 4.00am. They were shocked to be woken by a slave, whose master had insisted that his peremptory letter had to be delivered right away and that if there was no reply at their hotel room, the slave was to keep hammering at the door and then wait for the answer. They were very happy to leave Richmond early the next morning. The small party of now even-more-fervent abolitionists changed their intended route, and travelled back up north, in order to escape from the misery of travelling amongst slaves and slave owners.

Dickens wrote passionately about slavery in *American Notes*:

> The town of Richmond. There are pretty villas and cheerful houses in its streets, and Nature smiles upon the country round; but jostling its handsome residences, like slavery itself going hand in hand with many lofty virtues, are deplorable tenements, fences unrepaired, walls crumbling into ruinous heaps. Hinting gloomily at things below the surface, these, and many other tokens of the same description, force themselves upon the notice, and are remembered with depressing influence, when livelier features are forgotten.
>
> To those who are happily unaccustomed to them, the countenances in the streets and labouring-places, too, are shocking... . But the darkness – not of skin, but mind – which meets the stranger's eye at every turn; the brutalizing and blotting out of all fairer characters traced by Nature's hand; immeasurably outdo his worst belief... .

> I went upon my way with a grateful heart that I was not doomed to live where slavery was, and had never had my senses blunted to its wrongs and horrors in a slave-rocked cradle.

Their new schedule saw them return to Washington, DC (Dickens noting that there were two police constables on board their steamboat 'in pursuit of runaway slaves'). From there, Dickens wrote sadly to Forster:

> Richmond is a prettily situated town, but, like other towns in slave districts (as the planters themselves admit), has an aspect of decay and gloom which to an unaccustomed eye is most distressing. In the black car (for they don't let them sit with the whites), on the railroad as we went there, were a mother and family, whom the steamer was conveying away, to sell; retaining the man (the husband and father, I mean) on his plantation. The children cried the whole way.... On the bridge at Richmond there is a notice against fast driving over it, as it is rotten and crazy: penalty – for whites, five dollars; for slaves, fifteen stripes. My heart is lightened as if a great load had been taken from it, when I think that we are turning our backs on this accursed and detested system. I really don't think I could have borne it any longer. It is all very well to say 'be silent on the subject'. They won't let you be silent. They will ask you what you think of it; and will expatiate on slavery as if it were one of the greatest blessings of mankind. 'It's not,' said a hard, bad-looking fellow to me the other day, 'it's not the interest of a man to use his slaves ill. It's damned nonsense that you hear in England.' – I told him quietly that it was not a man's interest to get drunk, or to steal, or to game, or to indulge in any other vice, but he did indulge in it for all that; that cruelty, and the abuse of irresponsible power, were two of the bad passions of human nature, with the gratification of which, considerations of interest or of ruin, had nothing whatever to do; and that, while every candid man must admit that even a slave might be happy enough with a good master, all human beings knew that bad masters, cruel masters, and

masters who disgraced the form they bore, were matters of experience and history, whose existence was as undisputed as that of slaves themselves. He was a little taken aback by this, and asked me if I believed in the Bible. 'Yes,' I said, 'but if any man could prove to me that it sanctioned slavery, I would place no further credence in it.' 'Well then,' he said, 'by God, sir, the niggers must be kept down, and the whites have put down the colored people wherever they have found them.' 'That's the whole question,' said I. 'Yes, and by God,' says he, 'the British had better not stand out on that point when Lord Ashburton comes over, for I never felt so warlike as I do now, – and that's a fact.' I was obliged to accept a public supper in this Richmond, and I saw plainly enough there that the hatred which these Southern States bear to us as a nation has been fanned up and revived again by this Creole business, and can scarcely be exaggerated.

They left Washington for Baltimore, where they stayed at Barnum's, which Dickens would later praise as their 'most comfortable' hotel in America. He was cautiously nice about Baltimore. He visited the prison and praised it as 'very good'. Before leaving Baltimore, Charles, Catherine and Anne went through their vast luggage and took out anything they would not need before Canada, so they could travel with greater ease.

From Baltimore they took a train as far as York, in Pennsylvania, from where they continued their journey in a 'four-horse coach' to Harrisburg. It seems that, even in their country's infancy, Americans liked their methods of transport to be bigger than any in Europe. On seeing the approach of what seemed to him to be a very large coach, Dickens was surprised to hear the coachman say that 'the *big* coach' would be needed. As Dickens commented, 'the vehicle which was too small for our purpose was something larger than two English heavy night coaches.' Soon, however, he and Catherine witnessed the sight of an approaching carriage 'like a corpulent giant, a kind of barge on wheels'.

The scenery on their journey was beautiful:

Our road wound through the pleasant valley of the Susquehanna; the river, dotted with innumerable green islands, lay upon our right; and on the left, a steep ascent, craggy with broken rock, and dark with pine trees. The mist, wreathing itself into a hundred fantastic shapes, moved solemnly upon the water; and the gloom of evening gave to all an air of mystery and silence.

Harrisburg made a bad first impression, because it was raining when they arrived. Dickens's opinion of a place was frequently affected by the weather: when somewhere new was sunny, generally, he liked it, and when it was gloomy, he often took against it. Their impression of Harrisburg improved, however, when they met the landlord of their hotel, whom Dickens described with great affection in *American Notes*. He also wrote one of his most poignant passages in his travelogue about this little town:

> I walked out, after breakfast the next morning, to look about me; and was duly shown a model prison on the solitary system, just erected, and as yet without an inmate; the trunk of an old tree to which Harris, the first settler here (afterwards buried under it), was tied by hostile Indians, with his funeral pile about him, when he was saved by the timely appearance of a friendly party on the opposite shore of the river.... I was very much interested in looking over a number of treaties made from time to time with the poor Indians, signed by the different chiefs at the period of their ratification, and preserved in the office of the Secretary to the Commonwealth. These signatures, traced of course by their own hands, are rough drawings of the creatures or weapons they were called after. Thus, the Great Turtle makes a crooked pen-and-ink outline of a great turtle; the Buffalo sketches a buffalo; the War Hatchet sets a rough image of that weapon for his mark....
>
> I could not but think – as I looked at these feeble and tremulous productions of hands which could draw the longest arrow to the head in a stout elk-horn bow, or split a bead or feather with a rifle-ball – of Crabbe's musings over the Parish Register, and the irregular scratches made with a pen, by men who would plough a lengthy furrow

straight from end to end. Nor could I help bestowing many sorrowful thoughts upon the simple warriors whose hands and hearts were set there, in all truth and honesty; and who only learned in course of time from white men how to break their faith, and quibble out of forms and bonds. I wonder, too, how many times the credulous Big Turtle, or trusting Little Hatchet, had put his mark to treaties which were falsely read to him; and had signed away, he knew not what, until it went and cast him loose upon the new possessors of the land.

They left Harrisburg on a dismally raining night on a canal boat to Pittsburgh. In *American Notes*, Dickens writes about being astonished at the sleeping accommodation – the men, him included, slept on hammocks, slung in rows with one above the other. He wrote that he was on the lowest 'shelf' (as he worded it, comparing the men sleeping in hammocks to books reposing on library shelves) and 'there was a very heavy gentleman above me, whom the slender cords seemed quite incapable of holding.' Having survived to the morning, despite being plagued all night by his fellow passengers spitting from their hammocks onto the deck below (a large number of whom managed to spit onto his coat, which was lying beside his hammock), Dickens was shocked by the morning's ablutions:

> The washing accommodations were primitive. There was a tin ladle chained to the deck, with which every gentleman who thought it necessary to cleanse himself (many were superior to this weakness), fished the dirty water out of the canal, and poured it into a tin basin, secured in like manner. There was also a jack-towel. And, hanging up before a little looking-glass in the bar, in the immediate vicinity of the bread and cheese and biscuits, were a public comb and hair-brush.

One of the waiters then transformed himself into a barber and shaved any of the men who asked for it. The food on board was, according to Dickens, identical at every meal: 'tea, coffee, bread, butter, salmon, shad, liver, steak, potatoes, pickles, ham, chops, black-puddings, and sausages'.

In his book, Putnam related that, once the captain realised he had a celebrity on board, he gave his own cabin to Charles and Catherine. Putnam was pleased to see how much this new mode of travel pleased the English visitors, writing that the couple 'sat for hours' in two chairs on the little deck space in front of their cabin,

> greatly enjoying the absolute stillness of the scene... . Excepting when out upon the tow-path for exercise, Mr. Dickens spent most of his time while on the canal in this sheltered nook at the bow of the boat, sitting by the side of his wife, reading or conversing. The country through which we were passing was now exceedingly picturesque. The log-cabins of the settlers in that almost untrodden region, the little groups of houses which constituted the 'towns,' the homes of the 'lock-tenders,' and everything around us, was so unlike anything in the old country that our travellers were never weary. Each turn in the canal brought out new combinations of scenery; and when night came on, and the moon rose over the mountains, the prospect became still more charming and novel.

Dickens the dandy was also gratified by the keen attention paid to his clothing, especially his coat, by a fellow passenger who questioned him about it at length.

Their journey was broken to dine at an unnamed hotel, where Putnam was scathing about the food: a tiny quantity of veal and bread and butter. Their small party was amongst the first to arrive and managed to get a small portion for themselves, but those who disembarked later were offered only a dubious sounding 'pot pie' which the landlord tried valiantly to foist upon all arrivals. Putnam described it as 'a mass of bacon-rinds, pork-scraps, bits of gristle, and potatoes, and such odds and ends as usually go into the waste-tub, and which had probably been accumulating for several weeks.'

Dickens was transfixed by the beauty they passed. At night, under a sky of deep blue, studded with vivid stars, they saw the figures of men huddled around camp fires, with no sounds to be heard except the noise of the water as their boat glided along. During the day they were fascinated by the sight of new settlements being built, log cabins 'and lodgings for the pigs nearly as good as many of the human quarters', although Dickens mourned the changes that new settlements were making on the landscape. This was a land full of new settlers, new ideas and new technological advances. Dickens described in detail a hair-raising travelling experience:

> On Sunday morning we arrived at the foot of the mountain, which is crossed by railroad. There are ten inclined planes; five ascending, and five descending; the carriages are dragged up the former, and let slowly down the latter, by means of stationary engines; the comparatively level spaces between, being traversed, sometimes by horse, and sometimes by engine power, as the case demands. Occasionally the rails are laid upon the extreme verge of a giddy precipice; and looking from the carriage window, the traveller gazes sheer down, without a stone or scrap of fence between, into the mountain depths below.
>
> It was very pretty travelling thus, at a rapid pace along the heights of the mountain in a keen wind, to look down into a valley full of light and softness; catching glimpses, through the tree-tops, of scattered cabins; children running to the doors; dogs bursting out to bark, whom we could see without hearing: terrified pigs scampering homewards; families sitting out in their rude gardens; cows gazing upward with a stupid indifference; men in their shirt-sleeves looking on at their unfinished houses, planning out to-morrow's work; and we riding onward, high above them, like a whirlwind.

The following evening they arrived at Pittsburgh – or, to use Dickens's and Putnam's spelling, Pittsburg[8]. Charles, Catherine, Anne and Putnam spent three days there. By this time the group had settled into a symbiotic travelling regime. It's difficult to find out much about servants in Victorian England, as, so often, they are ignored by historians and contemporary commentators, even Anne Brown, who lived with the Dickens family for years, and was so invaluable that the whole family

---

8. The spelling of city's name has a long history of being changed between Pittsburgh and Pittsburg.

mourned when she left to get married. Putnam, however, wrote a brief description of Anne in his recollections:

> Ann [*sic*] – a warm-hearted English girl, – I believe London born and bred, – and devotedly attached to the family. Ann had many cockney notions, and it was pleasant to hear her comical expressions of surprise at our American words and ways. She had got a very strong impression of the wildness of our country, especially the West, which Mr. Dickens intended to visit, and anticipated no small danger from the Indians.

Dickens had heard Pittsburgh likened to Birmingham in England, but he struggled to see similarities. He wrote in *American Notes*, 'It is very beautifully situated on the Alleghany River, over which there are two bridges; and the villas of the wealthier citizens sprinkled about the high grounds in the neighbourhood, are pretty enough. We lodged at a most excellent hotel, and were admirably served.'

The travelling party left on 1 April 1868, on board the steamboat *Messenger*, bound for Cincinnati. The following day was Catherine and Charles's sixth wedding anniversary – and as they were on their temporary floating home, it was unlike any they had celebrated before. Once again, Dickens was amazed by how different travelling was in the USA compared to Britain:

> these western vessels are still more foreign to all the ideas we are accustomed to entertain of boats. I hardly know what to liken them to, or how to describe them.... In all modes of travelling, the American customs, with reference to the means of personal cleanliness and wholesome ablution, are extremely negligent and filthy.

He was also unimpressed by the food, something that was always a major consideration in his travel plans, and it was especially important on this journey, as they spent three days on board:

> There are three meals a day. Breakfast at seven, dinner at half-past twelve, supper about six. At each, there are a great

many small dishes and plates upon the table, with very little in them; so that although there is every appearance of a mighty 'spread,' there is seldom really more than a joint: except for those who fancy slices of beet-root, shreds of dried beef, complicated entanglements of yellow pickle; maize, Indian corn, apple-sauce, and pumpkin.

The food aside, the author found his imagination captivated by the Ohio River, but this also brought feelings of great sadness. He wrote of 'one's feelings of compassion for the extinct tribes who lived so pleasantly here, in their blessed ignorance of white existence, hundreds of years ago.' Perhaps these feelings explain why Dickens wrote so scathingly about many of his fellow passengers, especially the men. He was also angered by the sight of so many trees being burned to make way for more new homes:

The night is dark, and we proceed within the shadow of the wooded bank, which makes it darker. After gliding past the sombre maze of boughs for a long time, we come upon an open space where the tall trees are burning. The shape of every branch and twig is expressed in a deep red glow, and as the light wind stirs and ruffles it, they seem to vegetate in fire. It is such a sight as we read of in legends of enchanted forests: saving that it is sad to see these noble works wasting away so awfully, alone; and to think how many years must come and go before the magic that created them will rear their like upon this ground again.

In Cincinnati, Dickens's spirits rose: 'a beautiful city; cheerful, thriving and animated ... with its clean houses of red and white, its well-paved roads, and footways of bright tile.' One thing that impressed him most in Cincinnati was the free education offered to all children. Education was a subject always close to his heart and both he and Catherine ensured that their daughters received just as good an education as their sons. They witnessed several thousand men taking part in a Temperance march, complete with bands of musicians and a large number of Irish workers, carrying banners. The march was marshalled by mounted police escorts, who Dickens thought looked just as cheery as the marchers, because their horses were garlanded with brightly coloured ribbons. He admired the Irishmen for their spirit of adventure and independence at having moved halfway across the world to start a new life.

Ironically, given his strongly expressed opinion on the burning of native woods to make homes for the settlers, Dickens ended his glowing account of Cincinnati with the following words:

> The society with which I mingled, was intelligent, courteous, and agreeable. The inhabitants of Cincinnati are proud of their city as one of the most interesting in America: and with good reason: for beautiful and thriving as it is now, and containing, as it does, a population of fifty thousand souls, but two-and-fifty years have passed away since the ground on which it stands (bought at that time for a few dollars) was a wild wood, and its citizens were but a handful of dwellers in scattered log huts upon the river's shore.

The Dickens party left Cincinnati for Louisville in Kentucky, on a mail-carrying steamboat. On board they met a Native American chief. The meeting left a great impression on Dickens, which he recorded in *American Notes*:

> There chanced to be on board this boat, in addition to the usual dreary crowd of passengers, one Pitchlynn, a chief of the Choctaw tribe of Indians, who sent in his card to me, and with whom I had the pleasure of a long conversation.
>
> He spoke English perfectly well, though he had not begun to learn the language, he told me, until he was a young man grown. He had read many books; and Scott's poetry appeared to have left a strong impression on his mind: especially the opening of *The Lady of the Lake*, and the great battle scene in *Marmion*, in which, no doubt from the congeniality of the subjects to his own pursuits and tastes, he had great interest and delight. He appeared to understand correctly all he had read; and whatever fiction had enlisted his sympathy in its belief, had done so

keenly and earnestly. I might almost say fiercely. He was dressed in our ordinary everyday costume, which hung about his fine figure loosely, and with indifferent grace. On my telling him that I regretted not to see him in his own attire, he threw up his right arm, for a moment, as though he were brandishing some heavy weapon, and answered, as he let it fall again, that his race were losing many things besides their dress, and would soon be seen upon the earth no more: but he wore it at home, he added proudly.

He told me that he had been away from his home, west of the Mississippi, seventeen months: and was now returning. He had been chiefly at Washington on some negotiations pending between his Tribe and the Government: which were not settled yet (he said in a melancholy way), and he feared never would be: for what could a few poor Indians do, against such well-skilled men of business as the whites?... I asked him what he thought of Congress? He answered, with a smile, that it wanted dignity, in an Indian's eyes.

He would very much like, he said, to see England before he died; and spoke with much interest about the great things to be seen there. When I told him of that chamber in the British Museum wherein are preserved household memorials of a race that ceased to be, thousands of years ago, he was very attentive, and it was not hard to see that he had a reference in his mind to the gradual fading away of his own people... .

He was a remarkably handsome man; some years past forty, I should judge; with long black hair, an aquiline nose, broad cheek-bones, a sunburnt complexion, and a very bright, keen, dark, and piercing eye. There were but twenty thousand of the Choctaws left, he said, and their number was decreasing every day. A few of his brother chiefs had been obliged to become civilised, and to make themselves acquainted with what the whites knew, for it was their only chance of existence. But they were not many; and the rest were as they always had been. He dwelt on this: and said several times that unless they tried to assimilate themselves to their conquerors, they must be swept away before the strides of civilised society.

When we shook hands at parting, I told him he must come to England, as he longed to see the land so much: that I should hope to see him there, one day: and that I could promise him he would be well received and kindly treated. He was evidently pleased by this assurance, though he rejoined with a good-humoured smile and an arch shake of his head, that the English used to be very fond of the Red Men when they wanted their help, but had not cared much for them, since.

He took his leave; as stately and complete a gentleman of Nature's making, as ever I beheld; and moved among the people in the boat, another kind of being. He sent me a lithographed portrait of himself soon afterwards; very like, though scarcely handsome enough; which I have carefully preserved in memory of our brief acquaintance.

They spent only one night in Louisville, where they stayed in the Galt House, a splendid hotel. They were unimpressed by the city, of which Dickens made the wry comment,

> The interval, after breakfast, we devoted to riding through the town, which is regular and cheerful: the streets being laid out at right angles, and planted with young trees. The buildings are smoky and blackened, from the use of bituminous coal, but an Englishman is well used to that appearance, and indisposed to quarrel with it.

They left Louisville later that day, on the steamboat *Fulton*. On their way to join the boat, they passed a magistrate's office, an appellation Dickens put in inverted commas in his book, claiming it resembled a dame school: 'It was a perfect picture of justice retired from business for want of customers; her sword and scales sold off; napping comfortably with her legs upon the table.'

On this steamboat journey they met another noteworthy character. A 'Kentucky Giant' – 7'8" tall – named Porter. Aside from Porter,

Dickens and Travel: The Start of Modern Travel Writing

Dickens was as disgusted by his fellow passengers as he had been on their previous steamboat journeys:

> There was a magnetism of dulness [sic] in them which would have beaten down the most facetious companion that the earth ever knew.... Such deadly, leaden people; such systematic plodding, weary, insupportable heaviness.... Nor was the scenery, as we approached the junction of the Ohio and Mississippi rivers, at all inspiring.... The trees were stunted in their growth; the banks were low and flat.... No songs of birds were in the air, no pleasant scents, no moving lights and shadows from swift passing clouds. Hour after hour, the changeless glare of the hot, unwinking sky, shone upon the same monotonous objects. Hour after hour, the river rolled along, as wearily and slowly as the time itself.

On their third day of travelling they stopped at a place of which Dickens had heard much, but about which he was merciless:

> a spot so much more desolate than any we had yet beheld, that the forlornest places we had passed, were, in comparison with it, full of interest. At the junction of the two rivers, on ground so flat and low and marshy, that at certain seasons of the year it is inundated to the house-tops, lies a breeding-place of fever, ague, and death; vaunted in England as a mine of Golden Hope, and speculated in, on the faith of monstrous representations, to many people's ruin. A dismal swamp, on which the half-built houses rot away ... and teeming ... with rank unwholesome vegetation, in whose baleful shade the wretched wanderers who are tempted hither, droop, and die, and lay their bones; the hateful Mississippi circling and eddying before it, and turning off upon its southern course a slimy monster hideous to behold; a hotbed of disease, an ugly sepulchre, a grave uncheered by any gleam of promise: a place without one single quality, in earth or air or water, to commend it: such is this dismal Cairo.

After his return to England, Dickens would parody Cairo, Illinois, in *Martin Chuzzlewit*, as the sarcastically named Eden, the place to where the younger Martin Chuzzlewit and his friend Mark Tapley travel in order to seek their fortunes – instead, both catch malaria.

Dickens also offended American readers of his travelogue by his uncomplimentary comments about the Mississippi: 'an enormous ditch ... running liquid mud'. He was aghast at being expected to drink 'the muddy water of this river while we were upon it'. One thing he did praise, however, was the gorgeous sunsets 'tingeing the firmament deeply with red and gold'.

The boat arrived at St Louis on their fourth night and Dickens told the sweet story of a young woman on board, who had been in New York caring for her mother for a year, and was travelling with her baby. She had gone to New York a couple of months after her marriage when newly pregnant, and her baby had been born while she was away. All through the journey the woman was in a state of nervous agitation, in case her husband hadn't received her letter and might not be at the wharf to greet them and meet his child for the first time. The entire population of the boat was on tenterhooks with her, and rejoiced when a 'fine, good-looking, sturdy young fellow' appeared on deck and embraced her.

In St Louis, the Dickens party stayed at the Planter's House Hotel which Dickens described as 'built like an English hospital, with long passages and bare walls, and skylights above the room-doors for free circulation of air.... . It is an excellent house.... . Dining alone with my wife in our room, one day, I counted fourteen dishes on the table at once.' He was intrigued by St Louis and its French quarter and was keen to see the local area. So, leaving Catherine and Anne in St Louis, Dickens and Putnam joined an expedition of fourteen men on a trip to the Looking-Glass Prairie. Dickens described the collections of vehicles in which they travelled:

> one light carriage, with a very stout axletree; one something on wheels like an amateur carrier's cart; one double phaeton of great antiquity and unearthly construction; one gig with a great hole in its back and a broken head; and one rider on horseback who was to go on before. I got into the first coach with three companions; the rest bestowed themselves in the other vehicles; two large baskets were made fast to

the lightest; two large stone jars in wicker cases, technically known as demi-johns, were consigned to the 'least rowdy' of the party for safe-keeping; and the procession moved off to the ferryboat, in which it was to cross the river bodily, men, horses, carriages, and all, as the manner in these parts is... . We got over the river in due course ... and began to make our way through an ill-favoured Black Hollow, called, less expressively, the American Bottom.

They spent the night at a 'log-tavern on the edge of the prairie', returning to St Louis in the morning. In St Louis, as with most places they visited in North America, the Dickenses were greeted with great friendship, but it was in St Louis that Dickens finally lost his temper about slavery. Putnam wrote:

> One day a well-known literary gentleman called and was cordially received by Mr. Dickens. After conversing for some time he began to speak of the condition of society in America, and at last in a most bland and conciliating manner asked: 'Mr. Dickens, how do you like our domestic institution, sir?' 'Like what, sir?' said Mr. Dickens, rousing up and looking sharply at his visitor. 'Our domestic institution, sir, slavery!' said the gentleman. Dickens's eyes blazed as he answered promptly, 'Not at all, sir! I don't like it at all, sir!' 'Ah!' said his visitor, considerably abashed by the prompt and manly answer he had received, 'you probably have not seen it in its true character, and are prejudiced against it.' 'Yes, sir!' was the answer, 'I have seen it, sir! all I ever wish to see of it, and I detest it, sir!'
>
> The gentleman looked mortified, abashed, and offended, and, taking his hat, bade Mr. Dickens 'Good morning' which greeting was returned with promptness, and he left the room. Mr. Dickens then, in a towering passion, turned to me. 'Damn their impudence, Mr. P.! If they will not thrust their accursed "domestic institution" in my face, I will not attack it, for I did not come here for that purpose. But to tell me that a man is better off as a slave than as a freeman is an insult, and I will not endure it from any one! I will not bear it!'

To Washington and Beyond: Magnificent Intentions

Dickens had researched the USA carefully and something he was very keen to do was to 'strike the lakes', so they left St Louis for 'an old French village on the river, called Carondelet, and nicknamed Vide Poche', where they found almost nothing open, but were able to get a breakfast of 'ham and coffee' at a little tavern, which Dickens fancied had once been a Catholic chapel. The landlord talked to them about his time as a soldier, and expressed a desire to head to Texas and join the fighting. Dickens obviously liked him and his 'kind-hearted' wife, although he recorded wittily in *American Notes* that the man 'had seen all kinds of service, – except a battle.'

From St Louis, they returned to Cincinnati, from where they travelled to Columbus on a crowded stagecoach. Dickens took his 'favourite seat', up on the box with the driver, so he could see the landscape from the best vantage point. Putnam, who sat inside beside Catherine, was mortified by the behaviour of a fellow passenger, who continually 'poured out a rain of tobacco-spittle' which even Catherine's thick veil was unable to save her from.

At Carondelet, they boarded the steamboat *Messenger* on which, once again, they stopped at Cairo, Illinois:

> we came again in sight of the detestable morass called Cairo; and stopping there to take in wood, lay alongside a barge, whose starting timbers scarcely held together, ... on its side was painted 'Coffee House;' that being, I suppose, the floating paradise to which the people fly for shelter when they lose their houses for a month or two beneath the hideous waters of the Mississippi.

They disembarked at Louisville, spending the night at its 'excellent hotel', before joining the mailboat *Ben Franklin* to journey once again to Cincinnati, where they spent one night. Then they took a mail coach and a succession of stagecoaches to the little town of Sandusky. Charles and Catherine were relieved to find that the first part of their journey – 120 miles to Columbus – was tarmacked. Dickens wrote of the pleasure of being able to travel at the speed of six miles an hour on such a modern road and of his impressions of the countryside:

> Our way lies through a beautiful country, richly cultivated, and luxuriant in its promise of an abundant harvest.

> Sometimes we pass a field where the strong bristling stalks of Indian corn look like a crop of walking-sticks, and sometimes an enclosure where the green wheat is springing up among a labyrinth of stumps; the primitive worm-fence is universal, and an ugly thing it is; but the farms are neatly kept, and, save for these differences, one might be travelling just now in Kent.
>
> We often stop to water at a roadside inn, which is always dull and silent. The coachman dismounts and fills his bucket, and holds it to the horses' heads. There is scarcely ever any one to help him; there are seldom any loungers standing round; and never any stable-company with jokes to crack.

The journey was less agreeable, however, when it came to stopping for lunch – at a place Dickens disdains even to name:

> [The hotel has] nothing to drink but tea and coffee. As they are both very bad and the water is worse, I ask for brandy; but it is a Temperance Hotel, and spirits are not to be had for love or money. This preposterous forcing of unpleasant drinks down the reluctant throats of travellers is not at all uncommon in America.

Having changed coaches, they journeyed on until stopping for dinner, where they were surprised to be eating with a Welsh schoolteacher and his family, and then left in another coach. This pattern of spending several hours on a stagecoach, eating at an unimpressive coaching inn or hotel, then clambering onto yet another coach was continued for two days, until, on the evening of the second day, they arrived at Columbus, about which Dickens was very complimentary. Having rested for a night in a hotel, they hired a private carriage, together with an 'agent' who would ease them through all the necessary changes of horses and drivers – and who, to their great delight, arrived equipped with a handsome hamper of food and wine. Despite this propitious beginning, the journey was stressful and frightening:

> At one time we were all flung together in a heap at the bottom of the coach, and at another we were crushing our

heads against the roof. Now, one side was down deep in the mire, and we were holding on to the other.... The very slightest of the jolts with which the ponderous carriage fell from log to log, was enough, it seemed, to have dislocated all the bones in the human body. It would be impossible to experience a similar set of sensations, in any other circumstances, unless perhaps in attempting to go up to the top of St. Paul's in an omnibus. Never, never once, that day, was the coach in any position, attitude, or kind of motion to which we are accustomed in coaches.

Their only consolations were that the constant joltings meant it would have been impossible for the driver to fall asleep (a common danger on stagecoach journeys) and that the state of the roads meant their horses were unable to run, let alone bolt.

The change in temperature as they journeyed towards Sandusky and their much-anticipated destination, Niagara, was rapid. Dickens joked that they had left summer behind them and were 'fast leaving Spring'. Late at night they arrived at 'an Indian village', Upper Sandusky, where they stayed the night in a 'ghostly' inn. Dickens wrote about the sale of alcohol being prohibited in 'Indian settlements' and wrote sadly in a letter to John Forster:

> There was an old gentleman in the log inn at Lower Sandusky who treats with the Indians on the part of the American government, and has just concluded a treaty with the Wyandot Indians at that place to remove next year to some land provided for them west of the Mississippi, a little way beyond St. Louis. He described his negotiation to me, and their reluctance to go, exceedingly well. They are a fine people, but degraded and broken down.

The party left Upper Sandusky after an early breakfast, and travelled by coach to the town of Tiffin, and the expected joys of a railway, which proved to be 'very slow, its construction being indifferent, and the ground wet and marshy'. They travelled all afternoon, arriving in Sandusky on the shores of Lake Erie, in the evening. This was the beginning of Dickens's much-anticipated adventure on the lakes and he was restless at first, frustrated there were no steamboats until the following day. They dined at their hotel, where Charles and Catherine were disconcerted by one of the waitresses who brought their food, then sat in the most comfortable chair in the room and watched them eat, all the while picking food out of her teeth with the aid of a large pin, until their plates were ready to be cleared away.

After a frustrating twenty-four hours in the 'sluggish and uninteresting' Sandusky, Charles and Catherine, Anne and Putnam boarded the steamboat *Constitution*, 'a large vessel of five hundred tons, and handsomely fitted up, though with high-pressure engines'. This took them across Lake Erie. They reached Cleveland in the first minutes of Monday 25 April. Dickens and Putnam left the boat, which had docked overnight, to walk around the town. Despite it being just after midnight, Charles was an object of great interest and he was disconcerted to find so many people staring at him – either openly, on the street, or from their windows. It seems everyone knew there was a celebrity in town. According to the university archives, after the two men had returned to their cabins, the local mayor, Joshua Mills, boarded the boat in an attempt to meet Dickens, who refused unsurprisingly, considering it was, by then, the middle of the night. Allegedly, the mayor spent all night on the pier, but the boat left at 9.00am without him being able to meet the author.

On this boat journey – from Sandusky to Cleveland, Erie and Buffalo – Dickens was shown just how intrusive fame could be. He wrote in *American Notes*:

> There was a gentleman on board, to whom, as I unintentionally learned through the thin partition which divided our state-room from the cabin in which he and his wife conversed together, I was unwittingly the occasion of very great uneasiness. I don't know why or wherefore, but I appeared to run in his mind perpetually, and to dissatisfy him very much. First of all I heard him say: and the most ludicrous part of the business was, that he said it in my very ear, and could not have communicated more directly with me, if he had leaned upon my shoulder, and whispered me: 'Boz is on board still, my dear.' After a considerable pause, he added, complainingly, 'Boz keeps himself very close;'

which was true enough, for I was not very well, and was lying down, with a book. I thought he had done with me after this, but I was deceived; for a long interval having elapsed, during which I imagine him to have been turning restlessly from side to side, and trying to go to sleep; he broke out again, with 'I suppose that Boz will be writing a book by-and-by, and putting all our names in it!' at which imaginary consequence of being on board a boat with Boz, he groaned, and became silent.

They finally arrived in Buffalo, landing almost with the dawn, but spent only a couple of hours there, enough time for a good breakfast, as Dickens was so desperate to get on the train to Niagara:

It was a miserable day; chilly and raw; a damp mist falling; and the trees in that northern region quite bare and wintry. Whenever the train halted, I listened for the roar; and was constantly straining my eyes in the direction where I knew the Falls must be, from seeing the river rolling on towards them; every moment expecting to behold the spray. Within a few minutes of our stopping, not before, I saw two great white clouds rising up slowly and majestically from the depths of the earth. That was all. At length we alighted: and then for the first time, I heard the mighty rush of water, and felt the ground tremble underneath my feet.

He found Niagara a place of peacefulness, 'stamped upon my heart, an Image of Beauty'. He revelled in the chance to walk in solitude and to avoid meeting people, enraptured by the sight and sound of the Falls:

Oh, how the strife and trouble of daily life receded from my view, and lessened in the distance, during the ten memorable days we passed on that Enchanted Ground! What voices spoke from out the thundering water; ... I never stirred in all that time from the Canadian side, whither I had gone at first. I never crossed the river again; for I knew there were people on the other shore, and in such a place it is natural to shun strange company"

It is interesting to read *American Notes* and Dickens's letters from the time and to see his comments about Canada being 'British'. Once in Canada, he felt at home and seems to have realised that he had been quite homesick in the USA. They had actually spent a few hours in Canada before the USA, as their ship from Liverpool had docked briefly in Halifax before Boston. Both Charles and Catherine had suffered from terrible seasickness for most of the voyage. By the time they reached Halifax, Charles was feeling much better, but Catherine was still laid up, feeling dreadful. Dickens, however, was so rejuvenated that he left the ship, in the company of the ship's doctor, in order to feast on the famous local oysters – an idea that Catherine, in her queasiness, must have found stomach-churning. Charles was amazed to discover the great excitement amongst the local people that he was on board the ship. A local dignitary had sent his carriage, in the hopes that he could persuade Mr and Mrs Dickens to come and spend the day with him. Dickens was given a whistlestop tour of Halifax, including a visit to the home of the governor general and the houses of parliament. He ate and drank extremely well and was thrilled by his unexpected reception from the people of Halifax. He had written to Forster about the experience, using his nickname of 'The Inimitable':

> I wish you could have seen the crowds cheering the inimitable in the streets. I wish you could have seen the judges, law-officers, bishops, and law-makers welcoming the inimitable. I wish you could have seen the inimitable shown to a great elbow-chair by the Speaker's throne, and sitting alone in the middle of the floor of the house of commons."

Those few hours in Halifax had given Dickens a very favourable impression of Canada and the Canadians and now he was eager to discover more about the country. Their stay in Niagara also gave him time to work on a scheme he had been planning for some while: the chance for him and Catherine to perform onstage in Montreal, with a military theatrical society, The Garrison Amateurs. This occupied much of his concentration for their journey across Canada.

On 29 April 1842, Dickens wrote to Cornelius Felton about Niagara,

> To say anything about this wonderful place would be sheer nonsense. It far exceeds my most sanguine expectations,

though the impression on my mind has been, from the first, nothing by beauty and peace. I haven't drunk the water. Bearing in mind your caution, I have devoted myself to beer... . What do you say to my acting at the Montreal Theatre? ... We shall have a good house, they say. I am going to enact one Mr. Snobbington in a funny farce called A Good Night's Rest. I shall want a flaxen wig and eyebrows; and my nightly rest is broken by visions of there being no such commodities in Canada.

Charles, Catherine and Anne Brown left Niagara from Queenston. They arrived in Toronto after crossing Lake Ontario in a steamboat and arriving in Kingston. At the time of their visit, Kingston was still recovering from an enormous fire – caused by an explosion in a gunpowder warehouse – the previous year. Dickens described it in *American Notes*, 'one half of it appears to be burnt down, and the other half not to be built up.' Leaving Kingston, they headed for the centre of Toronto, where they stayed at Daley's Hotel[9], on the corner of Clarence Street and King Street. Dickens liked Toronto, but was shocked by the right-wing political feeling in the city, which he described as 'wild and rapid Toryism'. He was, however, very touched by the kindness of Canadians. He wrote to John Forster:

English [i.e. Canadian] kindness is very different from American. People send their horses and carriages for your use, but they don't exact as payment the right of being always under your nose. We had no less than *five* carriages at Kingston waiting our pleasure at one time; not to mention the commodore's barge and crew.

Dickens visited all the sights, including Fort Henry and the new Rideau Canal Waterway.

They travelled by steamboat along the St Lawrence River to Montreal, which they reached on 11 May 1842. There they stayed for almost three weeks, and much of their time was spent in rehearsing for their theatrical performances. They also took to a trip to Quebec City:

---

9. Daley's Hotel was later known as the British American Hotel and, later still, as the Sheraton.

we ... were charmed by its interest and beauty ... its giddy heights; its citadel suspended, as it were, in the air; its picturesque steep streets and frowning gateways; and the splendid views which burst upon the eye at every turn: is at once unique and lasting. It is a place not to be forgotten or mixed up in the mind with other places, or altered for a moment in the crowd of scenes a traveller can recall.

In Montreal, one of Dickens's favourite pastimes was to walk along the quay in the early morning and observe the newly arrived immigrants, most of whom came from England and Ireland. He was fascinated by them, wondering about the lives they had left behind and the new lives they had come to find. The more he observed them, the more he admired them and wrote of his awe for how much these couples and families loved one another, enough to face a frighteningly uncertain future in a new land. Most had been driven to migration by extreme poverty and Dickens was deeply moved by the faith couples had placed in one another to set out upon such a precarious adventure. He was, perhaps, even more disposed to view them as brave pioneers because he was feeling extremely homesick, longing to get back to his children, his friends and his life in London. After their great success onstage in Montreal, Dickens wrote to Forster that he and Catherine were in 'such a state of excitement' at the prospect of going home that he was unable to write a coherent letter.

On Wednesday 25 May, Charles and Catherine Dickens appeared in a private performance, to an invited audience, at what on the playbill was called the 'Queen's Theatre' – it seems this was actually the Theatre Royal, its identity being obscured to ensure the evening was kept strictly private, perhaps a testimony to Dickens's burgeoning fame and to reduce the risk of gatecrashers. That night, Charles and Catherine took part in a triple bill: in *A Roland for an Oliver* Charles played Alfred Highflyer; in *Past Two O'Clock in the Morning* (a play with only two characters) he played Mr Snobbington; and in *Deaf as a Post*, Catherine played Amy Templeton and Charles played Gallop.

On Saturday 28 May, the theatre was opened to the public and Catherine remained in the audience while Charles appeared in another triple bill. The first two plays were the same as in the private performance, but the concluding part of the programme was called *High Life Below Stairs*, in which he took the part of Phillip.

To Washington and Beyond: Magnificent Intentions

On 30 May, Catherine, Charles and their entourage reluctantly left Montreal and began a long journey back to New York. In *American Notes*, Dickens wrote wistfully:

> Canada has held, and always will retain, a foremost place in my remembrance. Few Englishmen are prepared to find it what it is. Advancing quietly; old differences settling down, and being fast forgotten; public feeling and private enterprise alike in a sound and wholesome state; nothing of flush or fever in its system, but health and vigour throbbing in its steady pulse: it is full of hope and promise.

He was so full of admiration for Canada, it is a great pity that he never visited again, even when he returned to the USA a quarter of a century after his first visit. This second visit took place during the winter and early spring, when the season and the Canadian climate conspired to make it too difficult for Dickens to travel to Canada.

They sailed from New York on 7 June 1842. On their journey home, Dickens was full of excitement and buoyed by his success and by his and Catherine's shared adventures. He became the ebullient public Dickens, full of the characteristic energy so frequently recorded in letters and diary entries by his contemporaries. On the voyage, he created a club, which he named the United Vagabonds. He described it in a letter to Cornelius Felton:

> This holy brotherhood committed all kinds of absurdities, and dined always, with a variety of solemn forms, at one end of the table, below the mast, away from all the rest. The captain being ill when were three or four days out, I produced my medicine-chest and recovered him. We had a few more sick men after that, and I went round 'the wards' every day in a great state, accompanied by two Vagabonds ... bearing enormous rolls of plaster and huge pairs of scissors. We were really very merry all the way, breakfasted as one party at Liverpool, shook hands, and parted most cordially.

The *George Washington* arrived back in Liverpool early on the morning of 29 June. After the communal breakfast, and the unloading of their luggage, Charles, Catherine and Anne took the first possible train to London, arriving home in the evening. The couple had missed the children so much that they swore never again to go on a long journey without their 'darlings'.

When Dickens began writing *American Notes*, he asked his friends to lend him the letters he had sent, to help him compose the manuscript. The book was never the commercial success he had hoped for, and even today it is one of his least well-known works. It offended many Americans, including Washington Irving. Although Dickens was very complimentary about Irving in the book, the American author felt Dickens had been rude by making angry comments about his country.

One of Dickens's London friends was also disappointed. The actor William Charles Macready had undertaken his own tour of the States in the 1820s and had been so enthusiastic about it that he had seriously considered moving there. Macready was fervently opposed to having a monarchy and admired America's republicanism. Although Dickens was never a staunch monarchist, he had been unimpressed by what he had seen of American democracy, particularly the racial inequalities. He wrote to Macready, trying to explain how he felt: 'I infinitely prefer a liberal Monarchy ... to such a Government as this. In every respect but that of National Education, the Country disappoints me.' He admitted he had started on his voyage expecting too much, that he had been seduced by the idea of such a 'young' country. Now, he considered the American press to be 'more mean and paltry and silly and disgraceful' than the journalism of anywhere else he had knowledge of, and he hoped Canada would resist the arrival of similar newspapers.

George Washington Putnam had said goodbye to the Dickens party when they departed America for Canada, but the two men kept in touch. In 1851, Dickens responded to a letter Putnam had sent to him about the birth of his daughter. It was a painful time for Charles and Catherine as their own baby daughter Dora (the ninth of their ten children) had died recently, but the letter he sent, written in Broadstairs, is one of warmth and nostalgia:

> My Dear Mr. Putnam.
> I have received your letter with very great pleasure.... I have often travelled, in fancy, over the old ground and water in America, and have over and over again beheld you coming

at dusk into the storm-gallery of a Western steamer, with a little jug of some warm mixture intended for my very little Cabin.... Whether we look as we used to look, I can't quite determine. I am much redder and browner, I believe, than I was in those times – more robust – less interesting – shorter haired – a more solid-looking personage – and not younger. But I take great exercise, and am very strong. Mrs. Dickens is stouter, though not quite so well in health as she used to be then. Anne, who has been with us in Italy and in Switzerland, is with us still, and looks (in my eyes) much the same.

I write from the sea side – from a fishing village and small watering-place to which we generally come at this time of the year.... We have eight children, and have had nine – a little girl died suddenly, not long ago. The picture of the four we had when we were in America, hangs in our dining room at home. It is in a gay round frame now, and has these many years forgotten the sliding lid of the box you used to take off, before you set it up on a side table at each of the four and twenty thousand Inns we stayed at. I wonder whether you recollect the Inn at Hartford where the 'Levee' wouldn't go away – or at Newhaven where they kicked the staircase, to express impatience – or at Columbus where they came in, arm in arm, at about midnight – or at St. Louis where we had (I think) a ball.... I feel as if I should like to see all those places again, so much – and to have another ride on a corduroy road, and to sit at another very long table with nothing particular to eat upon it, aboard the Messenger.

I see many Americans in London, and find them the old good-humoured kind-hearted people. We never quarrel, but 'get along' (as you would say) quite merrily and pleasantly. If I ever find one, in travelling about, I try to make him more at home, in remembrance of my old welcome. Sometimes he seems disposed to consider me a sort of Monster, at first, but he soon gets over it...

Always Faithfully Your friend.

The Journey to Italy

> *'And thus ever by day and night, under the sun and under the stars, climbing the dusty hills and toiling along the weary plains, journeying by land and journeying by sea, coming and going so strangely, to meet and to act and react on one another, move all we restless travellers through the pilgrimage of life.'*
>
> From *Little Dorrit* (1857)

On 1 November 1843, Dickens wrote to John Forster about his desire to leave England. He was in debt, which always brought back frightening memories from childhood, and he was exhausted by writing *Martin Chuzzlewit*. He was also under pressure from his publishers, Chapman and Hall, who thought his idea for a ghost story about Christmas would likely be a failure. Because of this, they had insisted he pay a large part of the production costs for *A Christmas Carol*.[10] Feeling overwhelmed by stress, he wrote:

> I shall let the house if I can; if not, leave it to be let. I shall take all the family, and two servants – three at most – to some place which I know beforehand to be CHEAP and in a delightful climate, in Normandy or Brittany, to which I shall go over, first, and where I shall rent some house for six or eight months. During that time, I shall walk through Switzerland, cross the Alps, travel through France and Italy; take Kate perhaps to Rome and Venice, but not elsewhere; and in short see everything that is to be seen. I shall write

---

[10]. This resulted in Dickens leaving Chapman and Hall for a new publisher, Bradbury and Evans.

my descriptions to you from time to time, exactly as I did in America; and you will be able to judge whether or not a new and attractive book may not be made on such ground.

In the same letter, Dickens mentioned his 'Italian master' Mr Mariotti, from whom he was attempting to learn the language, in preparation for his travels.

We know from a letter to Forster, that Dickens read the 1828 travelguide *Tour of Italy and Sicily*, by a M. Simonds, which he described as 'a most charming book ... remarkable for its excellent sense, and determination not to give in to conventional lies.' Perhaps he also read *Italy and Its Comforts: Manual of Tourists*, by Valery (the pseudonym of Antoine Claude Pasquin), published in 1841. Valery describes Italy as a dangerously exotic place and advises:

> The habits, customs and diet of the inhabitants, being instinctively adopted through the influence of the atmospheric constitution, should be conformed to as much as possible. However, the traveller would do well to refrain from taking supper, dangerous in places bordering on the sea, or in marshy lands, and which the ancients had wisely avoided.

Valery warns that Italians sleep more than the British and explains the habit of taking a siesta, advising travellers to do the same and not make the faux pas of calling on acquaintances during the afternoon when they might be in bed. If Charles and Catherine read Valery's book, they would have been cheered by his comment, 'In the *caffé*, an economical and wholesome breakfast may be made on chocolate, bread and butter, for less than ten sous... . The chocolates of Milan, Turin, Rome and Naples, are excellent.' He also recommended Rome for those interested in hunting birds, hares and wild boar.

On 15 January, Catherine gave birth to their fifth child, Francis Jeffrey Dickens ('Frank') and Charles felt his financial responsibility tighten even further. In the first half of 1844, in addition to all the preparations for his family's overseas adventure, he travelled around England. He visited Bath in January and again in June, and he took trips to Liverpool and Birmingham in February and Yorkshire in April.

On 2 July, two days after the publication of the final chapter of *Martin Chuzzlewit*, the Dickens family left London, in their new travelling carriage. Dickens had commissioned it to accommodate eleven people: himself, Catherine, Georgina, the five children, three servants and the dog, Timber. Although this seems like an expensive undertaking for a man concerned about finances, it was cheaper for the family to relocate to Italy for a year, renting out their home, than it was to stay living in London.

The family journeyed from London to Folkestone in Kent, from where they took the boat, known as the cross-Channel packet service, to Boulogne. Dickens once described Folkestone as 'one of the prettiest watering places on the south coast', and Boulogne would soon start to feature significantly in the family's life. Dickens was a keen scholar of French, mostly through reading French literature, and was eager to show off his skill. His first task in Boulogne was to change some money, so he went to a bank and proudly explained his needs, at great length, in French. He was deflated by the bank clerk replying in perfect English, 'How would you like to take it, sir?'

From Boulogne, they travelled to Paris for two days, which made Dickens determined to return. Dickens wrote about the journey in his second travelogue *Pictures from Italy*:

> On a fine Sunday morning in the Midsummer time … an English travelling-carriage of considerable proportions, fresh from the shady halls of the Pantechnicon near Belgrave Square, London, was observed (by a very small French soldier; for I saw him look at it) to issue from the gate of the Hôtel Meurice in the Rue Rivoli at Paris. …the English family travelling by this carriage … were going to live in fair Genoa for a year; and … the head of the family purposed, in that space of time, to stroll about, wherever his restless humour carried him.

In his novels, and travel articles, Dickens often wrote about the paraphernalia needed by travellers. Lucie Manette, in *A Tale of Two Cities*, is first encountered carrying a 'straw travelling-hat by its ribbon' and Mr Lorry and M. Defarge are described in a flurry of organising travelling papers, and 'travelling cloaks and wrappers, bread and meat, wine and hot coffee'. In *Little Dorrit,* the travellers going through Switzerland on their way to Italy ride mules strung about with 'lanterns, torches, sacks, provender, barrels, cheeses, kegs of honey and butter, straw bundles and packages of many shapes'.

From Paris the family travelled via Lyons, Valence, Avignon and Marseilles, from where they took a boat to Genoa. Dickens wrote to his friend Count D'Orsay enquiring, 'Were you ever at Lyons? *That's* the place. It's a great Nightmare – a bad conscience – a fit of indigestion – the recollection of having done a murder. An awful place!' Perhaps this was still in his mind several years later when writing *Little Dorrit,* in which the chilling murderer is a Frenchman. Although Dickens doesn't specify where Rigaud was born, perhaps it was this first impression of Lyons that helped to create his character. Rigaud, initially, seems to live a charmed life, as he moves with ease, fooling the gullible and bullying the weak to ease his own path in life. He states, 'I am a cosmopolitan gentleman. I own no particular country ... I am a citizen of the world.' In his Marseilles prison cell, Rigaud is able to sketch a perfect map of their surroundings to his cellmate:

> 'I was brought in here at night, and out of a boat, but I know where I am. See here! Marseilles harbour;' on his knees on the pavement, mapping it all out with a swarthy forefinger; 'Toulon (where the galleys are), Spain over there, Algiers over there. Creeping away to the left here, Nice. Round by the Cornice to Genoa. Genoa Mole and Harbour. Quarantine Ground. City there; terrace gardens blushing with the bella donna. Here, Porto Fino. Stand out for Leghorn. Out again for Civita Vecchia, so away to—hey! there's no room for Naples;' he had got to the wall by this time; 'but it's all one; it's in there!'

Accompanying the Dickens party throughout their journey was the indefatigable courier Louis Roche, a Frenchman from Avignon. A courier, at this time, was a type of tour guide, someone who spoke all the necessary languages, who understood the roads, the coaching inns, hotels and toll gates along the way, a person who guided the unwary safely through bandit country, haggled about the bill with hoteliers, found medical help if needed and ensured that every need was met. On the occasions when he and Dickens travelled alone, Roche also acted as a valet.

Dickens and Travel: The Start of Modern Travel Writing

Without a courier, all sorts of traps could be waiting for the unwary tourist. In an 1840 guidebook, *A Road-Book for Travellers in Central Italy*, written by Captain Jousiffe, the author warns:

> The Inns of Italy are, notwithstanding the great increase of travellers within these twenty years, still the worst of any country in Europe, excepting those of the great and most frequented towns…; it is a lamentable fact, that even at the present day the traveller is obliged, however short his stay is intended to be, to alight from his carriage and to bargain not only for the apartments he desires to occupy, but for the meals for himself and his servants, and indeed for every trifling thing he may want. Should he neglect this, he is presented with a bill upon his departure…. Couriers will add much to the ease of travellers…. Your courier will precede you on your journey, secure apartments, have the meals ready by the time you arrive, and pay the bill for you at your departure, not forgetting to exact a large share of the innkeeper's profit, for taking you to his hotel, besides having partaken of what is best in the house, and slept in a *best bed* for all of which he does not pay one farthing.

Dickens admired Louis Roche to such an extent that, in *Pictures from Italy*, he lovingly turns the courier into the swaggering hero of the journey:

> You have been travelling along, stupidly enough, as you generally do in the last stage of the day … and you have been thinking deeply about the dinner you will have at the next stage;… and here we are in the yard of the Hôtel de l'Ecu d'Or; used up, gone out, smoking, spent, exhausted;… . The landlord of the Hôtel de l'Ecu d'Or, dotes to that extent upon the Courier, that he can hardly wait for his coming down from the box, but embraces his very legs and boot-heels as he descends. 'My Courier! My brave Courier! My friend! My brother!' The landlady loves him, the femme de chambre blesses him, the garçon worships him. The Courier asks if his letter has been received? It has, it has. Are the

The Journey to Italy

rooms prepared? They are, they are. The best rooms for my noble Courier. The rooms of state for my gallant Courier; the whole house is at the service of my best of friends! ... He carries a green leathern purse outside his coat, suspended by a belt. The idlers look at it; one touches it. It is full of five-franc pieces. Murmurs of admiration are heard among the boys. The landlord falls upon the Courier's neck, and folds him to his breast. He is so much fatter than he was, he says! He looks so rosy and so well! ... The whole party are in motion. The brave Courier, in particular, is everywhere: looking after the beds, having wine poured down his throat by his dear brother the landlord, and picking up green cucumbers – always cucumbers; Heaven knows where he gets them – with which he walks about, one in each hand, like truncheons… . When it is nearly dark, the brave Courier, having eaten the two cucumbers, sliced up in the contents of a pretty large decanter of oil, and another of vinegar, emerges from his retreat below, and proposes a visit to the Cathedral, whose massive tower frowns down upon the court-yard of the inn. Off we go; and very solemn and grand it is, in the dim light.

Throughout *Pictures from Italy*, Dickens refers repeatedly to Roche as 'the brave Courier', an epithet with a tinge of mocking about it, but the teasing is gentle and his admiration for the courier was real. He wrote about Roche as 'the radiant embodiment of good humour who sat beside me in the person of a French Courier – best of servants and most beaming of men!' He even admits that any observers looking at the family would assume Roche was the patriarch, not Dickens, who felt he 'dwindled down to no account at all' in 'the shadow of his portly presence'.

In November 1844, when Dickens was preparing to return to London with the manuscript of his second Christmas book, *The Chimes*, he wrote to Thomas Mitton, 'Roche is my right hand. There never was such a fellow.' A few days later, Dickens wrote to Forster:

The brave C continues to be a prodigy. He puts out my clothes at every inn as if I were going to stay there twelve months; calls me to the instant every morning; lights the fire before I get up; gets hold of roast fowls and produces them in coaches at a distance from all other help, in hungry moments; and is invaluable.

After their year in Italy, whenever Dickens needed advice about travel in Europe, he would consult Louis Roche, and when Dickens was planning his family's trip to Switzerland in 1846, he ensured that Roche was available to act as their courier. Whenever Roche travelled to England, he was made welcome at the Dickens home, and when, in 1848, he became suddenly ill in London, Dickens found him a much-needed hospital bed. Sadly, the two men's travelling adventures were curtailed when Roche died young, in 1849. In his later years of travelling, Dickens missed this 'most faithful, affectionate, and devoted man'. In 1850, Dickens wrote a letter to an unnamed correspondent:

> Madam ... I can strongly recommend Roche to you. He is the brother of a deceased travelling servant of mine for whom I had a great regard and affection. He and his family are most respectable and trustworthy. He has been about my house for some months – is shrewd and clever – knows France, Italy, &c well – and is thoroughly honest, zealous, and good tempered. I believe you will find him everything you can desire; and if I were going abroad tomorrow, I would take him with me in the capacity in which he is to serve you.

In *The Uncommercial Traveller* (1860), Dickens's narrator wakes up in a carriage between England and France and is delighted to see Louis again:

> I must have fallen asleep after lunch, for when a bright face looked in at the window, I started, and said:
> 'Good God, Louis, I dreamed you were dead!'
>
> My cheerful servant laughed, and answered:
> 'Me? Not at all, sir.'
> 'How glad I am to wake! What are we doing, Louis?'
> 'We go to take relay of horses. Will you walk up the hill?'
> 'Certainly.'

On this first journey to Italy, the Dickens family and Louis Roche arrived in Marseilles on 14 July 1844, from where Dickens wrote to Forster that he was 'surrounded by strange and perfectly novel circumstances, I feel as if I had a new head on side by side with my old one.' Forster wrote in Dickens's biography that the journey, although more expensive than Dickens had anticipated, had been a success: 'The children had not cried in their worst troubles, the carriage had gone lightly over abominable roads, and the courier had proved himself a perfect gem.'

A century before the Dickens family travelled to Italy, Horace Walpole, author of *The Castle of Otranto*, also journeyed there. His letters provide a fascinating history of eighteenth-century travel. From Florence, he wrote:

> The farther I travel, the less I wonder at anything: a few days reconcile one to a new spot, or an unseen custome; and men are so much the same everywhere, that one scarce perceives any change of situation.... The most remarkable thing I have observed since I came abroad, is, that there are no people so obviously mad as the English. The French, the Italians, have great follies, great faults, but then they are so national, that they cease to be striking. In England, tempers vary so excessively, that almost every one's faults are peculiar to himself.
>
> (24 Jan 1740)

A month later Walpole wrote to his friend, Richard West, about Carnival in Italy:

> The end of the Carnival is frantic, Bacchanalian; all the morn one makes parties in mask to the shops and coffee-houses, and all the evening to the operas and balls.... What makes masquerading more agreeable here than in England, is the great deference that is showed to the disguised. Here they do not catch at those little dirty opportunities of saying any ill-natured thing they know of you, do not abuse you because they may, or talk gross bawdy to a woman of quality.
>
> (27 February 1740)

Dickens and Travel: The Start of Modern Travel Writing

Dickens would almost certainly have read the writings of Walpole before setting off on his own travels. When writing *Pictures from Italy*, he took pains to ensure his readers would be able to envisage the scenes he was recreating as vividly in their minds, as if they had been there. He wanted them to understand what the places smelt like, what sounds he had heard, how it felt to drink local Italian wines in Italy, and what it really meant to be a traveller in a country other than the one in which they had grown up and grown so very used to. Dickens wanted his readers to feel as if they had taken the journey with him.

A New Life in Genoa

*'The noble bay of Genoa, with the deep blue
Mediterranean, lies stretched out near at hand'*
     Charles Dickens, *Pictures from Italy* (1846)

The travelling party reached Albaro[11] on the evening of Tuesday 16 July, where they were met by the sculptor Angus Fletcher, the same friend who had travelled with Charles and Catherine around the Highlands of Scotland. Fletcher, who was now living in Genoa, had made great preparations for their arrival. When Dickens had asked him to find them a place to live, Fletcher had spoken to other migrant residents, including the Swiss banker Emile de la Rue and his English wife. They were living in a grand apartment inside the Palazzo Brignole Rosso and Emile had suggested Fletcher should arrange for the Dickens family to live in the nearby Palazzo Doria, just outside Genoa, but Fletcher had chosen a pretty pink-stoned villa instead, something he was convinced Dickens would prefer and which would make them neighbours.

The family's arrival was greeted by an extraordinary ceremony, as officials solemnly measured the travelling carriage of which Dickens was so proud. The streets in Genoa were so old and narrow – created long before Victorian travelling carriages – that the vehicle had to be measured before it could be ascertained whether it would be able to travel along the streets, especially as the journey to their new home was down some of the city's narrowest lanes. As Dickens commented wryly in *Pictures from Italy*:

> It was found to be a very tight fit, but just a possibility, and no more – as I am reminded every day, by the sight of

---
11. In Dickens's time, Albaro was outside Genoa, now it is part of the city.

various large holes which it punched in the walls on either side as it came along. We are more fortunate, I am told, than an old lady, who took a house in these parts not long ago, and who stuck fast in her carriage in a lane; and as it was impossible to open one of the doors, she was obliged to submit to the indignity of being hauled through one of the little front windows.

On 7 August 1844, Dickens wrote to his friend Count D'Orsay:

Do you remember Byron's old house? Yes? Well. It isn't that ... but keeping on, up the hill past Byron's house, you come to another large house at the corner of a lane, with a little tumble-down blackguard old green-grocer's shop at the other corner, on which is painted, if I recollect right, Croce di San Lorenzo. The Governor lives in the large house opposite the Green Grocer's now; and turning down between the Governor's *and* the Green Grocer's, you go down a long, straggling, very narrow lane until you come to mine: which is on the left hand, with the open Sea before it – a fort close by, on the left – a vineyard sloping down towards the short – and an old ruined church dedicated to St. John the Baptist ... blotting out just so much of the sea as its walls and towers can hide. It is properly called The Villa di Bella Vista; but I call it the Villa di Bagnerello – that being the name of an amiable but drunken butcher into whose hands it has fallen, and who, being universally known (in consequence of being carried home from some wine shop or other every night), is a famous address: which the dullest errandboy recognizes immediately.

Dickens described his house in *Pictures from Italy*, wanting his readers to have an idea of what it was really like to live in such an exotic country:

When you have got through these narrow lanes, you come to an archway, imperfectly stopped up by a rusty old gate – my gate. The rusty old gate has a bell to correspond, which you ring as long as you like, and which nobody answers, as it has no connection whatever with the house. But there is a rusty old knocker, too – very loose, so that it slides round when you touch it – and if you learn the trick of it, and knock long enough, somebody comes… . You walk into a seedy little garden, all wild and weedy, from which the vineyard opens; cross it, enter a square hall like a cellar, walk up a cracked marble staircase, and pass into a most enormous room with a vaulted roof and whitewashed walls: not unlike a great Methodist chapel. This is the *sala*… . The furniture of this *sala* is a sort of red brocade. All the chairs are immovable, and the sofa weighs several tons.

On the same floor, and opening out of this same chamber, are dining-room, drawing-room, and divers bedrooms: each with a multiplicity of doors and windows. Up-stairs are divers other gaunt chambers, and a kitchen; and down-stairs is another kitchen, which, with all sorts of strange contrivances for burning charcoal, looks like an alchemical laboratory. There are also some half-dozen small sitting-rooms, where the servants in this hot July, may escape from the heat of the fire…. A mighty old, wandering, ghostly, echoing, grim, bare house it is, as ever I beheld or thought of.

There is a little vine-covered terrace, opening from the drawing-room; and under this terrace, and forming one side of the little garden, is what used to be the stable. It is now a cow-house, and has three cows in it, so that we get new milk by the bucketful. There is no pasturage near, and they never go out, but are constantly lying down, and surfeiting themselves with vine-leaves—perfect Italian cows enjoying the *dolce far' niente* all day long. They are presided over, and slept with, by an old man named Antonio, and his son.

Unfortunately Dickens was not as enamoured of the villa as Angus Fletcher had been, despite its beautiful views and ancient frescoes, partly because of his unromantic discovery that its owner was the 'drunken butcher'. Dickens was also depressed by the unseasonally bad weather, as Forster related in his biography:

He opened his third letter (3rd of August) by telling me there was a thick November fog, that rain was pouring incessantly, and that he did not remember to have seen in his life, at that time of year, such cloudy weather as he had seen beneath Italian skies. 'The story goes that it is in autumn and winter, when other countries are dark and foggy, that the beauty and clearness of this are most observable. I hope it may prove so; for I have postponed going round the hills which encircle the city, or seeing any of the sights, until the weather is more favourable.... But the scenery is exquisite, and at certain periods of the evening and the morning the blue of the Mediterranean surpasses all conception or description. It is the most intense and wonderful colour, I do believe, in all nature.'

Dickens wrote about this initial disappointment in *Pictures from Italy*:

> The first impressions of such a place as Albaro, the suburb of Genoa, where I am now, as my American friends would say, 'located,' can hardly fail, I should imagine, to be mournful and disappointing. It requires a little time and use to overcome the feeling of depression consequent, at first, on so much ruin and neglect.

He also wrote wittily about the villa itself:

> The view, as I have said, is charming; but in the day you must keep the lattice-blinds close shut, or the sun would drive you mad; and when the sun goes down you must shut up all the windows, or the mosquitoes would tempt you to commit suicide. So at this time of the year, you don't see much of the prospect within doors. As for the flies, you don't mind them. Nor the fleas, whose size is prodigious, and whose name is Legion, and who populate the coach-house to that extent that I daily expect to see the carriage going off bodily, drawn by myriads of industrious fleas in harness. The rats are kept away, quite comfortably, by scores of lean cats, who roam about the garden for that purpose. The lizards, of course, nobody cares for; they play in the sun, and don't bite. The little scorpions are merely curious. The beetles

are rather late, and have not appeared yet. The frogs are company. There is a preserve of them in the grounds of the next villa; and after nightfall, one would think that scores upon scores of women in pattens were going up and down a wet stone pavement without a moment's cessation. That is exactly the noise they make.

Dickens loved discovering new things about Italy and observing the people. One day he saw 'the young men of the neighbourhood' wearing wreaths of vine leaves, and assumed that they were to keep away flies – it was some time before he discovered they had been dressed up to celebrate a saint's day. When they attended a celebration for another saint's day, Dickens noted that the women wore veils instead of bonnets: 'the most gauzy, ethereal-looking audience I ever saw.'

Dickens grew to know Albaro by walking. He explored tiny alleyways, ruined houses, churches, shops, abandoned gardens and busy piazzas and he discovered, after his early misgivings, that 'It is a place that "grows upon you" every day.' He made notes of Italian quirks, customs and traditions, and wrote of how grateful the waiters were for any tip, even a tiny one 'you would not offer to an English beggar'. He watched men playing bowls on the street and the ancient game of Morra, which Dickens described as the 'national game'. He wrote of it, in *Pictures from Italy*, 'On a holiday evening, standing at a window, or walking in a garden, or passing through the streets, or sauntering in any quiet place about the town, you will hear this game in progress in a score of wine-shops at once; and looking over any vineyard walk, or turning almost any corner, will come upon a knot of players in full cry.'

Dickens strove to improve his Italian, but early in their adventure he was put to shame by his cook. Within a short while of arriving in Genoa, while her employer was still struggling with the language, she was haggling with stallholders in the market and speaking with a surprisingly fluency. Dickens described her to Forster as 'a clever woman' without the 'ignorance' of so many of his servants – who, Dickens observed wryly, had the habit of speaking English more loudly, in an attempt to make themselves understood by Italians. At the end of August, however, Dickens wrote to Forster, 'The servants are beginning to pick up scraps of Italian; some of them go to a weekly *conversazione* of servants at the Governor's every Sunday night, having got over their consternation at the frequent introduction of quadrilles on these occasions; and I think they begin to like their foreigneering life.' Through striking up a friendship with a local woman sent to do the laundry, the cook started to speak Italian with increasing ease, quickly learning the names of all the foods she wanted to buy, and then instructing the rest of the staff.

Dickens wrote to friends that he was soon able to order whatever he wanted in a café or shop, and in September he wrote happily to Forster that the language was starting to come to him more naturally: 'The audacity with which one begins to speak when there is no help for it, is quite astonishing.'

Dickens also regularly wrote letters in French. To the French banker Emile de la Rue, Dickens commented, 'I read French as easily as English; and ... if it be pleasanter to you to write in that language (though I can hardly think it; you write English so well) it is all one to me.' After several months of living in Italy, Dickens was able to send a long letter to Clarkson Stanfield, written entirely in Italian.

Pictures from Italy moves between being an intimate insight into Dickens's daily life to being a travel guide he hopes will assist future tourists. He includes tips about where to visit, what food to eat and how to discover the 'real' Italy. In his chapters on Genoa, he writes:

> They who would know how beautiful the country immediately surrounding Genoa is, should climb (in clear weather) to the top of Monte Faccio, or, at least, ride round the city walls: a feat more easily performed. No prospect can be more diversified and lovely than the changing views of the harbour, and the valleys of the two rivers, the Polcevera and the Bizagno... . In not the least picturesque part of this ride, there is a fair specimen of a real Genoese tavern, where the visitor may derive good entertainment from real Genoese dishes, such as Tagliarini; Ravioli; German sausages, strong of garlic, sliced and eaten with fresh green figs; cocks' combs and sheep-kidneys, chopped up with mutton chops and liver; small pieces of some unknown part of a calf, twisted into small shreds, fried, and served up in a great dish like white-bait; and other curiosities of that kind. They often get wine at these suburban Trattorie, from France and Spain and Portugal, which is brought over by small captains

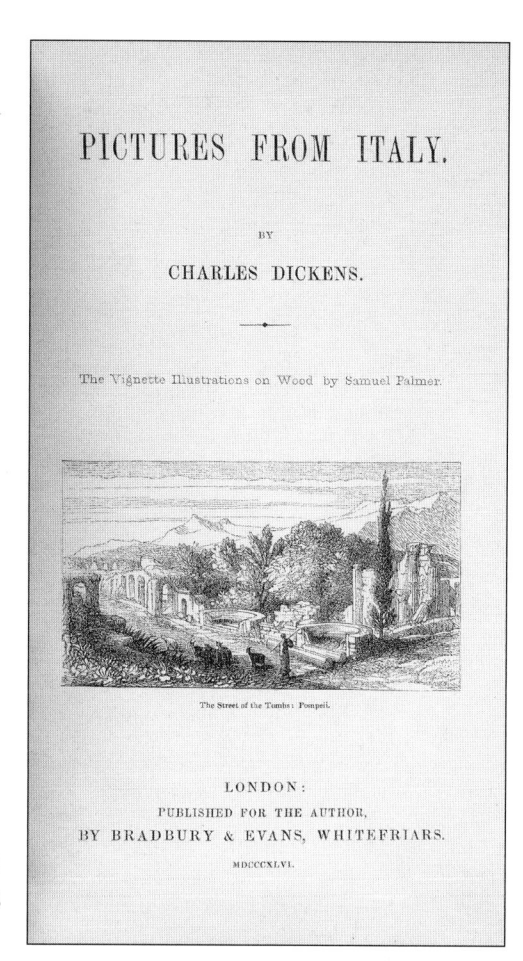

The title page for *Pictures from Italy*, published in 1846. This was Charles Dickens's second travelogue.

An illustration from *The Posthumous Papers of the Pickwick Club*, showing Bob Sawyer on the roof of a chaise (a type of carriage).

The Emigrants by Phiz (Hablot Knight Browne) from *David Copperfield*, showing Mr Micawber and Daniel Peggotty leaving for Australia.

Art critic and author John Ruskin was also in Italy in 1845. He documented his travels in his sketchbooks; this is his painting of the Basilica of San Frediano in Lucca.

Right: Condette, Allée Charles Dickens. This plaque commemorates the time Charles Dickens spent at this house in Condette, which he rented so he could live secretly with Ellen Ternan.

Below: Rotunda and new rooms, Dublin, 1795. Dickens's first readings at the Rotunda in Dublin took place in August of 1858. His tour was a great success and he visited Ireland again in 1867 and 1869.

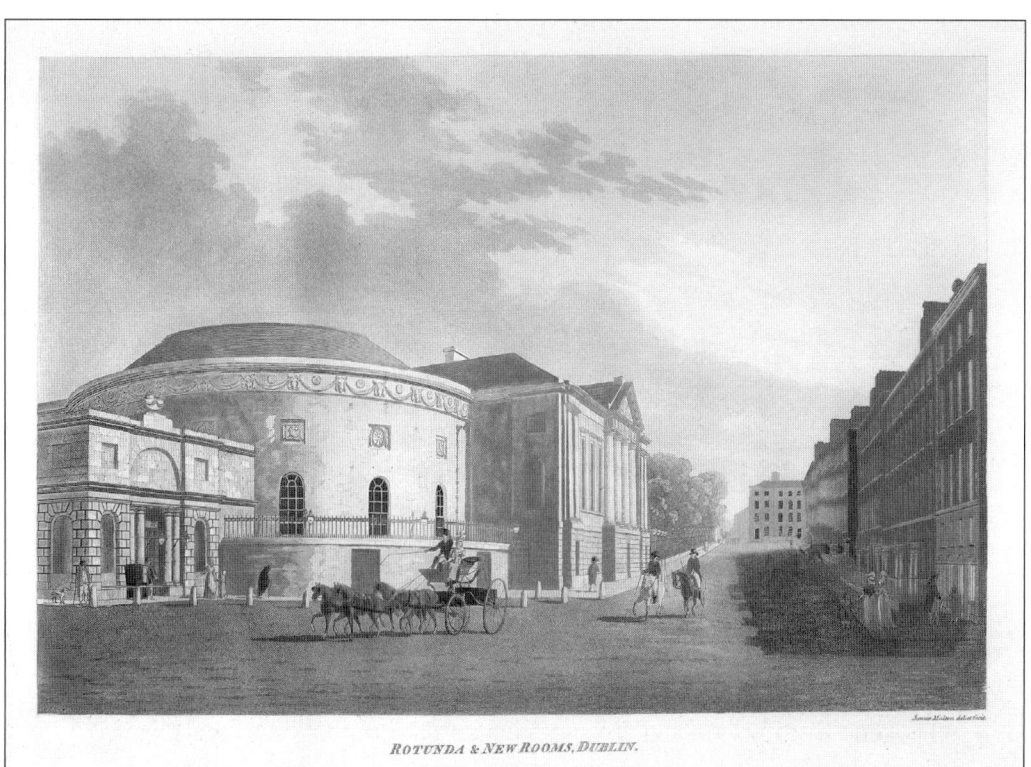

Venice in the nineteenth century, as Dickens would have seen it. He titled his Venetian chapter in *Pictures from Italy* 'An Italian Dream'.

Colosseum, Rome, c.1890. The bloody history of the Colosseum haunted Dickens from his first visit – yet he also felt compelled to walk past it every day.

In 1846, Charles Dickens and his family went to live in Lausanne, in Switzerland. Finding Lausanne too quiet, Dickens travelled to Geneva (seen above) so he could write amid the bustle of a city.

Glen Coe, c.1870. In 1841 Dickens wrote to his friend John Forster, 'Glencoe itself is perfectly terrible. The pass is an awful place.'

In Dickens's time, tourists were allowed to climb to the top of the Leaning Tower of Pisa (seen here in a nineteenth-century drawing). Dickens said it made him feel as though he were on a ship.

In June 1850, Dickens was a passenger on an exciting new route: the South Eastern Railway's overnight train from London Bridge Station (depicted here in 1851) to Paris.

New York, 1868. Dickens's second trip to America took place in the winter of 1867–1868; New Yorkers queued for hours to get tickets to his sold-out readings.

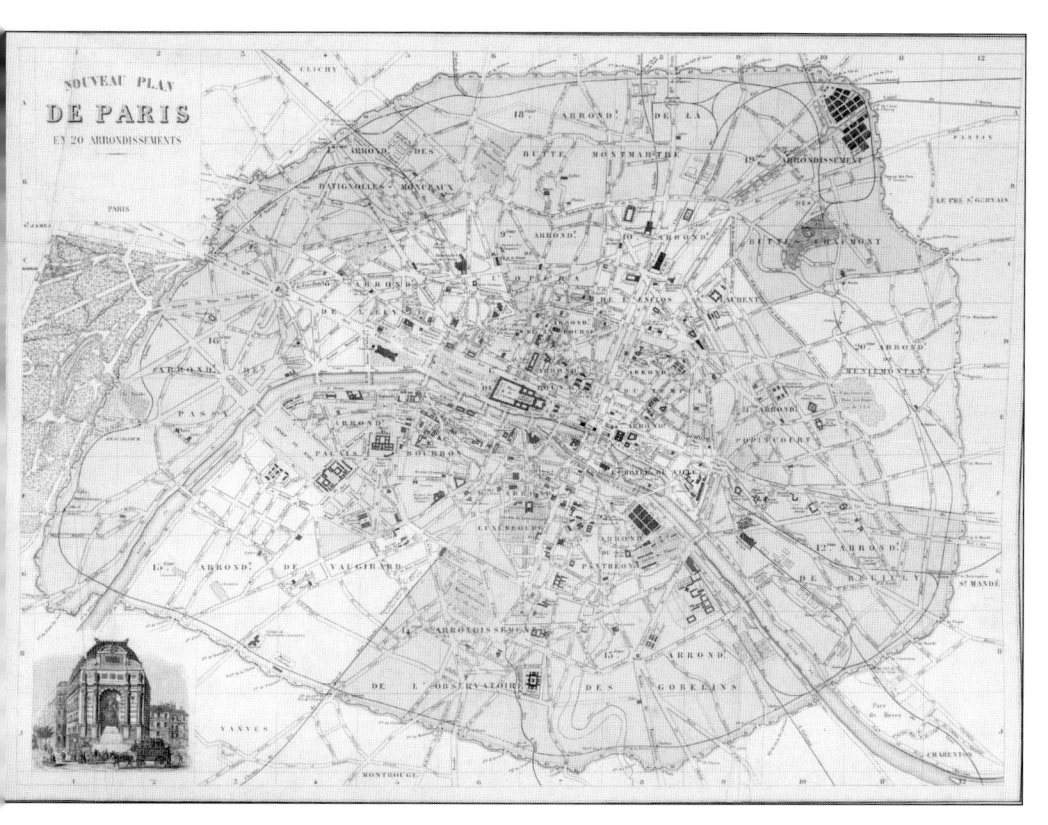

Map of Paris, 1850. Dickens grew to love Paris, a place he visited many times. His eldest child, Charley, once commented that his father should have been born in France.

Above: Staplehurst train crash, 1865. On 9 June 1865, Dickens was travelling on a train that crashed in Staplehurst in Kent; the accident left many passengers dead or injured.

Left: The Simplon Pass, nineteenth century. Dickens first travelled through the Simplon Pass in the 1840s. It continued to inspire his writing for the rest of his life.

in little trading-vessels. They buy it at so much a bottle, without asking what it is, or caring to remember if anybody tells them, and usually divide it into two heaps; of which they label one Champagne, and the other Madeira.

Valery had also written glowingly of Genoa:

[it] is very salubrious and is but rarely visited with burning summers or rigourous [sic] winters. The thermometer rarely rises above 24 degrees... . This coolness of the atmosphere is owing to the southerly and easterly winds that particularly reign during the months of July and August along the coast of Liguria. The water is excellent, the provisions wholesome, and the sobriety of the inhabitants contribute to their general good health... . Genoa possesses many splendid palaces, rich churches, admirable paintings…

He also praised the Genoese food:

The *paste* of Genoa are the best of Italy and are sent to all parts of Europe. The mushrooms that grow on the declivities of the Appenines are excellent and very plentiful. They are so abundant that there is a market appropriated for them.... Good preserves: Pears, lemons, and small green oranges called … *piccolo chinesi* are the most noted. Excellent figs and fruit.

Dickens's writing provides an insight into Italian life in the 1840s, such as this description of Albaro:

The great majority of the streets are as narrow as any thoroughfare can well be... . The houses are immensely high, painted in all sorts of colours, and are in every stage and state of damage, dirt, and lack of repair. They are commonly let off in floors, or flats... . As it is impossible for coaches to penetrate into these streets, there are sedan chairs, gilded and otherwise, for hire in divers places. A great many private chairs are also kept among the nobility and gentry; and at night these are trotted to and fro in all directions, preceded by bearers of great lanthorns, made of linen stretched upon a frame.

Despite nicknaming their first Italian home 'the pink jail', and searching for a new place to live, Dickens's letters show that he was not entirely immune to the charms of the Villa di Bagnerello. That summer of 1844, he wrote to his friend, the playwright Douglas Jerrold, tempting him with the words, 'come and see me in Italy. Let us smoke a pipe among the vines. I have taken a little house surrounded by them, and no man in the world should be more welcome to it than you.'

He wrote more expansively about his new home to Forster, a letter that evokes vividly what it was like to be living somewhere so unlike anywhere he had lived before. Today people travel so easily, and even those unable or unwilling to travel can witness the magnificence of scenery and nature far across the world on TV, films or the internet. In Dickens's time, however, people relied solely on the experiences of other travellers, or on descriptions of far-flung places in art and literature. In his letter, Dickens wrote:

> I address you, my friend with something of the lofty spirit of an exile, a banished commoner, a sort of Anglo-Pole. I don't exactly know what I have done for my country in coming away from it, but I feel it is something; something great; something virtuous and heroic. Lofty emotions rise within me, when I see the sun set on the blue Mediterranean.... In the south of France, at Avignon, at Aix, at Marseilles, I saw deep blue skies; and also in America.... But such green, green, green, as flutters in the vineyard down below the windows, *that* I never saw; nor yet such lilac and such purple as float between me and the distant hills; nor yet in anything, picture, book, or vestal boredom, such awful, solemn, impenetrable blue, as in that same sea.... When the sun sets clearly, then, by Heaven, it is majestic. From any one of eleven windows here, or from a terrace overgrown with grapes, you may behold the broad sea, villas, houses, mountains, forts, strewn with rose leaves. Strewn with them? Steeped in them! Dyed, through and through and through.... Everything is in extremes. There is an insect

here that chirps all day. There is one outside the window now. The chirp is very loud: something like a Brobdingnagian grasshopper... . The day gets brighter, brighter, brighter, till it's night. The summer gets hotter, hotter, hotter, till it explodes. The fruit gets riper, riper, riper, till it tumbles down and rots... . All the houses are painted in fresco, hereabout (the outside walls I mean, the fronts, backs, and sides), and all the colour has run into damp and green seediness; and the very design has straggled away into the component atoms of the plaster. Beware of fresco! Sometimes (but not often) I can make out a Virgin with a mildewed glory round her head, holding nothing in an undiscernible lap with invisible arms; and occasionally the leg or arm of a cherub. But it is very melancholy and dim. There are two old fresco-painted vases outside my own gate, one on either hand, which are so faint that I never saw them till last night; and only then, because I was looking over the wall after a lizard who had come upon me while I was smoking a cigar above, and crawled over one of these embellishments in his retreat...

To Daniel Maclise, in July 1844, Dickens wrote of their daily routine:

We breakfast about half past nine or ten – dine about four – and go to bed about eleven. We are much courted by the visiting people of course; and I very much resort to my old habit of bolting from callers, and leaving their reception to Kate. Green figs I have already learnt to like. Green almonds (we have them at dessert every day) are the most delicious fruit in the world. And green lemons, combined with some rare Hollands that is to be got here, make prodigious Punch, I assure you.

Despite his growing fondness for Albaro, Dickens was determined to find his family a new home – one not owned by a drunken butcher – and this led the family to an exciting experience unlike anything they could have had in London. On 7 August, Dickens wrote to his friend Count D'Orsay that the villa 'would never do for a winter residence' so he had found somewhere more suitable in which to spent the colder months: the beautiful Palazzo Peschiere. As he explained to the count, 'I have the whole Palace except the Ground Piano. I don't know whether you ever saw the rooms. They are very splendid indeed; and every inch of the walls is painted in fresco. The Gardens also, are beautiful.' Dickens told D'Orsay that he had grown to have a great interest in Italy:

> [I] walk about, or ride about, the [town] when I go there in a dreamy sort of way, which is very comfortable. I seem [to be] thinking, but I don't know what about – I haven't the least idea. I can sit down in a church, or stand at the end of a narrow Vico, zig-zagging uphill like a dirty snake: and not feel the least desire for any further entertainment.

He also warned his friend not to address letters to his house: 'P.S. Address to the Poste Restante. The Albaro postman gets drunk – loses letters – and goes down on his knees in sober repentance.' This simple postscript invokes a time when everyone who was able wrote regular letters, long letters filled with evocative descriptions of everyday life and gossip about family, friends and acquaintances; letters which were so vital to the traveller, exiled from home – albeit willingly – in an era before telephones and emails. It was a time when every letter and postcard received was a welcome link to a faraway world of home and connections.

At this date, Albaro was outside the city gates of Genoa. At the end of August, Dickens wrote to Forster about what an inconvenience this could be. One evening, he was invited to a dinner at the French consul's residence, followed by a party at the home of the Marquis de Negro – both of which were in the city. Dickens's carriage had been ordered to fetch him from the party once the dancing was over, but then he realised that the dancing was going to continue into the early hours of the morning and that the gates of Genoa closed at midnight,

> I had barely time to reach the gate before midnight; and was running as hard as I could go, downhill, over uneven ground, along a new street called the strada Sevra, when I came to a pole fastened straight across the street, nearly breast high, without any light or watchman – quite in the Italian style. I went over it, headlong, with such force that I rolled myself completely white in the dust; but although I tore my clothes

to shreds, I hardly scratched myself except in one place on the knee. I had no time to think of it then, for I was up directly and off again to save the gate: but when I got outside the wall, and saw the state I was in, I wondered I had not broken my neck. I 'took it easy' after this, and walked home, by lonely ways enough, without meeting a single soul. But there is nothing to be feared, I believe, from midnight walks in this part of Italy. In other places you incur the danger of being stabbed by mistake; whereas the people here are quiet and good-tempered, and very rarely commit any outrage.

The travel writer Valery left an evocative description of what Genoa was like in the early 1840s. The attractions, shops and merchants he lists include theatres, 'booksellers and reading rooms', a pharmacy, a maker of artificial flowers, two florists, a manufacturer of objects made from fig wood (whom he recommends for the making of snuff boxes), goldsmiths, a silk mercer, 'The velvets of Genoa still retain their ancient superiority', tobacconists including those who sell 'real Havannah cigars', public bathhouses including 'floating sea baths' (even though Valery feels public baths are unnecessary as 'every house is supplied with water to the highest story and every hotel keeps chamberbaths that are got ready in a few minutes').

One local amenity with which the Dickens family was unimpressed, however, was the laundry service, in which clothes were 'washed in a pond, beaten with gourds, and whitened with a preparation of lime so that what between the beating and the burning they fall into holes unexpectedly, and my white trowsers, after six weeks' washing, would make very good fishing-nets', as Dickens wrote to Forster.

Valery also wrote of how regularly the 'diligences' (a type of carriage) travelled between Genoa and Turin. There were also steamboats to Livorno (known then as 'Leghorn'), Civita Vecchia, Naples and Marseilles. This ease of travel was what encouraged Dickens to keep inviting friends and family to join them.

Almost as soon as they had arrived in Italy, Dickens had started asking his younger brother Fred to visit, including writing to him in July 1844,

> I am assured that the journey, straight through, can be very well done in something less than a week, for £15 each way.

> If you should decide to come, I will very gladly stand £10 of this Thirty. And I can answer for your seeing all manner of novelties, and being very much entertained in this New World. I believe (but I will enquire further into this, if you decide to come) that you would cross the Alps, and not steam it. In that case; or indeed in any, most probably; I would come on to some point to meet you. Such French phrases as you would want, I could give you in a letter; but you can book yourself to Paris, in London; and very nearly to this place, in Paris. And one word *'combien'* – how much? – would carry you further than you are ever likely to go, in Foreign Parts.

In the same letter, Dickens tells his brother that boots are much cheaper to buy in Italy than London, but adds, 'I don't know what you would do on the pavements; which are very trying. It is like walking on marbles.' He also told Fred that his children had been so entranced by the Genoese women wearing veils 'instead of bonnets' that they were insistent their dolls needed veils as well. It is touching to think of Charles and Catherine scouring Genoese shops for dolls' clothing.

There was great excitement in the household when 'Uncle Fred' announced he had made his travelling plans. In the autumn of 1844, Dickens travelled to Marseilles to meet him and bring him back to Genoa for a two-week holiday. He wrote to Catherine on 7 September to say Fred had arrived safely, sporting a natty new moustache, and that he did not appear 'to be at all tired'. He wrote wittily to Forster about their experience of travelling back from Marseilles (via Nice), and the ironically named, Grand Hotel of the Post:

> We lay last night … in an inn … . The house of call for fleas and vermin in general… . There was nothing to eat in it and nothing to drink. They had lost the teapot; and when they found it, they couldn't make out what had become of the lid, which, turning up at last and being fixed onto the teapot, couldn't be got off again for the pouring in of more water. Fleas of elephantine dimensions were gambolling boldly in the dirty beds; and the mosquitoes! – But let me here draw a curtain (as I would have done if there had been any)…

A New Life in Genoa

While living in Italy, Dickens surprised even himself by his new-found desire to swim in the sea. In August he wrote to Count D'Orsay, 'There is a delicious air here – almost always a sea breeze – and very good bathing.' He was, however, disconcerted by Italian swimwear, writing to his friend and solicitor Thomas Mitton about their mutual friend, Angus Fletcher:

> to see him; with his very bald head & his very fat body; limping over the sharp rocks in a small, short, tight pair of striped drawers – such as they wear in Masaniello on the stage; which is the dress you are expected to wear here, in bathing – is one of the most ridiculous sights I ever beheld in my life.

A couple of weeks before Fred's arrival, Dickens had written to Clarkson Stanfield:

> What do you think of my suddenly finding myself a Swimmer? But I have really made the discovery; and skim about a little blue bay just below the house here, like a fish in high spirits. I hope to preserve my bathing dress for your inspection and approval – or possibly to enrich your collection of Italian Costumes – on my return.

He took Fred out one day rather too ambitiously. Fred got into difficulties and had to be rescued by a passing fishing boat.

Shortly after his brother's departure from Albaro, the Dickens family left the Villa di Bagnerello for the Palazzo Peschiere. On 11 August 1844, Dickens had written to Mitton:

> I have taken the unexpired term of an English colonel who is going away, in the Palazzo Peschiere (pronounced Peskeeairy): which I enter on the possession of, on the 1st. of October, and hold until the sixteenth of March, at 5 Guineas a week – one more than this place. To remain here in the winter would have been impossible, for there are no fire-places; and the coach-hire into Genoa is very expensive, besides being very damnable, and jolting one to death. The Peschiere is

greatly esteemed as being perfectly healthy – in the midst of the most splendid prospects – within the walls of Genoa – in the heart of all the Mountain walks – and surrounded by the most delicious gardens (filled with fountains, orange trees, and all sorts of lovely things) you can conceive… . Within, it is painted: walls and ceilings, every inch: in the most gorgeous manner. There are ten rooms on one floor: few smaller than the largest habitable rooms in Hampton Court Palace: and one quite as long and wide as the Saloon of Drury Lane Theatre; with a great vaulted roof higher than that of the Waterloo Gallery in Windsor Castle – I think again, and can safely add very much higher.

Dickens also loved the luxuriousness of the palazzo's marble bath 'from which in all weathers, cold or warm, wet or dry, the heels of the Inimitable B[oz] may be beheld protruding, as the clock strikes 8 every morning', as he wrote to Thomas Beard. In a letter to Forster he noted the 'miraculously splendid' fireflies. 'They get into the bedrooms, and fly about, all night, like beautiful little lamps.'

The palazzo provided everything Dickens needed to make him feel like a success: he had taken his family out of the dreariness he had been struggling with in London and housed them in a palace. In November, he wrote to his friend the Countess of Blessington, 'We like Italy more and more, every day. We are splendidly lodged – have a noble Sala – fifty feet high, and splendidly painted – and beautiful gardens. Mrs. Dickens and the children are as well as possible; our servants (contrary to all predictions) as contented and orderly as at home.'

The Dickens family and their servants were very loyal and kind to one another. At the very end of their time at the Palazzo Peschiere, Dickens wrote sadly to Forster about an English couple, friends of a mutual friend, who had moved into apartments in the palazzo. Dickens's servants told him the couple's servant was deeply unhappy and was locked up at night 'in a basement room with iron bars to the window'. They agreed that, when the English couple were in bed, Dickens's servants would visit the man, taking him food and wine and sitting talking to him.

Living in a palazzo fired Dickens's imagination. He wrote to friends of his haunting dreams and of ghost stories he had been told about their new home. Although the description of the fictional palace in his 1852

A New Life in Genoa

short story *To Be Read At Dusk* was very different from the real palace, Dickens's belief in the Palazzo Peschiere being haunted helped to inspire the Italian palace in the story:

> We all know what an old palace in or near Genoa is – how time and the sea air have blotted it – how the drapery painted on the outer walls has peeled off in great flakes of plaster – how the lower windows are darkened with rusty bars of iron – how the courtyard is overgrown with grass – how the outer buildings are dilapidated – how the whole pile seems devoted to ruin.

Their palazzo was a short distance from the de la Rues' home, and this led to an increasingly intimate relationship between the two families, with Dickens urging the banker and his wife, Augusta, to treat his home as their own. Augusta was exhibiting signs of anxiety, including a facial tic, which Dickens believed he could cure. Dickens remained fascinated by the practice of mesmerism, which he had used with such great success to help cure his friend John Leech on their Isle of Wight holiday. Mesmerism was a method of healing by hypnotic trance, pioneered by the German doctor Franz Anton Mesmer (1734–1815). In London, Dickens had attended lectures about mesmerism given by his friend Dr John Elliotson (the first doctor in Britain to use a stethoscope). Elliotson had taught Dickens the art of mesmerism and Dickens was now convinced he could use it to heal Mme de la Rue. She was obviously enthralled by Dickens, something Emile de la Rue, either affected not to mind or was genuinely unconcerned about. He actively promoted his wife's close friendship with the celebrated author. Catherine, however, was much less happy about it.

On 6 November 1844, Dickens and Louis Roche went on an adventure. Their first stop was Piacenza, which they reached via Alessandria and Stradella. In *Pictures from Italy*, Dickens includes amusing observations about their fellow travellers and his amazement at how much gossip Louis managed to amass during their coach journey. He described Piacenza as

> A brown, decayed, old town ...[a] deserted, solitary, grass-grown place, with ruined ramparts; half filled-up trenches ... and streets of stern houses, moodily frowning at the other

houses over the way. The sleepiest and shabbiest of soldiery go wandering about, with the double curse of laziness and poverty, uncouthly wrinkling their misfitting regimentals; the dirtiest of children play with their impromptu toys (pigs and mud) in the feeblest of gutters; and the gauntest of dogs trot in and out of the dullest of archways, in perpetual search of something to eat, which they never seem to find.... What a strange, half-sorrowful and half-delicious doze it is, to ramble through these places gone to sleep and basking in the sun! ... Sitting on this hillock where a bastion used to be, and where a noisy fortress was, in the time of the old Roman station here, I became aware that I have never known till now, what it is to be lazy.

They travelled on to Parma, a place of 'cheerful, stirring streets'. Dickens, still in a contemplative state of mind, relished the silence and noted that

the Cathedral, Baptistery, and Campanile ... are clustered in a noble and magnificent repose. Their silent presence was only invaded, when I saw them, by the twittering of the many birds that were flying in and out of the crevices in the stones and little nooks in the architecture, where they had made their nests.

He was less impressed with the interiors of the buildings, finding them far too Roman Catholic and gloomy.

They arrived at Modena in 'the most delicious weather ... the bright sky, so wonderfully blue'. Dickens's mood, however, was lowered by entering the cathedral. He was a religious man, a practising Unitarian, but in Italy he visited churches as a tourist, and usually found leaving the rich sunshine to enter the oppressive gloom of a cathedral or church lowered his spirits rather than elevated them. He described the Italian style of religion as a 'torpid, listless system'. As they left Modena's cathedral, a procession of circus performers passed them, complete with unfortunate lions and tigers, advertising a show that evening.

Dickens and Roche travelled rapidly, spending just a short time in each place before speeding on to the next: 'Indeed, we were at Bologna, before … we had half done justice to the wonders of Modena. But it is such a delight to me to leave new scenes behind, and still go on, encountering newer scenes.' As Italian roads had become notorious for travellers' stories of being robbed, the journey to Bologna was marked by constant stopping of the carriage to check their luggage was still in place. After that experience, Dickens and Roche agreed to try and travel in daylight.

In Bologna, Dickens was recommended to tip a 'very smart official', but he considered him so very grand in his uniform that he feared the man would be offended by the idea of a tip. Having been persuaded that it was the right thing to do, Dickens was gratified to see how magnificently the official accepted it, and then became his guide around the cemetery. Dickens liked Bologna, 'an ancient sombre town, under the brilliant sky… . There is a grave, a learned air about the city, and a pleasant gloom upon it.' He marvelled over the city's art collection, but was disappointed to find the city 'very full of tourists', because flooding had closed roads between Bologna and Florence.

Dickens stayed 'at the top of an hotel, in an out-of-the-way room which I never could find: containing a bed, big enough for a boarding-school, which I couldn't fall asleep in' and with a waiter who appeared to be a bigger fan of Lord Byron than Dickens. He managed to bring 'Milor Beeron' into every conversation, as Dickens reported:

> I made the discovery by accidentally remarking to him, at breakfast, that the matting with which the floor was covered, was very comfortable at that season, when he immediately replied that Milor Beeron had been much attached to that kind of matting. Observing, at the same moment, that I took no milk, he exclaimed with enthusiasm, that Milor Beeron had never touched it.

Dickens assumed the waiter had been one of Lord Byron's servants when he lived in Italy, but it turned out he was just 'in the habit' of talking about Lord Byron with all English tourists.

From Bologna, they travelled to Ferrara, today a UNESCO world heritage site, but which Dickens described as 'More solitary, more depopulated, more deserted' than any of the cities they had visited. He was uncomplimentary about the town which, during the Renaissance, had been the grand home of the aristocratic Este family. Dicken's limited experience of Ferrara was recorded in *Pictures from Italy* with the words 'the sun shines with diminished cheerfulness in grim Ferrara … this dreary town.'

They had travelled to Ferrara to cross the River Po, whereupon they entered 'Austrian territory'. Here, Roche argued furiously with the Austrian official, stubbornly refusing to tip, despite Dickens's entreaties to do so. The official was defeated and Roche and Dickens continued their journey to Padua, a 'pleasant city', before arriving at Dickens's much-desired destination: Venice.

The chapter on Venice in *Pictures from Italy* is written in a very different style from the others. The others have functional titles, such as 'Genoa and its Neighbourhood' or 'Through Bologna and Ferrara', but the chapter on Venice is called 'An Italian Dream'. It is written as if it were merely a fantastic dream, a magical place too perfect to exist, and Dickens doesn't mention the name of the place until the very last word of the chapter.

> It was now quite night, and we were at the waterside. There lay here, a black boat … paddled, by two men, towards a great light, lying in the distance on the sea… . I could not but think how strange it was, to be floating away at that hour: leaving the land behind… . Before I knew by what, or how, I found that we were gliding up a street – a phantom street; the houses rising on both sides, from the water, and the black boat gliding on beneath their windows. Lights were shining from some of these casements, plumbing the depth of the black stream with their reflected rays, but all was profoundly silent.
>
> So we advanced into this ghostly city, continuing to hold our course through narrow streets and lanes, all filled and flowing with water… . I saw some figures coming down a gloomy archway from the interior of a palace: gaily dressed, and attended by torch-bearers. It was but a glimpse I had of them; for a bridge, so low and close upon the boat that it seemed ready to fall down and crush us: one of the many bridges that perplexed the Dream: blotted them out, instantly. On we went, floating towards the heart of this

A New Life in Genoa

strange place.... Going down upon the margin of the green sea, rolling on before the door, and filling all the streets, I came upon a place of such surpassing beauty, and such grandeur, that all the rest was poor and faded, in comparison with its absorbing loveliness...

Floating down narrow lanes, where carpenters, at work with plane and chisel in their shops, tossed the light shaving straight upon the water, where it lay like weed, or ebbed away before me in a tangled heap... . Past quays and terraces, where women, gracefully veiled, were passing and repassing, and where idlers were reclining in the sunshine, on flag-stones and on flights of steps. Past bridges, where there were idlers too; loitering and looking over... . There, in the errant fancy of my dream, I saw old Shylock passing to and fro upon a bridge, all built upon with shops and humming with the tongues of men; a form I seemed to know for Desdemona's, leaned down through a latticed blind to pluck a flower. And, in the dream, I thought that Shakespeare's spirit was abroad upon the water somewhere: stealing through the city ... close about the quays and churches, palaces and prisons sucking at their walls, and welling up into the secret places of the town: crept the water always. Noiseless and watchful: coiled round and round it, in its many folds, like an old serpent... . Thus it floated me away, until I awoke in the old market-place at Verona. I have, many and many a time, thought since, of this strange Dream upon the water: half-wondering if it lie there yet, and if its name be VENICE.

Dickens wrote to Forster,

my dear fellow, nothing in the world that ever you have heard of Venice, is equal to the magnificent and stupendous reality. The wildest visions of the Arabian Nights are nothing to the piazza of Saint Mark... . The gorgeous and wonderful reality of Venice is beyond the fancy of the wildest dreamer. Opium couldn't build such a place, and enchantment couldn't shadow it forth in a vision... . You

> know that I am liable to disappointment in such things from over-expectation, but Venice is above, beyond, out of all reach of coming near, the imagination of a man. It has never been rated high enough. It is a thing you would shed tears to see.

One of the things that thrilled Dickens so much, was to see a place immortalised by Shakespeare. Before Dickens had ever even glimpsed Italy, his opinions of the country had been coloured by his knowledge of Shakespeare's plays (despite there being no evidence that Shakespeare ever visited Italy). Because of this, Dickens had become quite concerned about visiting Verona. He had such expectations about the home of Romeo and Juliet – a place inextricably linked with William Shakespeare – that he was worried he would find it a disappointment. He did not, although he was unimpressed by the state of the House of the Capulets

> now degenerated into a most miserable little inn ... the yard ... was ankle-deep in dirt, with a brood of splashed and bespattered geese; and there was a grim-visaged dog, viciously panting in a doorway, who would certainly have had Romeo by the leg, the moment he put it over the wall.

Perhaps it was this wittily remembered scene that gave Dickens such fervour to take part in the 'saving' of Shakespeare's birthplace. In 1846, the year after Dickens returned to England from Italy, the home in which Shakespeare had been born almost 300 years earlier was put up for sale. Amongst the rumoured interested purchasers was P.T. Barnum, the American circus owner. In his autobiography, Barnum revealed that he had planned to buy it, then have it taken down and shipped, piece by piece, to America, where it would be recreated in New York:

> I soon despatched a trusty agent to Stratford-on-Avon armed with cash and full powers to buy the Shakespeare house, if possible, and have it carefully taken down, packed in boxes and shipped to New York. He was cautioned not to mention my name, and to give no hint that the building was ever to leave England.

Somehow, however, Barnum's plans did get found out and, for a year, the story of the house sale fascinated the media and the public, and a panic started to set in that the Bard's birthplace was in jeopardy of being taken to America. Dickens was a member of the Shakespeare's Birthplace Committee; the other members included Queen Victoria's husband, Prince Albert. When an auction date was set for 1847, Dickens employed his usually hyperactive energy to raise funds, offering events such as benefit readings. The committee managed to raise £3,000, which enabled them to buy the property and ensure Shakespeare's Birthplace remained safely in Stratford-upon-Avon.

In 1844, Dickens found something pleasing in just how dirty and unromantic the Capulets' house was, and his writing about Verona is amusing and enthusiastic. He visited all the touristy sights that he could, including the impressive Roman amphitheatre 'so well preserved, and carefully maintained', and enjoyed himself immensely, praising the city in *Pictures from Italy* as

> Pleasant Verona! With its beautiful old palaces, and charming country in the distance, seen from terrace walks, and stately, balustraded galleries. With its Roman gates, still spanning the fair street, and casting, on the sunlight of to-day, the shade of fifteen hundred years ago. With its marble-fitted churches, lofty towers, rich architecture, and quaint old quiet thoroughfares, where shouts of Montagues and Capulets once resounded.... With its fast-rushing river, picturesque old bridge, great castle, waving cypresses, and prospect so delightful, and so cheerful! Pleasant Verona!... I walked through and through the town all the rest of the day, and could have walked there until now, I think.

That night, Dickens sat in his hotel room and re-read *Romeo and Juliet*, knowing he was enacting a cliché by doing so. As he and Roche continued their journey to Mantua, Dickens mused whether a person of Shakespeare's time would have seen the same sights they were seeing:

> Was the way to Mantua as beautiful, in his time, I wonder! Did it wind through pasture land as green, bright with the

same glancing streams, and dotted with fresh clumps of graceful trees! Those purple mountains lay on the horizon, then, for certain; and the dresses of these peasant girls, who wear a great, knobbed, silver pin like an English 'life-preserver' through their hair behind, can hardly be much changed.

He was surprised, though, to discover how close Mantua was to Verona, writing to his friend, the playwright Douglas Jerrold, 'I was rather shocked, yesterday (I am not strong in geographical details) to find that Romeo was only banished twenty five miles. That is the distance between Mantua and Verona.'

When Dickens and Roche were in the author's hotel room in Mantua working out their schedule, they were surprised to hear a knock at the door. Standing outside it was 'an intensely shabby little man … there was so much poverty expressed in his faded suit and little pinched hat'. He asked whether the tourists wanted a *cicerone*, or tour guide. Dickens hired him immediately and was taken on an amusingly terrible tour of the town. When Dickens asked politely if there was much to see, the man said apologetically, 'Truly, no.'

Dickens recalled his impressions of Mantua in *Pictures from Italy*:

> Our walk … showed us, in almost every street, some suppressed church: now used for a warehouse, now for nothing at all: all as crazy and dismantled as they could be, short of tumbling down bodily. The marshy town was so intensely dull and flat, that the dirt upon it seemed not to have come there in the ordinary course, but to have settled and mantled on its surface as on standing water.

Early the next morning, as soon as the city gates were opened, Dickens and Roche left Mantua in a hired carriage. Their driver, who had faithfully promised the journey to Milan would take two and a half days, soon showed himself ignorant of how to get there. They made their way through the poverty-stricken town of Bozzolo, where Dickens was deeply moved at witnessing the landlord of the town's 'miserable inn' carrying out his weekly custom of giving money to those poorer than himself, 'a clamorous herd of women and children, whose rags were fluttering in the wind and rain'. They spent their first night in the old Roman outpost of Cremona and the second in Lodi, famous in the Victorian mind as the site of a 1796 battle, in which the troops of Napoleon Bonaparte defeated the Austrian Army. By this time, winter was starting to set in and Dickens was depressed by the relentless 'mud, mist, and rain, and marshy ground'. He declared that no fog in England could surpass that of the fog that enshrouded Milan, when they finally arrived. As a result, this first visit to Milan did not impress him, although when he returned, the following summer, he found the city much more to his liking.

The thick Milanese fog, however, was nothing compared to the gathering fury with which Dickens contemplated Leonardo da Vinci's *The Last Supper*:

> I would simply observe, that in its beautiful composition and arrangement, there it is, at Milan, a wonderful picture; and that, in its original colouring, or in its original expression of any single face or feature, there it is not. Apart from the damage it has sustained from damp, decay, or neglect, it has been … so retouched upon, and repainted, and that so clumsily, that many of the heads are, now, positive deformities, with patches of paint and plaster sticking upon them like wens, and utterly distorting the expression. Where the original artist set that impress of his genius on a face, which, almost in a line or touch, separated him from meaner painters and made him what he was, succeeding bunglers, filling up, or painting across seams and cracks, have been quite unable to imitate his hand; and putting in some scowls, or frowns, or wrinkles, of their own, have blotched and spoiled the work.

Catherine and her sister Georgina travelled to meet Dickens and Roche in Milan, and brought with them everything Dickens would need for the rest of his journey, and the post that had arrived for him. After leaving Milan, the two men travelled on to Lago Maggiore: 'the Alps, stupendously confused in lofty peaks and ridges, clouds and snow, were towering in our path… . The beautiful day was just declining when we came upon the Lago Maggiore, with its lovely islands.' From there they headed to the Simplon Pass, a place that would stay in Dickens's imagination and appear in his writing for years to come, including in the Christmas story of 1867, *No Thoroughfare*.

By the time they reached the pass, it was late November, there was snow on the ground and the air 'was piercing cold'. Dickens found the experience 'sublime'. He wrote to Catherine:

> we began the ascent of the Simplon that same night... . Most favourable state of circumstances for journeying up that tremendous Pass! The brightest moon I ever saw, all night; and daybreak on the summit. The Glory of which: making great wastes of snow, a rosy red: exceeds all telling. We sledged through the snow on the summit, for two hours or so. The weather was perfectly fair and bright; and there was neither difficulty nor danger – except the danger that there always must be in such a place, of a horse stumbling on the brink of an immeasurable precipice. In which case, no piece of the unfortunate traveller would be left, large enough, to tell his story... . Glencoe, well-sprinkled with Snow, would be very like the ascent. But the top itself, so wild, and bleak, and lonely, is a thing by itself, and not to be likened to any other sight.

Although he loved being with his children and was still happily married, Dickens always enjoyed the chance to escape from his familial responsibilities and go travelling by himself or with male friends, and on this journey, it was as if he and Roche were explorers, discovering new places – new at least to Dickens – and having experiences he would always remember. Dickens's writing in *Pictures from Italy* evokes so strongly what it was like to be a traveller in Europe at that time: the sharpness of the cold air, the sight of 'calm Italian villages ... sleeping in the moonlight', sinuous roads winding up mountainsides lit by a strong moon, the experience of travelling by carriage or on horse- or mule-back, the clause expected in every carriage hire contract that no matter what the urgency of the journey, the carriage will stop for a couple of hours in the middle of the day to give the horses a rest. He describes what it was like when he and Roche suddenly lost sight of the moon and stars as their carriage entered into the folds of a mountain tunnel, and they could see nothing, surrounded as they were by an encasing of black rock with the sound of angrily rushing water thundering overhead. When the road become too difficult for their carriage, the travellers were moved onto a horse-drawn sledge through which they ascended up a snowy track, surrounded by what Dickens described as a 'great white desert'.

This journey was an adventurous way for Dickens to return to London for a business trip. After Switzerland, Dickens and Roche travelled through France, via Strasbourg to Paris, where they stayed at the Hotel Bristol. Dickens wrote to Macready, 'I have been travelling for weeks, and have not been five minutes in Paris, on my way to London – after a 50 hours' spell in a horrible coach.... . I go on to London at 8 tomorrow morning.' In that December of 1844 'the road to Paris, was one sea of mud, and thence to the coast, a little better for a hard frost ... the cliffs of Dover were a pleasant sight, and England was so wonderfully neat.' Yet he wrote to Catherine with a homesickness for Italy and a longing to 'return to our Italian Bowers'.

Dickens was travelling with a precious manuscript of his second Christmas book, *The Chimes*. In the months Dickens had been living in Italy, he had done comparatively little writing for an author who was usually intensively prolific. Instead, he had concentrated on recording his impressions of Italy, seeing new places, spending time with his family and friends and recovering his mental equilibrium after the exhausting and depressing year that had been 1843. Now, *A Christmas Carol*, the book in which his publisher had had so little faith, was a confirmed success. Dickens was not only increasingly famous, but his finances were finally out of danger, and he could stop panicking that his children were going to witness the fear and heartbreak he had experienced as the child of an unrepentant debtor.

By the time he returned to London, less than six months after leaving it, Dickens's mood was entirely different from that in which he had left. He was greeted warmly by the friends who had missed his ebullient presence at their parties and delivered the manuscript of *The Chimes* to his publisher. He also gave pre-publication readings to small groups of his close friends.

Dickens was still trying to persuade Douglas Jerrold to come to Italy, and, prior to his journey home, wrote beseechingly to the playwright about his life in the palazzo:

> You rather entertained the notion once, of coming to see me at Genoa. I shall return straight on the ninth of December,

limiting my stay in town to one week. Now, couldn't you come back with me? The journey that way is very cheap, and I am sure the gratification to you would be high. I am lodged in quite a wonderful place, and would put you in a painted room as big as a church, and much more comfortable. There are pens and ink upon the premises; orange trees, gardens, battledores and shuttlecocks, rousing wood fires for evenings, and a welcome worth having.

After a triumphant week in London, Dickens and Louis Roche began their return journey, beginning with a cold voyage across the English Channel, 'with ice upon the decks'. They travelled through deep snow towards Paris, and Dickens was saddened by the sight of people wearing only rags searching through the snow with sticks. They stopped in Paris for a couple of days, where Dickens met up with Macready, before continuing their journey to Marseilles. As they headed south, the snow was starting to thaw – but this led to flooded roads and a tense journey for the mail coach on which they were travelling, culminating in a broken spring which needed to be repaired before they could continue. Dickens wrote how they, the sole passengers on the coach, were sent to an inn while the repairs were being effected, spending their time 'in miserable billiard-rooms, where hairy company, collected about stoves, were playing cards; the cards being very like themselves – extremely limp and dirty.'

The intention had been to reach his family in time for Christmas, but after being detained at Marseilles by bad weather, with the ships threatening not to sail to Genoa, Dickens became worried he was going to miss the festivities altogether. Eventually, he was able to find a berth on the *Charlemagne*, despite dire warnings that the adverse weather would probably mean going no further than Nice. He was gratified to be recognised by a group of American travellers and wrote with wry amusement to his friends about how the Americans had just one foreign language dictionary between them, which was kept jealously in the cabin of a man who was constantly seasick, but who refused to part with it. Dickens could hear his friends repeatedly going in to beg to look up a word, so they could ask for a pillow, or sugar, or some other necessity of life on board. Dickens listened with amusement through the thin walls, but he was also forced to spend the entire voyage listening to the less pleasant aural accompaniments of his seasick neighbour.

A New Life in Genoa

At last, the boat arrived in Genoa – whereupon it transpired that Dickens's passport did not have the correct visa, so he was not given permission to leave the ship. On 20 December, Dickens wrote a desperate letter to Timothy Yeats Brown, the British Consul in Genoa, explaining:

> Through my passport having fallen into the hands of a rival boat at Marseilles, which promised to sail, and didn't ... and through my having only rescued it from those Sharks by main force, in time to leap on board this Vessel – it has not the visa of the Sardinian Minister at Marseilles upon it: which ought to have been obtained.

The consul, it appears, intervened, and Dickens made it back to Palazzo Peschiere in time for an Italian Christmas.

Pictures from Italy

'The wines of Italy are generally very fine, exceedingly wholesome, and some are of great celebrity; there is scarcely a hut in the mountains, or villages, but where they may be obtained.'
Captain Jousiffe from
A Road Book for Travellers in Central Italy (1840)

Soon after his arrival in Italy, in the summer of 1844, Dickens had written to his friend Count D'Orsay of his plans for future travels:

> ...I shall come back here for Christmas, and remain here through January. In February, I think I shall start ... and taking the Steamboat to Civita Vecchia, go to Rome – from Rome to Naples – and from Naples to Mount Aetna, which I very much desire to see. Then I purpose returning to Naples, and coming back here, by Steamer. For Easter Week, I design returning to Rome again; taking Mrs. Dickens and her sister with me, that time; then coming back here, picking up my caravan, starting off to Paris, and remaining there a month or so, before I return to England.

After spending Christmas with his family, Dickens put some of this plan into action. In the January of 1845, Charles and Catherine left the children in Albaro and began travelling. Dickens wrote of the start of their journey with hyperbole:

> There is nothing in Italy, more beautiful to me, than the coast-road between Genoa and Spezzia. On one side: sometimes far below, sometimes nearly on a level with the road, and often

skirted by broken rocks of many shapes: there is the free blue sea, with here and there a picturesque felucca gliding slowly on; on the other side are lofty hills, ravines besprinkled with white cottages, patches of dark olive woods, country churches with their light open towers, and country houses gaily painted. On every bank and knoll by the wayside, the wild cactus and aloe flourish in exuberant profusion; and the gardens of the bright villages along the road, are seen, all blushing in the summer-time with clusters of the Belladonna, and are fragrant in the autumn and winter with golden oranges and lemons.

On this journey between Genoa and La Spezia, Dickens was echoing the travels of earlier British writers. Mary Shelley and her husband, Percy Shelley, lived in the pretty harbour town of Lerici. Lord Byron swam regularly across the bay from Portovenere to visit them. It was while travelling by boat back to Lerici that Percy was caught in a storm and drowned. The area, which also has connections with the Italian poets Petrarch and Dante Alighieri, has become known as 'Golfo dei Poeti' or the Gulf (or Bay) of the Poets.

The area they were travelling through is now one of the most overly visited tourist regions in Italy, the area known as Cinque Terre. Today, it is so crowded, with walking routes packed with people and every side street filled with row upon row of shops aimed solely at tourists, that it is difficult to imagine what it was like when Dickens marvelled over its solitude:

> Some of the villages are inhabited, almost exclusively, by fishermen; and it is pleasant to see their great boats hauled up on the beach, making little patches of shade, where they lie asleep, or where the women and children sit romping and looking out to sea, while they mend their nets upon the shore. There is one town, Camoglia .... Seen from the road above, it is like a tiny model on the margin of the dimpled water, shining in the sun. Descended into, by the winding mule-tracks, it is a perfect miniature of a primitive seafaring town; the saltest, roughest, most piratical little place that ever was seen.

This description was written in nostalgic hindsight, about a journey Dickens became accustomed to making during his year in Italy. On the journey that Charles and Catherine took together, however, it was a cold and wet January, where the beautiful views described above were shrouded in mist under lowering wintry skies. 'There might have been no Mediterranean in the world, for anything that we saw of it,' complained Dickens in a letter. 'The rain was incessant; every brook and torrent was greatly swollen ... I never heard the like of in my life.' They rushed past, because the intention on this particular journey was to get to Rome.

In La Spezia, the ferry across the River Magra was delayed by bad weather, so they were forced to wait for a day, which Dickens decided was a good thing as

> Spezzia [sic] ... is a good place to tarry at; by reason, firstly, of its beautiful bay; secondly, of its ghostly Inn; thirdly, of the head-dress of the women, who wear, on one side of their head, a small doll's straw hat, stuck on to the hair; which is certainly the oddest and most roguish head-gear that ever was invented.

Safely across the swollen river, they travelled on horseback to Carrara, renowned as the place from which Michelangelo bought the marble for his statue of *David*. Dickens marvelled at the pretty Tuscan town surrounded by quarries:

> They are four or five great glens, running up into a range of lofty hills, until they can run no longer, and are stopped by being abruptly strangled by Nature. The quarries, 'or caves,' as they call them there, are so many openings, high up in the hills, on either side of these passes, where they blast and excavate for marble.... . Some of these caves were opened by the ancient Romans, and remain as they left them to this hour. Many others are being worked at this moment; others are to be begun to-morrow, next week, next month; others are unbought, unthought of; and marble enough for more ages than have passed since the place was resorted to, lies hidden everywhere: patiently awaiting its time of discovery.

Although he was impressed by the grandeur of the quarries, Dickens was concerned about the health of the workers and deeply distressed by the plight of the oxen used to haul the heavily laden carts. When he and Catherine visited marble workers' studios, they admired the sculptures, but to Dickens, 'it seemed … so strange to me that those exquisite shapes, replete with grace, and thought, and delicate repose, should grow out of all this toil, and sweat, and torture!'

Despite these worries, Dickens liked Carrara, which he described as 'very picturesque and bold'. He noted with the satisfaction of one who believes himself a traveller, not a mere tourist, that few tourists ever stayed in the town. Angus Fletcher was also in Carrara at the time; as a sculptor he was a regular visitor and knew the town well. He was the guest of an English marble merchant who also invited Charles and Catherine to stay in his home. Dickens described the merchant, in a letter to Forster on 25 January, as

> A Yorkshireman, who talks Yorkshire Italian with the drollest and pleasantest effect; a jolly, hospitable, excellent fellow; as odd yet kindly a mixture of shrewdness and simplicity as I have ever seen. He is the only Englishman in these parts who has been able to erect an English household out of Italian servants, but he has done it to admiration. It would be a capital country-house at home; and for staying in 'first-rate'. Mr. Walton is a man of an extraordinarily kind heart, and has a compassionate regard for Fletcher, to whom his house is open as a home, which is half affecting and half ludicrous. He paid the other day a hundred pounds for him, which he knows he will never see a penny of again.

Mr Walton took his guests to an opera at Carrara's new theatre (which was 'crammed to excess'). The chorus was made up of labourers from the marble quarries, 'who are self-taught and sing by ear … and acquitted themselves very well,' noted Dickens. The people of Carrara made a special effort for the visiting author and his wife, and Dickens recorded with great pleasure how the theatre had been 'illuminated that night in my honour', of the reception that they attended after the performance and of how the orchestra arrived to 'serenade' them later that night at Mr Walton's house.

Today, the town of Carrara continues to honour Dickens. In 2013, the very first Italian branch of the Dickens Fellowship was founded in

Carrara. In 2020, to mark the 175th anniversary of the Dickenses' visit, the town named a road in his honour: the Viale Charles Dickens.

From Carrara, they travelled to Pisa, a place Dickens visited several times and by which he was enchanted and disappointed in equal measure. They arrived on a beautiful moonlit night, when the town was celebrating the 300th anniversary of the cathedral and leaning tower. Dickens experienced the 'Mona Lisa effect': when he saw the famed leaning tower, a place he had seen illustrations of many times and dreamt about seeing, it was 'too small ... a short reality'. He was also surprised by how quiet Pisa was, expecting it to be thronged with people. At that time it was possible to climb up to the top of the tower, which gave Dickens a giddy feeling as though he were on board a listing ship. He soon grew to admire it, writing in *Pictures from Italy*,

> It was a surprise to me to find [the leaning tower] in a grave retired place, apart from the general resort, and carpeted with smooth green turf. But, the group of buildings, clustered on and about this verdant carpet: comprising the Tower, the Baptistery, the Cathedral, and the Church of the Campo Santo: is perhaps the most remarkable and beautiful in the whole world; and from being clustered there, together, away from the ordinary transactions and details of the town, they have a singularly venerable and impressive character. It is the architectural essence of a rich old city, with all its common life and common habitations pressed out, and filtered away.

Dickens loved the architecture and the art of the town, praising in particular a painting by Andrea del Sarto, writing approvingly of ancient frescoes and of Pisa's long and interesting history. He was also grudgingly impressed by the skill of the beggars: 'They waylay the unhappy visitor at every turn.... . The beggars seem to embody all the trade and enterprise of Pisa. Nothing else is stirring, but warm air.'

From Pisa they took a trip by railway, which Dickens praised as 'good' and 'punctual', to the bustling, business-oriented town of Livorno. There they visited the grave of the Scottish writer Tobias Smollett and listened to tales of when Livorno was held in the grip of terror by an 'assassination club', whose gang members were notorious for carrying out night-time stabbings of strangers. They returned by rail to Pisa, where they hired a carriage driver to take them to Rome, 'through pleasant Tuscan villages and cheerful scenery all day'. Dickens made a note of the many and varied roadside shrines and crosses, 'repeated every four or five miles, all along the highway'.

In Siena, where they stopped on the evening of their second day, they had been told they were in time to witness the carnival, but they found it disappointing, comprising 'a score or two of melancholy people walking up and down the principal street in common toy-shop masks, and being more melancholy, if possible, than the same sort of people in England.' The following morning, they toured the town, a place which Dickens found 'wonderfully picturesque ... ancient ... dreamy and fantastic, and most interesting'.

The journey from Siena took them through wine-growing country onto 'a region gradually becoming bleaker and wilder, until it became as bare and desolate as any Scottish moors.' There they stopped for another night, at a 'perfectly lone house' with a lethally smoking fireplace. The talk that night was of bands of thieves attacking carriages, of the recent robbery from a mail coach, and of a group of tourists who had been robbed while climbing Mount Vesuvius. Charles and Catherine comforted themselves with the knowledge that they had brought with them almost nothing worth being robbed for and set themselves to enjoy the dinner, and especially the wine. Dickens's descriptions of food in *Pictures from Italy* give an interesting insight of how British people felt about Italian cuisine at that date:

> We had the usual dinner in this solitary house; and a very good dinner it is, when you are used to it. There is something with a vegetable or some rice in it which is a sort of shorthand or arbitrary character for soup, and which tastes very well, when you have flavoured it with plenty of grated cheese, lots of salt, and abundance of pepper. There is the half fowl of which this soup has been made. There is a stewed pigeon, with the gizzards and livers of himself and other birds stuck all round him. There is a bit of roast beef, the size of a small French roll. There are a scrap of Parmesan cheese, and five little withered apples, all huddled together on a small plate, and crowding one upon the other, as if each were trying to save itself from the chance of being eaten. Then there is

coffee; and then there is bed.... . If you are good-humoured to the people about you, and speak pleasantly, and look cheerful, take my word for it you may be well entertained in the very worst Italian Inn, and always in the most obliging manner, and may go from one end of the country to the other (despite all stories to the contrary) without any great trial of your patience anywhere. Especially, when you get such wine in flasks, as the Orvieto, and the Monte Pulciano.

Their next stop was a few miles away from their solitary hotel, across a landscape that Dickens described as being 'as barren, as stony, and as wild, as Cornwall'. Despite their assurances to one another that they were carrying nothing of value, they had no choice but to travel with all the money they needed for their journey. Dickens wrote to Forster that he wished he was able to carry pistols.

Unmolested by bandits, they made it safely to Radicofani, where they stayed at an inn, formerly an aristocratic hunting lodge. This fired Dickens's imagination with visions of ghosts and goblins (the latter very much on his mind, having just published *The Chimes*, a goblin story). This spooky feeling was compounded on their continuing journey, by a ferocious storm that blew up as they crossed a mountain pass. Both he and Catherine were told to get out of the carriage and walk alongside it, holding on to it as tightly as they could to try and prevent it from being blown over; if they had remained inside, they risked being blown, along with the carriage, down the mountainside.

Dickens related how they couldn't stop laughing as they struggled to walk through the winds whilst trying to keep hold of the carriage. Catherine's voluminous skirts and petticoats would have been swept up and danced around by the wind, making her task harder than the men's. As they looked from the treacherous mountain pass down onto the sea, Dickens commented,

> There was snow, and hail, and rain, and lightning, and thunder; and there were rolling mists, travelling with incredible velocity. It was dark, awful, and solitary to the last degree; there were mountains above mountains, veiled in angry clouds; and there was such a wrathful, rapid, violent, tumultuous hurry, everywhere ... unspeakably exciting and grand.

The Ghosts of Rome

*'Here was Rome indeed at last; and such a Rome
as no one can imagine in its
full and awful grandeur!'*

Charles Dickens,
Pictures from Italy (1846)

At last, they were in the vicinity of Rome, having crossed what Dickens called the 'dismal, dirty Papal Frontier', although the outskirts of the city proved less than impressive. They witnessed another 'carnival' in Acquapendente, the procession of which Dickens claimed was made up solely of one man dressed up as a woman and one woman dressed up as a man, both walking 'in a very melancholy manner' through mud that sloshed up to their ankles. Then their carriage took them past Lake Bolsena, which Dickens noted was 'much celebrated for malaria'. They were both, by this time, thoroughly fed up with the journey, and the weather, and the scenery, and were finding everything 'intolerable'. The landscape seemed to limp past in a mire of bleakness, with Dickens descrying ghost stories in the sight of ancient towns, tiny villages, forgotten lakes and images of historic earthquakes. Their final stop for the night before arriving in Rome was Ronciglione, 'a little town like a large pig-sty'.

They left Ronciglione at 7.00am and travelled across the Campagna Romana, which Dickens found depressingly monotonous and lonely, a place marked by centuries of graves, where he envisaged howling men possessed of devils had been sent when banished from the city. Desperate to get down from the carriage, to stretch their screaming muscles and ease their aching limbs, they sought for the first sight of Rome:

> We began, in a perfect fever to strain our eyes for Rome; and when, after another mile or two, the Eternal City appeared,

at length, in the distance; it looked like – I am half afraid to write the word – like LONDON!!! There it lay, under a thick cloud, with innumerable towers, and steeples, and roofs of houses, rising up into the sky, and high above them all, one Dome.

They arrived in Rome on a cold, grey and rainy evening, feeling uncomfortable and miserable, and, as is so often the case when travelling into a large city today, they passed through the most unaesthetic parts of the city on their journey. Carnival was in full swing, but all they saw were a few stragglers trying to catch up to the main procession. Having been so disappointed by their small-town carnivals, they mistakenly thought this was the sum total of the famed Roman carnival, so went to their hotel in a bad humour. They had entered by a gate some distance from the ancient heart of the city, so instead of immediately seeing ancient monuments and fabled buildings, Dickens was disgusted to encounter 'long streets of commonplace shops and houses, such as are to be found in any European town'.

In the morning, refreshed by a good night's sleep and a comfortable hotel, they set out to discover the Rome they had read about. Although impressed by the beauty of St Peter's Basilica, Dickens found it less emotionally affecting than his favourite churches in London and it compared unfavourably to St Mark's in Venice. Their tour guide kept them inside the basilica for much too long, after which they jumped back into their cab gladly and asked to be driven to the Colosseum. There, Dickens experienced the horror of the writer's imagination. As soon as he entered, he could feel the pain and terror of those who had been killed there and his mind created horrifying images of all the misery. As he wrote in *Pictures from Italy*,

> they who will, may have the whole great pile before them, as it used to be, with thousands of eager faces staring down into the arena, and such a whirl of strife, and blood, and dust going on there, as no language can describe. Its solitude, its awful beauty, and its utter desolation, strike upon the stranger the next moment, like a softened sorrow... . To see it crumbling there, an inch a year; its walls and arches overgrown with green; its corridors open to the day ... is to

see the ghost of old Rome, wicked, wonderful old city, haunting the very ground on which its people trod. It is the most impressive, the most stately, the most solemn, grand, majestic, mournful sight, conceivable. Never, in its bloodiest prime, can the sight of the gigantic Coliseum, full and running over with the lustiest life, have moved one's heart, as it must move all who look upon it now, a ruin. GOD be thanked: a ruin!

From the Colosseum, they embarked on one of Dickens's favourite pastimes, walking. His mood was affected by the visions of death and sadness he had found crowding unbidden upon his mind and the rest of Rome seemed to him to be a place of ruin and decay, invoking a feeling of desolation. The city of the ancient Romans seemed to haunt him. Dickens had read so much about Rome, had perused books and gazed at old illustrations, so the reality – with modern-day Romans living amongst the antiquity, just as in modern London – was a shock. In his preconceptions about the city, Dickens seems to have envisaged an ancient city kept as a shrine to antiquity. It took him some time, and several visits to Rome, to appreciate it precisely for its mixture of the ancient with the contemporary.

On the Sunday, they returned to St Peter's to watch the 'performance' of a papal mass. Dickens was unimpressed, writing that the experience was 'not religiously impressive or affecting'. He wrote with disdain of how 'gaudy' he found the clothing of the cardinals and priests, and the uniforms of the Pope's famous Swiss Guards, whom Dickens likened to overdressed bit-part actors. He disliked the singing at the Vatican, which he described as 'atrocious' and the ornate decoration of St Peter's, which he compared to an 'exploded cracker'.

Dickens shows an intense dislike of Catholicism in *Pictures from Italy*, particularly in his writing about Rome. This is very strange for the man who had written so passionately on behalf of Catholics in *Barnaby Rudge*. In Rome, after watching the Pope being carried in a sedan chair, blessing the crowd as he passed, Dickens wrote satirically that it put him in mind of Bonfire Night and that 'a bundle of matches and a lantern would have made it perfect'. Dickens intended to be funny, but *Pictures from Italy* offended his Catholic friend Clarkson Stanfield, whom Dickens had hoped would be the book's illustrator. Stanfield refused.

At last Charles and Catherine were to experience a proper carnival. After taking advice about how to take part, they had duly bought 'little wire masks' and hired a barouche – a fashionable open carriage – into which they climbed, having to navigate their way over the sacks of sugar plums and posies of flowers already inside the carriage, which they had bought to throw out at the crowds. Dickens's description of the carnival seems to have been written in a breathless excitement, a stark contrast to the despondent mini carnival processions they had witnessed during their journey:

> On the Monday afternoon at one or two o'clock, there began to be a great rattling of carriages into the court-yard of the hotel; a hurrying to and fro of all the servants in it; and, now and then, a swift shooting across some doorway or balcony, of a straggling stranger in a fancy dress. All the carriages were open, and had the linings carefully covered with white cotton or calico, to prevent their proper decorations from being spoiled by the incessant pelting of sugar-plums; and people were packing and cramming into every vehicle as it waited for its occupants, enormous sacks and baskets full of these confétti, together with such heaps of flowers, tied up in little nosegays, that some carriages were not only brimful of flowers, but literally running over.... Accordingly, we fell into the string of coaches.... If any impetuous carriage dashed out of the rank and clattered forward, with the wild idea of getting on faster, it was suddenly met, or overtaken, by a trooper on horseback, who ... immediately escorted it back to the very end of the row...
>
> Presently, we came into a narrow street, where, besides one line of carriages going, there was another line of carriages returning. Here the sugar-plums and the nosegays began to fly about, pretty smartly; and I was fortunate enough to observe one gentleman attired as a Greek warrior, catch a light-whiskered brigand on the nose (he was in the very act of tossing up a bouquet to a young lady in a first-floor window) with a precision that was much applauded by the bystanders. As this victorious Greek was exchanging a facetious remark with a stout gentleman in a doorway –

The Ghosts of Rome

one-half black and one-half white, as if he had been peeled up the middle – who had offered him his congratulations on this achievement, he received an orange from a housetop, full on his left ear, and was much surprised, not to say discomfited. Especially, as he was standing up at the time; and in consequence of the carriage moving on suddenly, at the same moment, staggered ignominiously, and buried himself among his flowers... . From all the innumerable balconies: from the remotest and highest, no less than from the lowest and nearest: hangings of bright red, bright green, bright blue, white and gold, were fluttering in the brilliant sunlight. From windows, and from parapets, and tops of houses, streamers of the richest colours, and draperies of the gaudiest and most sparkling hues, were floating out upon the street. The buildings seemed to have been literally turned inside out, and to have all their gaiety towards the highway... . Every sort of bewitching madness of dress was there. Little preposterous scarlet jackets; quaint old stomachers, more wicked than the smartest bodices; Polish pelisses, strained and tight as ripe gooseberries; tiny Greek caps, all awry, and clinging to the dark hair, Heaven knows how...

Some [carriages] were driven by coachmen with enormous double faces ... . Other drivers were attired as women, wearing long ringlets and no bonnets,... . Still, carriages on carriages, dresses on dresses, colours on colours, crowds upon crowds, without end. Men and boys clinging to the wheels of coaches, and holding on behind, and following in their wake, and diving in among the horses' feet to pick up scattered flowers to sell again;... a man-monkey on a pole, surrounded by strange animals with pigs' faces, and lions' tails, carried under their arms, or worn gracefully over their shoulders; carriages on carriages, dresses on dresses, colours on colours, crowds upon crowds, without end ... an abandonment so perfect, so contagious, so irresistible, that the steadiest foreigner fights up to his middle in flowers and sugar-plums, like the wildest Roman of them all, and thinks of nothing else till half-past four o'clock, when he is suddenly reminded (to his great regret) that this is not the whole business of his existence.

At 5.00pm, the procession came to an end and the Via Del Corso became a racetrack, with unfortunate horses – riderless but goaded by being dressed in costumes that included spurs to make them run faster – raced along the street, accompanied by the shouts and calls of the over-excited crowd. As the evening drew in, the entertainment turned into a street-wide game with tapering candles being sold to put in every window and house and shop and balcony and carriage and rooftop – the game being to try and extinguish everyone else's candle while protecting one's own flame from being put out by anyone else. 'The spectacle,' wrote Dickens, 'is one of the most extraordinary that can be imagined.'

The signal for the end of the carnival, all across the city, was when the sound of *Ave Maria* was played on church bells. Dickens was amazed at how rapidly the revellers stopped and the celebrations came to an end. After the exuberance and colour and excitement of the street carnival, he and Catherine were less than impressed by the after party: a masquerade ball at the theatre, 'as dull and senseless as a London one'. The street party had been much more to their taste, an experience that had enchanted them both. Dickens pondered what was it that had made the carnival so wondrous, especially the evening candle game, which he connected with the ancient Roman festival of Saturnalia. He loved the childlike enjoyment of everyone concerned, the easy mingling of both genders and all classes and the 'unbroken good humour of all concerned'.

Every morning, Catherine and her husband left their hotel early, to walk and walk, arriving back footsore but happy late in the evening. They also travelled out into the surrounding countryside, in an attempt to see everything they possibly could – except more churches. Dickens wrote that it was impossible to visit every church in the city. They found the nearby town of Tivoli 'squalid', but were enchanted by its Temple of the Sibyl (also known as the Temple of Vesta). Dickens also loved Albano (site of the Pope's summer residence Castel Gandolfo) 'with its lovely lake and wooded shore', although was less than enthusiastic about the local wine. He and Catherine, with two unnamed friends, went in search of Horace and

Cicero and Cato, and marvelled over Roman amphitheatres, deserted villas and ruined aqueducts.

Dickens observed carefully the local people, as well as the tourists, all of which proved great research for his novels and satirical magazine articles in years to come. He wrote of his bemusement whenever he passed the crowds of locals standing around Spanish Steps, because he became convinced that he recognised them but had no idea how he knew them. This nagged away at him for several days, until he realised that they were artists' models, waiting to be chosen for their day's work:

> There is one old gentleman, with long white hair and an immense beard, who, to my knowledge, has gone half through the catalogue of the Royal Academy. This is the venerable, or patriarchal model… . There is another man in a blue cloak, who always pretends to be asleep in the sun … the *dolce far' niente* model. There is another man in a brown cloak, who leans against a wall, with his arms folded in his mantle, and looks out of the corners of his eyes: which are just visible beneath his broad slouched hat. This is the assassin model. There is another man, who constantly looks over his own shoulder, and is always going away, but never does. This is the haughty, or scornful model. As to Domestic Happiness, and Holy Families, they should come very cheap, for there are lumps of them, all up the steps.

Although Dickens found much to marvel over in Rome, he had mixed feelings about the city. When he discovered how expensive it was to live there, he wrote happily to Thomas Mitton of his perspicacity in settling in Genoa:

> there is no palace like the Peschiere for architecture, situation, gardens, or rooms. It is a great triumph to me, too, to find how cheap it is. At Rome, the English people live in dirty little fourth, fifth, and sixth floors, with not one room as large as your own drawing-room, and pay, commonly, seven or eight pounds a week.

The bloody history of the Colosseum continued to play upon his mind, yet it was such a fascinating horror that he found himself compelled to walk past it every day. He was also haunted by the idea of the colossal crypts under all the churches in Rome, and the famous Roman catacombs became 'ghastly passages ... a chain of labyrinths'. One moonlit evening, he walked past the Jewish quarter: 'The little town of miserable houses, walled, and shut in by barred gates, is the quarter where the Jews are locked up nightly, when the clock strikes eight – a miserable place, densely populated, and reeking with bad odours.' Added to this depressing experience was the horror of witnessing the execution of a murderer. Although public hangings were still common in Britain at this time, in Rome, the execution was a beheading. The head was then paraded around the gathered crowd before being placed on a pole in front of the scaffold.

What is particularly strange about this episode is that Dickens chose to attend the execution. He arrived early and waited hours for it to begin, even though it was something he had very strong feelings against. Was it his investigative journalist's self that made him attend something he knew he would hate? His motivation is difficult to interpret. Dickens's writing about it in *Pictures from Italy* seems quite detached, a description of the full timeline of the event in a dispassionate style, and a cynical look at what drove other people to want to watch the man's death. Dickens wrote about the vendors of cigars and pastries selling their wares to the arriving spectators, who gathered early and waited for several hours to watch a man die. He examined the scene in the same way a modern forensic investigator might do, going up after the death to see the scaffolding and to look closely at the severed neck. He noted with a sense of irony that the executioner was himself an outlaw, one who dared not cross the bridge into the centre of Rome except when in the course of his work, or he would be in danger of his life. Despite his seemingly dispassionate writing about the execution, Dickens finished with the comments:

> Nobody cared, or was at all affected. There was no manifestation of disgust, or pity, or indignation, or sorrow. My empty pockets were tried, several times, in the crowd immediately below the scaffold, as the corpse was being

put into its coffin. It was an ugly, filthy, careless, sickening spectacle; meaning nothing but butchery beyond the momentary interest, to the one wretched actor.

As early as in his writing of *Oliver Twist*, Dickens showed anger about the death penalty. In the chapter, 'Fagin's Last Night Alive', the writing imparts a feeling of claustrophobic fear to the reader: a terrifying sense of listening to the hours count down towards one's death. He also writes with contempt about the crowd baying outside for the blood of a man they've never met, looking forward to the theatre of a public execution.

In Dickens's time, public executions had a holiday atmosphere, with tour companies putting on special coaches to take tourists to watch the hangings and parties of friends and families travelling to watch the criminal's final moments. For decades, Dickens campaigned vociferously against the practice and his articles and opinions reached such a wide audience that his celebrity helped to bring about an end to public executions in Britain. It would be almost a century after Dickens's death before Britain abolished the death penalty altogether, but after 1868 executions were carried out inside a prison, hidden from the ghoulish eyes of the public.

Catherine and Charles stayed in Rome for some time so they could experience Holy Week, which Dickens later advised his readers to avoid: 'The ceremonies, in general, are of the most tedious and wearisome kind; the heat and crowd at every one of them, painfully oppressive; the noise, hubbub, and confusion, quite distracting. We abandoned the pursuit of these shows, very early in the proceedings.'

It is interesting to realise how international Roman tourism was by that date. When Dickens wrote about the ceremony of the Pope washing the feet of thirteen men (representing Jesus washing the feet of the Apostles), he commented that 'the eyes of Heaven knows how many English, French, Americans, Swiss, Germans, Russians, Swedes, Norwegians, and other foreigners' were watching them. There was also a recreation of the Last Supper, at which Dickens noted with glee:

> The gentlemen about me were remarkably anxious to see what was on the table; and one Englishman seemed to have embarked the whole energy of his nature in the determination to discover whether there was any mustard.

'By Jupiter there's vinegar!' I heard him say to his friend, after he had stood on tiptoe an immense time, and had been crushed and beaten on all sides. 'And there's oil! I saw them distinctly, in cruets! Can any gentleman, in front there, see mustard on the table? Sir, will you oblige me! Do you see a Mustard-Pot?'

Dickens himself was pleased to see there was both red and white wine for Jesus to drink and that 'the dinner looked very good ... chiefly composed of fish and vegetables.'

On Easter Sunday, they drove out of the city to escape the crowds. It was a beautiful sunny day, and Dickens noted that the River Tiber 'was no longer yellow, but blue'. This burst of gorgeous sunshine, bathing the city in light as their carriage bore them away, seemed to make Rome look more beautiful to them than it had before. It had taken a while for Dickens to fall in love with Rome, but just as they were about to end their time there, he felt a rush of affection for the city.

They watched the Easter Monday fireworks from the window of a rented room opposite the Castel Sant'Angelo and took a last moonlit journey around Rome. One of their final destinations was yet another visit to the Colosseum: 'I had seen it by moonlight before (I could never get through a day without going back to it), but its tremendous solitude that night is past all telling.' The following morning, they left on their journey towards Naples. As they travelled, they discovered a little wooden cross, marking the spot where a 'Pilgrim Contessa' had been murdered. This was the victim of the man whose execution Dickens had witnessed. It was a fittingly sombre ending to a place in which he had found himself thinking deeply about life, death and how the scars of history can shape a city.

Charles and Catherine were soothed by the sight and scent of the sea, as their carriage rolled along cliff paths and the southern Italian coastline unfurled ahead of them. When travelling at night they heard 'the murmur of the sea beneath the stars' and woke up to their first glimpse of Naples in the distance, and the sight of Vesuvius 'spouting fire!', a glimpse so brief before it disappeared behind clouds that they had to question whether it were real or merely a vision. They had to cross a border to enter the Neapolitan region, something they found unpleasant and which was achieved only with bribery. Their first Neapolitan town, Fondi, was 'filthy' and an unromantic disappointment, steeped as Dickens felt in decay and poverty, with the street dogs so thin he marvelled that they were still alive. He later wrote to Forster, 'Except Fondi, there is nothing on earth that I have seen so dirty as Naples.' He believed the poverty in Naples was worse than any he had seen in London: 'There is probably no country in the world where [beggars] are treated with such frightful cruelty. It is universal.'

He was intrigued by the use of what he called 'pantomime' [sign language] that he witnessed all over the Neapolitan area and was tantalised by the views from Naples of the island of Capri, but the famed Bay of Naples compared unfavourably with the Bay of Genoa, 'which is the most lovely thing I have ever seen'. He wrote to Thomas Mitton:

> I am as badly off in this place as in America – beset by visitors at all times and seasons, and forced to dine out every day. I have found, however, an excellent man for me – an Englishman, who has lived here many years, and is well acquainted with the people, whom he doctored in the bad time of the cholera, when the priests and everybody else fled in terror. Under his auspices, I have got to understand the low life of Naples (among the Fishermen and Idlers) almost as well as I do ... of my own country; always excepting the language, which is very peculiar and extremely difficult, and would require a year's constant practice at least. It is no more like Italian than English is to Welsh.

Catherine's sister Georgina joined them in Naples to visit the eerily preserved ruins of Herculaneum and Pompeii. When Mount Vesuvius had erupted in the late summer of AD79, the eruption was so intense and so rapid that its two nearby settlements, Herculaneum and Pompeii, were smothered – Pompeii with ash and Herculaneum with mud – leaving their inhabitants little time to escape. For almost two millennia, the cities and their long-dead occupants had lain mostly undisturbed, until a major archaeological excavation had begun in the eighteenth century.

Georgina, Catherine and Charles found the experience of these ruined towns, complete with the preserved remains of their ancient inhabitants, deeply moving. Dickens noted how sobering it was to encounter a group of skeletons huddled together, and a wine cellar, seemingly beautifully preserved – but with all the wine replaced by centuries-old ash from the volcano. He marvelled to find walls still standing, with their paintings still visible, eighteen centuries after the eruption; to find furniture, eating utensils, musical instruments and other everyday possessions all seemingly waiting for their owners to return; to walk around the ruins of Herculaneum's theatre, which still looked so similar to how it would have looked to its contemporary audiences; and of discovering a temple dedicated to a religion that no longer existed anywhere on earth. Dickens wrote of the experience in *Pictures from Italy*:

> Stand at the bottom of the great market-place of Pompeii, and look up the silent streets, through the ruined temples of Jupiter and Isis, over the broken houses with their inmost sanctuaries open to the day, away to Mount Vesuvius, bright and snowy in the peaceful distance; and lose all count of time, and heed of other things, in the strange and melancholy sensation of seeing the Destroyed and the Destroyer making this quiet picture in the sun. Then, ramble on, and see, at every turn, the little familiar tokens of human habitation and every-day pursuits; the chafing of the bucket-rope in the stone rim of the exhausted well; the track of carriage-wheels in the pavement of the street; the marks of drinking-vessels on the stone counter of the wine-shop; the amphoræ in private cellars, stored away so many hundred years ago, and undisturbed to this hour.

That night, they journeyed through the sunset for a very cold night-time tour of Mount Vesuvius, which was both covered in snow and gently erupting. They were accompanied by a tumult of guides, all wanting to take this curious trio of tourists on their extraordinary journey, as well as a 'rather heavy gentleman'. The guides told Dickens the weather was more severe than it had been for twenty years, with the snow concealing a thick layer of ice. Dickens took a stout stick and walked up the mountain alongside the guides, while Catherine, Georgina and the portly gentleman were borne up the mountainside in 'litters' (a type of sedan chair). As they climbed in the dark, with the air around them bitingly cold, they could see almost nothing of Vesuvius, until the moon suddenly appeared from behind clouds. They stumbled their way upwards and, when Catherine and Georgina climbed out of their litters, Charles and some of the guides helped them as far as they could go. He wrote with wonder of how they crawled on their hands and knees to try and get as close to the crater as possible, wanting to be able to reach the summit and look inside! Louis Roche was furious with Dickens and the guides, 'tearing his hair like a madman, and crying that we should all three be killed.' They then 'came rolling down' from the crater, with stray gobbets of lava setting their clothes on fire, and patting themselves constantly to extinguish the little flames.

From the heat of the lava, they soon encountered the chill of the layer of ice. In a frightening descent, surrounded by guides, the party slipped and tripped their way back down the ice until they were back in the safety of the nearby village, where, Dickens claimed, everyone had assumed they had all come to grief. He summed it up to Thomas Mitton, 'A pretty unusual trip for a pleasure expedition, I think! I am rather stiff to-day but am quite unhurt, except a slight scrape on my right hand. My clothes are burnt to pieces. My ladies are the wonder of Naples, and everybody is open-mouthed.'

To the Countess of Blessington, Dickens wrote, 'Who can forget Herculaneum and Pompeii? As to Vesuvius, it burns away, in my thoughts, beside the roaring waters of Niagara; and not a splash of the water extinguishes a spark of the fire; but there they go on tumbling and flaming, night and day, each in its fullest glory.'

In *Pictures from Italy*, Naples is summed up as

> macaroni-eating at sunset, and flower-selling all day long, and begging and stealing everywhere and at all hours, ... the bright sea-shore, where the waves of the bay sparkle merrily. But, lovers and hunters of the picturesque, let us not keep too studiously out of view the miserable depravity, degradation, and wretchedness, with which this gay Neapolitan life is inseparably associated!

They left the city willingly and travelled on to visit the ruins of the ancient Greek city of Paestum. This was the most southerly point in Italy Dickens was able to visit. His plans to travel to Sicily and see Mount Etna remained sadly unrealised. Soon they were in their hired carriage heading north, going home to Genoa and the children.

Their journey took them via Capua, Monte Cassino – where they visited the monastery on mule back – and a multitude of tiny villages, which Dickens called 'the most shattered and tattered' of places, although he loved the little inns they stopped at along the way, describing them as 'such hobgoblin places, that they are infinitely more attractive and amusing than the best hotels in Paris.' They stopped for a few days in Rome, from where Dickens wrote to Angela Burdett-Coutts: 'I do not think I ever felt it so cold as between this place and Naples, about a Month ago... . I have certainly seen more Sun in England, between the end of December and the middle of March, than I have seen in Italy in that time.' A few weeks later, Dickens was still griping about the weather in a letter to Thomas Beard: 'Said Writer [is] purporting to leave the Sunny clime of Italy (respecting which clime, much Gammon is afloat among the subjects of her Britannic Majesty).'

From Rome, they travelled to Terni, where they visited the famous Marmore Waterfalls, to Perugia 'strongly fortified by art and nature', to Castiglione and Arezzo, and then to Florence. This was a city that Dickens adored:

> how much beauty of another kind is here, when, on a fair clear morning, we look, from the summit of a hill, on Florence! See where it lies before us in a sun-lighted valley, bright with the winding Arno, and shut in by swelling hills; its domes, and towers, and palaces, rising from the rich country in a glittering heap, and shining in the sun like gold!
>
> Magnificently stern and sombre are the streets of beautiful Florence; and the strong old piles of building make such heaps of shadow, on the ground and in the river, that there is another and a different city of rich forms and fancies, always lying at our feet... . Among the four old bridges that span the river, the Ponte Vecchio – that bridge which is covered with the shops of Jewellers and Goldsmiths – is a most enchanting feature in the scene. The space of one house, in the centre, being left open, the view beyond is shown as in a frame; and that precious glimpse of sky, and water, and rich buildings, shining so quietly among the huddled roofs and gables on the bridge, is exquisite.

As always, even when surrounded by beauty, Dickens felt compelled to visit the local prison, which he condemned as a 'foul and dismal place, where some men are shut up close, in small cells like ovens.' While he was there, a new inmate was brought in: an 80-year-old man convicted of stabbing a teenage girl to death in the middle of the flower market.

In Rome, Dickens had visited the Non-Catholic Cemetery and seen the graves of John Keats and Percy Bysshe Shelley. In Florence, Dickens's literary pilgrimage took him to the houses of Giovanni Boccaccio and the Stone of Dante Alighieri, where Dickens mused how Dante must have felt about the city he had loved, but from which he had been banished. He also visited the grave of Michelangelo in the Basilica of Sante Croce and took a day trip to the ancient Etruscan town of Fiesole. In *Pictures from Italy,* Dickens wrote fondly, 'Let us look back on Florence while we may, and when its shining Dome is seen no more, go travelling through cheerful Tuscany, with a bright remembrance of it; for Italy will be the fairer for the recollection.'

From Florence, Charles and Catherine journeyed home via Modena, arriving in Albaro in early April. There the family stayed for two months, enjoying the splendours of the Palazzo Peschiere, until it was time to return to life in London. By June of 1845 they had packed up their Italian life and the journey home began, but they were not being accompanied by their cook. On 9 May 1845, a few weeks before the family left the palazzo, Dickens wrote to Daniel Maclise:

> You recollect our Cook, our nice Cook, our good-looking Cook; the best Servant as ever trod (excuse my being nautical) twixt stem and stern your Honor? Yesterday she came up to her Mistress, and announced that was not going to return to England, but intended to be married, and to settle here!!!
>
> The Bridegroom is the Governor's Cook: who has been visiting in the kitchen ever since our first arrival. The Governor's servants have a weekly ball in the Summer, and there they first met – 'twas in a Crowd, I believe. He is a Frenchman by birth, but has been here a long time. They have courted in Italian, as he knows no English, and she no French. They are to be married as soon as her Baptism Certificate can arrive from England (at Leghorn; they must

go there, for the purpose; it is not legal here: she being a Protestant) – and intend opening a Restaurant in Genoa. It is a great venture on her part, for she is well brought-up: quite delicate in her ideas: full of English notions of comfort and cleanliness and decency – and must, for some time at all events, live in some miserable rooms in some miserable neighborhood, of which you can form no idea, without seeing the ordinary residences of an Italian Town. I do not remember a single English person of her own station who will be here, after we have left. But she is resolved. And [all] I can do, is to take care that the Marriage is lawfully and properly solemnized before we depart.

This is the second of them who has found a lover here; the Nurse, Charlotte, having 'provided herself' with that commodity the other day.

Dickens also wrote to Forster about the wedding, expressing more misgivings, and worrying the marriage would not be recognised legally as she was a Protestant, and saying all he could do was ensure she had enough money to return to England should she ever need an escape route. He wrote to Thomas Mitton shortly before they returned home, 'we are still in hopes that she will return. Not only on her own account (for she would certainly be unhappy) but because she is a most capital Servant. I have some misgivings that she speaks Italian better than I do, or at least more fluently.' His worries did not prove prophetic. In 1851, Dickens wrote to Emile de la Rue, 'A thousand thanks for your kindness to our old Cook... . She is now happily married... . They have been married in both churches, and are (I suppose) doubly blessed.'

Before the family's year in Italy was over, there was great local commotion about an upcoming double execution, of a pair of murderers. Two men were to be hanged for strangling a woman, the servant of a priest. The men – one of whom was the priest's nephew – had robbed the priest's home and because the servant had been at home when they entered, they had murdered her. The hangings took place on the sea wall, and Dickens wrote of the boats that gathered ghoulishly in the harbour, offering paying passengers a good view. Dickens wrote to Maclise, 'I was afraid to go, for I know how they manage things here: and knew

I should be horrified. It was very dreadful, I understand ... Roche went – and could eat nothing for a long time afterwards.'

Louis Roche accompanied the family on their journey to England, via Stradella, Milan, Lake Como and the Swiss village of Faido, before travelling through the St Gotthard Pass to Lucerne and Zurich. The party stopped in Brussels, where they were met by John Forster, Douglas Jerrold and Daniel Maclise. The journey was continued via Ghent and Bruges, to the harbour at Ostend. They arrived back in London at the start of July – and within just a few weeks were back in Broadstairs for their summer holiday.

Aside from *The Chimes*, much of Dickens's writing in Italy had been devoted to composing letters home, to be turned into his second travelogue. He had used his time abroad to heal his mind, to recover from the exhaustion of the previous year and to enjoy life in a new country. His written observations of Italy in the 1840s are fascinating to anyone who knows the country in the twenty-first century, not least because so many of the things which Dickens saw remain the same today, in a country where the 1840s are, really, very recent history.

His descriptions include this one of the Via del Corso, one of Rome's main streets:

> a mile long; a street of shops, and palaces, and private houses, sometimes opening into a broad piazza. There are verandahs and balconies, of all shapes and sizes, to almost every house – not on one story alone, but often to one room or another on every story – put there in general with so little order or regularity, that if, year after year, and season after season, it had rained balconies, hailed balconies, snowed balconies, blown balconies, they could scarcely have come into existence in a more disorderly manner.

During their drive from Rome to Naples, Dickens described the constant procession of wine carts, 'each driven by a shaggy peasant reclining beneath a little gipsy-fashioned canopy of sheep-skin.' He was fascinated by the homes he passed all over Italy, from elegant villas to 'hovels', and with the many types of people: gun-toting horsemen, shepherds, boat dwellers, hungry soldiers and ragged beggars.

Dickens and Travel: The Start of Modern Travel Writing

This type of travel writing, although not yet common, was a fashionable new form of literature. In the year the Dickens family left for Italy, Mary Shelley published her travelogue *Rambles in Germany and Italy in 1840, 1842, and 1843* (her mother, Mary Wollstonecraft, had published an account of travelling in Scandinavia in 1796). Shelley wrote:

> I love the Italians. It is impossible to live among them and not love them. Their faults are many – the faults of the oppressed – love of pleasure, disregard of truth, indolence, and violence of temper. But their falsehood is on the surface – it is not deceit... . They are affectionate, simple, and earnestly desirous to please. There is life, energy, and talent in every look and word; grace and refinement in every act and gesture. They are a noble race of men – a beautiful race of women ... the country of Dante and Michael Angelo and Raphael still exists.

The Continuing Influence of Italy

*'I have become attached to the country and I
don't care who knows it.'*
Letter from Charles Dickens to
John Forster, 25 January 1845

Dickens left Italy considerably happier, wealthier (thanks to the success of *A Christmas Carol*) and rested, yet it was inevitable that on his return to London he felt a lowering of spirits. He attributes similar feelings to both David Copperfield and Arthur Clennam on their return from travelling:

> My health, severely impaired when I left England, was quite restored. I had seen much. I had been in many countries, and I hope I had improved my store of knowledge... .
> I landed in London on a wintry autumn evening. It was dark and raining, and I saw more fog and mud in a minute than I had seen in a year. I walked from the Custom House to the Monument before I found a coach; and although the very house-fronts, looking on the swollen gutters, were like old friends to me, I could not but admit that they were very dingy friends. (*David Copperfield*)
>
> It was a Sunday evening in London, gloomy, close, and stale. Maddening church bells of all degrees of dissonance, sharp and flat, cracked and clear, fast and slow, made the brick-and-mortar echoes hideous. Melancholy streets, in a penitential garb of soot, steeped the souls of the people who were condemned to look at them out of windows, in dire despondency. In every thoroughfare, up almost every alley, and down almost every turning, some doleful bell

was throbbing, jerking, tolling, as if the Plague were in the city and the dead-carts were going round. Everything was bolted and barred that could by possibility furnish relief to an overworked people... . Nothing to see but streets, streets, streets. Nothing to breathe but streets, streets, streets. Nothing to change the brooding mind, or raise it up. Nothing for the spent toiler to do, but to compare the monotony of his seventh day with the monotony of his six days, think what a weary life he led, and make the best of it—or the worst, according to the probabilities.

...Mr Arthur Clennam, newly arrived from Marseilles by way of Dover, and by Dover coach the Blue-eyed Maid, sat in the window of a coffee-house on Ludgate Hill. Ten thousand responsible houses surrounded him, frowning ... heavily on the streets... . Miles of close wells and pits of houses, where the inhabitants gasped for air, stretched far away towards every point of the compass. Through the heart of the town a deadly sewer ebbed and flowed, in the place of a fine fresh river... . (*Little Dorrit*)

Pictures from Italy was published in May of 1846. Although many Dickens fans had been bemused by *American Notes*, this second travelogue was more fashionable – for the simple reason that Italy was more fashionable as a tourist destination than the USA.

Dickens's sharp observations about tourists and tourism that didn't necessarily find their way into his non-fiction often appeared in his novels. Although he spent very little time in Italy after 1845, the country continued to inspire him. When Dickens was writing *Little Dorrit*, in 1857, he returned to his memories of the country that had welcomed his family so hospitably, and he created the Dorrit family's Italian journey. The Dorrits journey through France, Switzerland and Italy, meeting other travellers, and talking about their routes and travel difficulties, and boasting about visiting the sights that most Victorian readers aspired to see. Dickens gently poked fun at the 'professional tourist' in his description of the Meagles' home and the souvenirs they had amassed:

Mr Meagles led the way into the house... . Some traces of the migratory habits of the family were to be observed in the covered frames and furniture.... Of articles collected on his various expeditions, there ... were antiquities from Central Italy, made by the best modern houses...; bits of mummy from Egypt (and perhaps Birmingham); model gondolas from Venice; model villages from Switzerland; morsels of tesselated pavement from Herculaneum and Pompeii ... and lava out of Vesuvius; Spanish fans, Spezzian straw hats, Moorish slippers, Tuscan hairpins, Carrara sculpture, Trastaverini scarves, Genoese velvets and filigree, Neapolitan coral, Roman cameos, Geneva jewellery, Arab lanterns, rosaries blest all round by the Pope himself, and an infinite variety of lumber.

Dickens's initial feelings that Rome was a rather terrifying, barbaric city is also attributed to the Dorrits. As the family journeys from Venice to Rome, there's a feeling of impending decay:

The period of the family's stay at Venice came, in its course, to an end, and they moved, with their retinue, to Rome. Through a repetition of the former Italian scenes, growing more dirty and more haggard as they went on, and bringing them at length to where the very air was diseased, they passed to their destination. A fine residence had been taken for them on the Corso, and there they took up their abode, in a city where everything seemed to be trying to stand still for ever on the ruins of something else.... Little Dorrit would often ride out in a hired carriage ... and wander among the ruins of old Rome. The ruins of the vast old Amphitheatre, of the old Temples, of the old commemorative Arches, of the old trodden highways, of the old tombs.

Amy Dorrit is depressed by the ancient monuments, as they bring to mind only 'the ruins of her own life'. Much of her thoughts are Dickens voicing his own opinion of travelling and the people he had met. Just as the author had discovered, Amy Dorrit comes to an awareness that many of her fellow tourists are visiting places purely to be able to say that they have been there, not to really see or to get to know the place itself. The Dorrits hire carriages to take them around the tourist sites and the people they mix with are not Italians, but other tourists, all visiting the same things and wanting the food and comforts they are used to at home. When the Dorrits were travelling to Italy via the Alps, one of their travelling companions, the unforgettably 'genteel' widow Mrs General, remarks that 'like other inconvenient places, it must be seen. As a place much spoken of, it is necessary to see it.' This attitude towards travelling is common to almost everyone in the party, Amy alone appears to be bemused by it.

Dickens always liked to believe that he was a traveller not a tourist. He wrote scornfully to Count D'Orsay, in March 1845 from Rome:

> The Holy Week is in full force at this time; and hundreds of English people with hundreds of Murray's Guide Books ... in their hands are chattering in all the silent places, worrying the professional Ciceroni to death, and doubting the authenticity of everything on the spot – to defend it to the last gasp, when they get home again ... everybody says that everything is not worth seeing; and everybody goes to see everything else notwithstanding, by day and by night, with unabated vigour.

By the end of their time in Genoa, Dickens was very sad to leave his Italian idyll. He later claimed – perhaps with a nostalgic dose of hindsight – that he would have been content to remain living in Italy, but that Catherine had been homesick and longing to leave. Despite these protestations, he went back to Italy remarkably seldom in his life, becoming instead more enamoured with France. Yet he remained staunchly interested in Italy and the Italians, and kept up with Italian politics.

In London he became friends with the exiled politician and journalist Giuseppe Mazzini. Dickens went with Mazzini to visit his school in Clerkenwell (the Italian area of London) for the education of Italian boys. Dickens admired Mazzini's vision and became vociferous in his support for exiled Italians.

In 1846, when editing the *Daily News*, Dickens made his support of Mazzini's cause, 'Italy for the Italians', explicit . In 1847, Dickens joined The People's International League, whose ideals were 'freedom' and progressive politics for people around the world. Following the 1848 revolution in Italy, Dickens wrote an article entitled 'An Appeal to the English People on Behalf of the Italian Refugees', which was published in *The Examiner*[12] on 8 September 1849, and then taken up by several other publications. Some years later, when he took his family to live in Paris in the mid-1850s, Dickens hired another exiled Italian revolutionary, Daniele Manin, to be his daughters' Italian tutor. In 1860, in his collection of essays known as *The Uncommercial Traveller*, Dickens wrote the short story 'The Italian Prisoner', allegedly based on a true story about a political prisoner in Italy and the tender-hearted Englishman who saves and befriends him.

In October 1853, Dickens returned to Genoa, on a two-month journey with the novelist Wilkie Collins and the artist Augustus Egg. Dickens, fresh from finishing the manuscript of *Bleak House*, was spending a long summer in Boulogne with his family. He enjoyed planning the holiday and deciding what route he and his friends would take to Italy, writing to Angela Burdett-Coutts:

> I particularly want Mr. Egg, who is so fine and picturesque an artist and has never been farther than Holland, to see some good Swiss interiors and backgrounds. And with this view, if the season should be tolerably open, we shall make a push for Chamounix and try to get the short way through the snow thence to the Simplon.

He also wrote to Simon Winckworth, who ran a warehouse providing travellers' essentials, often used by people planning to emigrate. His letter gives an intriguing insight into nineteenth-century travel preparations:

> Mr. Charles Dickens begs Mr. Winckworth to be so good as to fill the accompanying case of bottles; one with Laudanum, one with sal volatile, and one with the best powdered ginger. He also begs to have a large box – as it is to travel with, it should be strong – of the pills according to Dr. Southwood Smith's prescription which is in Mr. Winckworth's possession.

Collins and Egg travelled together from England to Boulogne to meet Dickens. They were accompanied by a new courier whose name was

---
12. John Forster was the editor of *The Examiner*.

Edward, although, for Dickens, no one could ever replace the inimitable Louis Roche. As they embarked on this male-only adventure, Collins wrote home that they were 'in a state of mad good spirits'.

It was a very difficult time, politically, for travelling through Europe, following the revolutions and upheavals of 1848 and much of the continent was still in chaos, with conspiracy theories being whispered everywhere. The friends' planned route was almost disrupted after Dickens was warned by 'a prince' (a friend of Angela Burdett-Coutts) about a dispute between Switzerland and Austria, which was affecting travellers passing through the two countries. This they discussed at great length, but as Wilkie wrote to his mother, Harriet Collins on 28th October:

> The arrival of Dickens produced a prodigious sensation in the English colony at Lausanne, which practically expressed itself by a grand dinner and a grand evening party.... . All the resident gentlemen whom we consulted about the best route to take to get into Italy were unanimous in declaring that the 'French Prince' who had solemnly assured us that we should not be let into Italy by the Austrians if we went by the Simplon Pass was utterly wrong – so by the Simplon we determined to go – and here we are without having experienced the smallest hindrance in crossing the dreaded frontier. I shall never believe in a diplomatic nobleman again as long as I live.

In his letters home – which he had already warned his wife and friends might be censored – Dickens was fulsome in his praise of the border officials.

The friends and their courier travelled by steam boat, and by public and private carriages. They walked whenever they could and in Chamonix, they went mountain climbing (a very popular pursuit in the nineteenth century). Their travels took them through 'all the magnificent scenery' of Switzerland, as Collins told his mother – although for him, the beauty was ruined by the amount of disease, deformity and poverty they witnessed amongst the Swiss people.

They reached an Italy bathed in warm weather, with sunlight sparkling on lakes and lighting to beautiful effect vineyards, snow-capped mountains and picturesque villages. When they stopped for their first night at an Italian hotel, Wilkie Collins, who was very happy to be back in Italy, wrote of 'the vast rooms, and the dirt and the screaming servants with their pleasant Italian manners – all unchanged since I had last seen them.' Dickens sent a letter to Angela Burdett-Coutts saying, 'It is so strange and like a dream to me to hear the delicate Italian once again – so beautiful to see the delightful sky and all the picturesque wonders of the country.' Yet the trio had arrived in a new Italy. The country had undergone a vast political change in the almost-decade since Dickens and his family had made it their home. Dickens scholar Professor Francesca Orestano writes: 'Dickens could not ignore the different powers parcelling Italy: Sardinia in Piedmont; Austria ruling Lombardy and the North-East; the Papal State in Central Italy; Bourbons in Naples and the whole South; their satellites and relatives in smaller regions.'

The author seemed to find both Italy and himself in a more depressed state on this second visit. They visited Turin and Milan – of which Wilkie Collins was scathing, not least because he was robbed by a pickpocket – and then to Genoa, where they were greeted with great excitement by Dickens's friends and enjoyed several days of lavish hospitality.

Dickens took them around all his favourite sights, but on taking his friends to see the Palazzo Peschiere, he was saddened to discover it had been turned into a school, and all the beautiful frescoes, of which he had been so proud, were covered up. Genoa was renowned for its silver and artisan silversmiths, and Collins wrote home that he had bought a silver bracelet for his mother and a silver snuff box for a friend. He also bought himself a new snuff box to replace the one stolen in Milan.

On 29 October, Dickens wrote to his sister-in-law Georgina Hogarth from Genoa:

> We ... arrived here in a rather damaged condition. We live at the top of this immense house, overlooking the port and sea ... the apartment is rather vast and faded.
>
> The old walks are pretty much the same as ever, except that they have built behind the Peschiere on the San Bartolomeo hill, and changed the whole town towards San Pietro d'Arena, where we seldom went. The Bisagno looks just the same, strong just now, and with very little water in it. 'Vicoli' stink exactly as they used to, and are fragrant with the same old flavour of very rotten cheese kept in very hot blankets... . The old Jesuit college in the Strada Nuova is under the present

government the Hôtel de Ville; and a very splendid caffé with a terrace garden has arisen between it and Palavacini's old palace. Another new and handsome caffé has been built in the Piazza Carlo Felice, between the old caffé and the Strada Carlo Felice. The old beastly gate and guard-house on the Albaro road are still in their dear old beastly state, and the whole of the road is just as it was. The man without legs is still in the Strada Nuova; but the beggars in general are all cleared off.... . The puppets are here, and the opera is open, but only with a buffo company, and without a buffet. We went to the Scala, where they did an opera of Verdi's, called 'Il Trovatore,' and a poor enough ballet. The whole performance miserable indeed. I wish you were here to take some of the old walks. It is quite strange to walk about alone.

They left Genoa on a steamship and Dickens wrote to Georgina again on 4 November, after they arrived in Naples:

we found the steamer more than full of passengers from Marseilles, and in a state of confusion.... . We could get no places at the table, got our dinners how we could on deck, had no berths or sleeping accommodation of any kind, and had paid heavy first-class fares! To add to this, we got to Leghorn too late to steam away again that night ... and we lay off the lighthouse all night long. The scene on board beggars description. Ladies on the tables, gentlemen under the tables, and ladies and gentlemen lying indiscriminately on the open deck, arrayed like spoons on a sideboard. No mattress, no blankets, nothing. Towards midnight, attempts were made by means of an awning and flag to make this latter scene remotely approach an Australian encampment; and we three lay together on the bare planks covered with overcoats. We were all gradually dozing off when a perfectly tropical rain fell, and in a moment drowned the whole ship. The rest of the night was passed upon the stairs, with an immense jumble of men and women.... . There were excellent officers aboard, and the first mate lent me his cabin to wash in in the morning, which I afterwards lent to

Egg and Collins. Then we ... went off on a jaunt together to
Pisa, as the ship was to lie at Leghorn all day.

On this day trip to Pisa, with the captain, the ship's doctor, the second officer and the Irish politician Sir James Emerson Tennent and his family. Dickens managed to arrange accommodation on board the boat for when they returned. The Emerson Tennents' son offered to give Dickens his bed (the letter doesn't explain where the son slept instead) and the captain agreed to let Augustus Egg and Wilkie Collins sleep in the store room. Dickens wrote with glee to Georgina that his two friends 'slept with the moist sugar, the cheese in cut, the spices, the cruets, the apples and pears', as well as another poor passenger, who had become so wet and cold on the previous night that the doctor feared for his health, the ship's cat and the steward 'who dozed in an armchair, and all night long fell headforemost, once in every five minutes, on Egg, who slept on the counter or dresser.' The following night, Dickens was given the steward's cabin, because the previous occupier had disembarked at Civita Vecchia. A few years later, Dickens wrote in *Little Dorrit*: 'Mr Dorrit and his matchless castle were disembarked among the dirty white houses and dirtier felons of Civita Vecchia, and thence scrambled on to Rome as they could, through the filth that festered on the way.'

On his watery journey, Dickens estimated there were around 200 people (including the crew) on a boat intended to carry half that amount. He wrote of incessant heavy rain and constant lightning, though the seas were mercifully calm. He wrote disparagingly of the crew, 'I could not help thinking what would happen if we met with any accident; the crew being chiefly Maltese, and evidently fellows who would cut off alone in the largest boat on the least alarm.'

He was also irritated at the ship's officers' inability to speak any language but English: 'The absence of any knowledge of anything not English on the part of the officers and stewards was most ridiculous. I met an Italian gentleman on the cabin steps, yesterday morning, vainly endeavouring to explain that he wanted a cup of tea for his sick wife.' He also related how ridiculous the chief officer had looked, when they were at Genoa, barking instructions in English to the passing Italian boats.

From Naples, they visited Pompeii, where they 'picknicked among the ruins' with the Emerson Tennents. They had planned a day trip to Sorrento, but on the appointed day the weather turned cold and rainy, so they stayed in Naples instead. They spent two days back on the road, in a hired carriage, before arriving in Rome. From there, Collins wrote to his brother Charlie[13] how much he loved being back in 'this wonderful and mournful place' after a gap of sixteen years:

> All the other places we have visited in Italy have seemed more or less changed to me. This place seems, and really is, unaltered... . I saw the same Bishops, in purple stockings, followed by servants in gaudy liveries – the same importunately impudent beggars – the same men with pointed hats and women with red petticoats and tightly swaddled babies that I remembered so well... . Genoa I did not know again, till I got to the great street of palaces – Naples I found altered in one of two important respects ... but Rome is what it was when we saw it.

During this Italian trip, Dickens grew ever more proud of his moustache and wrote to his friends and family about the efforts made by Collins, Egg and their courier, Edward, to grow moustaches of their own. In a letter to Georgina, Dickens described his friends' whiskery efforts as 'more distressing, more comic, more sparse and meagre, more straggling, wandering, wiry, stubbly, formless ... than anything nature ever produced', smugly secure in his own superior lip hair. It seems this sudden fad amongst the friends to be hirsute was because Italian men were renowned for their moustaches and the Englishmen didn't want to look like tourists.

Dickens's letters are not all nostalgic and witty, however. He also became quite panicked about what he believed was a plague of malaria, writing that it lurked all around Rome waiting to 'swallow it up', and while Collins and Egg lost themselves in the beauty of Venice, just as Dickens had done a few years earlier, he felt battered because he had been questioned by the occupying Austrian police. Suddenly that bullying bureaucracy seemed everywhere in a city he had once so loved for its romance.

It seems Dickens also found himself too often as the odd man out within the trio. Having assumed initially that it would be he and Collins

---

13. Wilkie Collins's younger brother was the Pre-Raphaelite artist Charles Allston Collins. In 1860, he became Charles and Catherine Dickens's son-in-law, by marrying their artist daughter, Katey.

who would form the most important duo, he found himself being irritated by Egg (an artist) and Collins (the son and brother of artists) bonding over their shared love of Italian art. On 25 November, Collins wrote to his mother, 'I am more struck than I could have imagined possible, with a sense of the superiority of the Venetian painters – and especially of Tintoretto, to my mind the chief and greatest of them all.... . These Venetians ... are the most *original* race of painters that the world has yet seen.'

Initially, the three friends had planned on travelling to Sicily, but they decided the journey was too arduous, so gave up the plan. Or, as Dickens confided in a letter home, he had been unable to persuade his friends to agree to spend nights in a travelling carriage. Collins and Egg were not as adventurous as Dickens and were insistent they would need to stop each night at a hotel, which meant they did not have the time to get to Sicily. It is a great loss to travel writing that Dickens didn't make it to Sicily, and it was especially frustrating for him, as this was the second time his desire to travel there had been thwarted. During his year in Italy, Dickens had written to Thomas Mitton that they had needed to change their itinerary because 'The weather is so atrocious (rain, snow, wind, darkness, hail, and cold) that I can't get over into Sicily.'

In early December 1853, the three travellers returned to England via Paris, where they collected Dickens's eldest child Charley, who was travelling home from school in Germany. They were back in London on time for Christmas.

At the start of 1854, Dickens wrote to his friend William De Cerjat in Lausanne, whom he had seen in the October, apologising that he had not had time to send a letter during his Italian trip:

> The accused pleads guilty, but throws himself upon the mercy of the Court. He humbly represents that his usual hour for getting up, in the course of his travels, was three o'Clock in the morning, and his usual hour for going to bed, nine or ten the next night. That the places in which he chiefly deviated from these rules of hardship, were Rome and Venice; and that at those cities of Fame he shut himself up in solitude, and wrote Christmas papers for the incomparable publication known as *Household Words*... . We had only three bad days out of the whole time. After Naples, which was very hot, we had very cold, clear, bright weather. When we got to Chamounix, we found the greater

part of the Inns shut up and the people gone – no visitors whatsoever – and plenty of snow. These were the very best circumstances under which to see the place, and we stayed a couple of days at the Hotel de Londres (hastily re-furbished for our entertainment) and climbed through the snow to the Mer de Glace, and thoroughly enjoyed it. Then we went, in Mule procession (I walking) to the old hotel at Martigny, where Collins was ill, and I suppose I bored Egg to death by talking all the evening about the time when you and I were there together. Naples (a place always painful to me, in the intense degradation of the people) seems to have only three classes of inhabitants left in it – priests, soldiers (standing army one hundred thousand strong) and spies. Of Maccaroni we ate very considerable quantities everywhere; also, for the benefit of Italy, we took our share of every description of Wine. At Naples I found Layard the Nineveh Traveller, who is a friend of mine and an admirable fellow; so we fraternised and went up Vesuvius together, and ate more Maccaroni and drank more Wine. At Rome, the day after our arrival, they were making a Saint at St. Peters: on which occasion I was surprised to find what an immense number of pounds of wax candles it takes to make the regular, genuine article. From Turin to Paris, over the Mont Cenis, we made only one journey. The Rhone being frozen and foggy was not to be navigated, so we posted from Lyons to Chalons – and everybody else was doing the like – and there were no horses to be got – and we were stranded at midnight in amazing little cabarets, with nothing worth mentioning to eat in them, except the iron stove – which was rusty, and the billiard table – which was musty. We left Turin on a Tuesday evening, and arrived in Paris on the Friday evening; where I found my son Charley.... Leaving Calais on the evening of Sunday the 10th. of December, fact of distinguished author's being aboard was telegraphed to Dover, whereupon authorities of Dover Railway detained Train to London for distinguished author's arrival – rather to the exasperation of British public. D. A. arrived home between 10 and 11 that night thankful, and found all well and happy.

'My Hat Shall Ever Be Ready to Be Thrown Up For ... Switzerland'

> *'The mountain in the sunset had stopped the five couriers in a conversation. It is a sublime sight, likely to stop conversation.'*
> From *To Be Read at Dusk* (1852)

Dickens first visited Switzerland when travelling through it during his year in Italy. He wrote to Catherine during his journey with Louis Roche in November 1844, 'The cold in Switzerland ... has been something quite indescribable. My eyes are tingling tonight, as one may suppose cymbals to tingle when they have been lustily played. – It is positive purgatory to me to write.' On the family's return to England, in the summer of 1845, he wrote to John Forster,

> If the Swiss villages looked beautiful to me in winter, their summer aspect is most charming: most fascinating: most delicious. Shut in by high mountains capped with perpetual snow; and dotting a rich carpet of the softest turf, overshadowed by great trees; they seem so many little havens of refuge from the roubles and miseries of great towns. The cleanliness of the little baby-houses of inns is wonderful to those who come from Italy.

The year after leaving Italy, when Dickens was, once again, keen to get away from England and write in another country, his initial thought was to return to Genoa, but he had been seized with a compulsion. As happened so frequently with Dickens, once he had an idea, he needed to act on it quickly. This latest compulsion was to discover what it would be like to live beside mountains, so he moved his family to Switzerland. The following year, when he wrote to his friend the Reverend Edward Taggart, he explained that the family's move to Switzerland had been prompted by the need to 'recover from an uncommon depression of spirits'.

So, in the summer of 1846, Dickens and Roche travelled for several days, through Neuchâtel, Strasbourg and Basel, before arriving in Lausanne. Despite having convinced himself he wanted mountains, countryside and peace in which to write, as always when he was away from the London he alternately loved and loathed, Dickens began to panic in case he was too far away from a city. Now he soothed himself with the knowledge that Geneva was only a short journey away. They began their stay in Lausanne, in a clemently warm June, at the Hotel Gibbon, the former home of author Edward Gibbon (1737–1794). It was while living in Lausanne that Gibbon had written *The Decline and Fall of the Roman Empire*, a book Dickens referenced in his own work, most notably in *Our Mutual Friend*. In the novel, Dickens uses Gibbon's work to great comic effect, when Silas Wegg is hired to read the book aloud to the newly wealthy but illiterate Noddy Boffin.

During his two days at the hotel, Dickens searched feverishly for a home suitable to rent for his family. In his biography, Forster recalled that Dickens found many of the houses already let out to other English travellers, and that he found most of them annoyingly reminiscent of 'small villas in the Regent's-park, with verandahs, [and] glass-doors opening on lawns'. Dickens wanted to live somewhere unlike anywhere he could afford in London. He set his heart on a hilltop house, until he accepted how impractical it would be, especially during a Swiss winter.

In the end he chose the first house he had been shown, the Villa Rosemont[14], writing to his brother Fred,

> We pay £10 per month for the house, for the first 6 months, and £8 for the second six, supposing we should remain here. I am not sufficiently experienced yet, to say what market prices are, but I should think they were about the Genoa mark, and not so cheap as English people suppose. Some things are much cheaper than in Genoa, as, for instance,

---

14. Sadly, the Villa Rosemont was demolished in 1938.

> Piano hire. We have really a very good German Piano, for which we pay but ten francs (eight and fourpence) per month. House rent too is much cheaper. I could have got a very splendid house indeed (as large as the Peschiere) for £150 pr. year. But the largest houses are the cheapest, because they involve the necessity of a large establishment of servants.

As always, Dickens also sent his brothers and several friends precise travel instructions, should they wish to visit:

> The best Hotel at Ostend, is the Hotel de la Cour Imperiale. From Ostend to Cologne, straight through, by Railway. Fare, 27 francs (extra charge for luggage, which is weighed). Time 15 hours. At Cologne, you sleep. Any hotel will serve your turn… . Next day you pay your fare, and take your ticket, at the office of any of the Steam Packet Companies (the Cologne Company is the best, but they are all good) through to Mannheim. Fare, 22 francs. At the office, as well as everywhere else upon the Rhine, there is some one who can speak English. The boat will probably start at about 10 or half past 10 in the morning, and allow you to sleep at Coblentz that night: either going on next morning in the same boat, or in another boat belonging to the same company. The time from Cologne to Coblentz is about 8 hours. Any hotel at Coblentz, except the Giant… . From Coblentz to Mannheim is about 14 hours. Hotel at Mannheim, the Hotel de l'Europe. Very good, and close to the wharf. Sleep there. You will have dined on board: paying extra for your dinner. Next day, from Mannheim to Kehl, by Railway. Time about 6 hours. Fare, 1st. class, 14 francs. From Kehl to Strasburg (two or three miles) by Omnibus. The french custom house is on the road, where luggage is examined. (It is also examined on the Railroad between Ostend and Cologne. But all you have to do, is, to go into the room you are shewn; wait until you see your Portmanteau brought in; cry 'halloa' at sight of it, open it, and afterwards lock it up again.) Hotel at Strasburg, the Hotel de la Ville de Paris,

> very good. You can sleep there, or go on to Bâle, also by Railway, by the next Train. Fare, 1st. class, 17 francs. Time, about 4 hours. Hotel at Bâle, the Hotel of the Three Kings, one of the very best on the Continent. At Bâle, there are the Mail, and at least two Diligences, starting, every day and evening, for Lausanne. Fare about 26 francs. Time, about 24 hours.
>
> Returning; the Journey by the Rhine, being with the Stream, is performed in half the time. All along the Rhine, English is understood and spoken – French, everywhere.

Forster wrote that the Villa Rosemont was 'quite a doll's house; with two pretty little salons, a dining-room, hall, and kitchen, on the ground floor; and with just enough bedrooms upstairs to leave the family one to spare.' Dickens rented it for five months. He loved his children to be surrounded by beauty, and at the villa they had large gardens to play in and a view of both the Alps and Lake Geneva. As Dickens explained to Forster,

> It is beautifully situated on the hill that rises from the lake, within ten minutes' walk of this hotel, and furnished, though scantily as all here are, better than others ... on account of its having being built and fitted up (the little salons in the Parisian way) by the landlady and her husband for themselves... . A portion of the grounds is farmed by a farmer, and he lives close by; so that, while it is secluded, it is not at all lonely.

Not being lonely, especially at the times he would be there without his family, was key. Dickens may have believed he needed solitude in order to write, but at those times when he was not at his desk, he craved company and excitement. His brother-in-law, Henry Burnett, remembered an instance very early in Dickens's career, at his home in London, when Dickens had left the company to go and work, but was incapable of staying away from the presence of his wife and their guests. So he returned to the drawing room, where he wrote quite contentedly in a corner, with the sounds of a party going on around him.

'My Hat Shall Ever Be Ready to Be Thrown Up For ... Switzerland'

Despite writing to Thomas Mitton that 'The town of Lausanne is prodigious if ugly, and (I should hope) the dullest in all the world', his new home pleased Dickens. He wrote to Forster:

> There are all manner of walks, vineyards, green lanes, cornfields, and pastures full of hay. The general neatness is as remarkable as in England. There are no priests or monks in the streets, and the people appear to be industrious and thriving. French (and very intelligible and pleasant French) seems to be the universal language. I never saw so many booksellers' shops crammed within the same space, as in the steep up-and-down streets of Lausanne.

To Mitton, Dickens wrote happily, 'The native wine is something between vinegar and pickled cucumbers, and makes you wink and cry when you taste it. But I get very good French wine (red) at ten pence the bottle. This we drink as you would drink Beer in England.'

Perhaps knowing himself well enough, however, to realise he would get bored, despite the beauty and the availability of French wine, Dickens tried to persuade friends to come and join him. To Douglas Jerrold he wrote, 'I wish you would seriously consider the expediency and feasibility of coming to Lausanne in the summer or early autumn. It is a wonderful place to see.' Once settled in the villa, Dickens wrote again to Jerrold, with full instructions for how to travel from London to Lausanne, writing:

> We are established here in a perfect doll's house, which could be put bodily into the hall of our Italian palazzo. But it is in the most lovely and delicious situation imaginable, and there is a spare bedroom wherein we could make you as comfortable as need be. Bowers of roses for cigar-smoking, arbours for cool punch-drinking, mountain and Tyrolean countries close at hand, piled-up Alps before the windows...

Dickens may have been promoting the relaxation of Lausanne, but he was also excited by what he felt was the spirit of revolution in Switzerland. He had come to Switzerland to enjoy mellow writing time, but it turned out to be a turbulent few months for the country. On 24 October he was staying in a hotel in Geneva, having been plagued by a long-lasting headache and needing a break from the noise of family life. From there, he wrote to William Charles Macready,

> I am ... lodging for a week in the Hôtel de l'Écu de Genève, wherein there is a large mirror shattered by a cannon-ball in the late revolution. A revolution, whatever its merits, achieved by free spirits, nobly generous and moderate, even in the first transports of victory, elevated by a splendid popular education, and bent on freedom from all tyrants, whether their crowns be shaven or golden. The newspapers may tell you what they please. I believe there is no country on earth but Switzerland in which such a violent change could have been effected in the Christian spirit shown in this place, or in the same proud, independent, gallant style. Not one halfpennyworth of property was lost, stolen, or strayed. Not one atom of party malice survived the smoke of the last gun. Nothing is expressed in the government addresses to the citizens but a regard for the general happiness and injunctions to forget all animosities...

A couple of weeks earlier he had written to Forster, 'We heard the guns (they shook this house) all day.... It is a horribly ungentlemanly thing to say here, though I do say it without the least reserve – but my sympathy is all with the radicals.'

On 1 May, the poet Elizabeth Barrett Browning wrote a letter to her husband, in which she related a conversation she had been told about:

> [Tennyson] had been dining at Dickens's, and meeting various celebrities, and Dickens had asked him to go with him (Dickens) to Switzerland, where he [is] going, to write his new work: 'but' laughed Tennyson, 'if I went, I should be entreating him to dismiss his sentimentality, and so we should quarrel and part, and never see one another any more. It was better to decline – and I have declined.'

Despite these protestations, Tennyson was obviously intrigued by Dickens's plan, and he did travel to Switzerland that year. In August,

Dickens wrote to Forster of 'walking up and down under the little colonnade in the garden, racking my brain about *Dombeys* and *Battles of Lives*, when two travel-stained-looking men approached, of whom one, in a very limp and melancholy straw hat, ducked perpetually to me as he came up the walk.' The two men were Alfred, Lord Tennyson and the publisher and poet Edward Moxon.

Charles and Catherine's son, Charley Dickens, wrote in his memoirs of that memorable Lausanne moment:

> One evening in the twilight when my sister Mamie was sitting at the piano and singing *The May Queen*, Alfred Tennyson[15] unexpectedly strolled in among us through the window that opened on to the lawn, as if the odd coincidence were quite a matter of course.

Music was always of vital importance in the Dickens family. When they were living in Albaro in 1844, Dickens rented a piano for their new home within days of moving into the villa.

Wherever they travelled, the children's education was also of paramount importance. Charles and Catherine ensured their children had excellent tutors and governesses. Dickens had written to Mitton from Italy, 'Charley has a Writing Master every day – and a French Master. He and his sisters are to be waited on, by a Professor of the noble art of Dancing, next Week.' From Switzerland, Dickens wrote again to Mitton:

> Charley goes to a school, kept by a German, about a quarter of a mile off. He is a weekly boarder, and comes home every Saturday. There are one or two other English boys, so I hope he will be set up in French for life, before he comes home. He speaks the language always, now, and can make himself understood anywhere; but does not speak correctly, yet.

He wrote proudly to Angela Burdett-Coutts that Charley Dickens, her godson, 'has won a Geneva watch by speaking French in three months. I rashly pledged myself to make that desperate present in the event of

---

15. A few months earlier, Tennyson had become godfather to the sixth of the Dickens children, Alfred D'Orsay Tennyson Dickens (born in October 1845).

his succeeding – and as he has succeeded.' To Forster, Dickens wrote of 'an annual child's fête at the Signal the other night: given by the town. It was beautiful to see perhaps a hundred couple of children dancing in an immense ring in a green wood. Our three eldest were among them.' The children's time in Lausanne was also enlivened rather strangely, as Dickens wrote to Forster: 'a crocodile is said to have escaped from the Zoological Gardens at Geneva, and to be now "zig-zag-zigging" about the lake. But I can't make out whether this is a great fact, or whether it is a pious fraud to prevent too much bathing and liability to accidents.'

Surrounded by such gorgeous nature at the Villa Rosemont, Dickens intended to work on his fourth Christmas book, *The Battle of Life*, and to grapple with the writing of *Dombey and Son* which he was finding a challenge. The first few weeks were difficult, which he found frustrating and worrying, but by November, he was writing contentedly to John Forster, 'I am at work at *Dombey* with good speed, thank God. All well here. Country stupendously beautiful. Mountains covered with snow. Rich, crisp weather.' He could not, however, leave behind him his worries about life in England, writing to his brother Fred about 'a poor woman named Greenwood, who lodges in Blenheim Street Oxford Street, at a little Cobbler's' and asking Fred to go and visit her, see how she was and give her some money: 'She is very industrious, and has suffered a great deal.'

Dickens worked on the first four chapters and the overarching plot of *Dombey and Son* in Switzerland, but was feeling a desperate need to be back in a city. In September 1846 he wrote to Forster:

> The absence of any accessible streets continues to worry me, now that I have so much to do, in a most singular manner. It is quite a little mental phenomenon. I should not walk in them in the day time, if they were here, I dare say: but at night I want them beyond description. I don't seem able to get rid of my spectres unless I can lose them in crowds. However, as you say, there are streets in Paris.

In October, Catherine and Georgina accompanied Dickens to Geneva, from where he wrote to Forster mockingly that he had 'trembled at the noise in the streets, which was fully equal to the uproar of Richmond in

Surrey.' He had been struggling with depression and admitted to Forster that he felt moving from such a quiet place back to a city had saved him from sinking into 'some bad low fever'. Dickens was disappointed by the lack of signs of the recent revolution, saying that the streets were 'as quiet by ten o'clock as Lincoln's-inn-fields' (the sedate London square on which John Forster lived).

In the middle of November, Dickens moved his family to the inspirational chaos of Paris – the beauties of Lausanne having proved too relaxing for his active writing mind. The journey took five days, which was longer than they had expected, and Dickens was full of praise for how well his children, even the baby (Alfred), behaved on the journey. He wrote to Forster:

> We have been up at five every morning, and on the road before seven. We were three carriages: a sort of wagon, with a cabriolet attached, for the luggage; a ramshackle villainous old swing upon wheels (hired at Geneva), for the children; and for ourselves, that travelling chariot.... . It was very cold indeed crossing the Jura – nothing but fog and frost; but when we were out of Switzerland and across the French frontier, it became warmer, and continued so. We stopped at between six and seven each evening; had two rather queer inns, wild French country inns; but the rest good. They were three hours and a half examining the luggage at the frontier custom-house – atop of a mountain, in a hard and biting frost; where Anne and Roche had sharp work I assure you, and the latter insisted on volunteering the most astonishing and unnecessary lies about my books, for the mere pleasure of deceiving the officials. When we were out of the mountain country, we came at a good pace, but were a day late in getting to our hotel here.

In the 1867 preface to *Dombey and Son*, Dickens wrote:

> I began this book by the Lake of Geneva, and went on with it for some months in France, before pursuing it in England. The association between the writing and the place of writing is so curiously strong in my mind, that at this

day, although I know, in my fancy, every stair in the little midshipman's house, and could swear to every pew in the church in which Florence was married, or to every young gentleman's bedstead in Doctor Blimber's establishment, I yet confusedly imagine Captain Cuttle as secluding himself from Mrs MacStinger among the mountains of Switzerland. Similarly, when I am reminded by any chance of what it was that the waves were always saying, my remembrance wanders for a whole winter night about the streets of Paris – as I restlessly did with a heavy heart, on the night when I had written the chapter in which my little friend and I parted company.

From Paris on 22 November, he wrote to his friend, the poet Walter Savage Landor, 'Don't be hard upon the Swiss. They are a thorn in the sides of European despots, and a good wholesome people… . My hat shall ever be ready to be thrown up, and my glove ever ready to be thrown down for Switzerland.' When *The Battle of Life* was published in December 1846, its dedication read: 'This Christmas book is cordially inscribed to my English friends in Switzerland.'

Although in future years Dickens only visited Switzerland very briefly, the country and especially its landscape haunted his imagination. In *David Copperfield* Dickens wrote about David's travels:

I was in Switzerland. I had come out of Italy, over one of the great passes of the Alps, and had since wandered with a guide among the by-ways of the mountains… . I had found sublimity and wonder in the dread heights and precipices, in the roaring torrents, and the wastes of ice and snow…. I came, one evening before sunset, down into a valley, where I was to rest… . I came into the valley, as the evening sun was shining on the remote heights of snow, that closed it in, like eternal clouds. The bases of the mountains forming the gorge in which the little village lay, were richly green; and high above this gentler vegetation, grew forests of dark fir, cleaving the wintry snow-drift, wedge-like, and stemming the avalanche. Above these, were range upon range of craggy steeps, grey rock, bright ice, and smooth verdure-specks of pasture, all gradually blending with the crowning snow. Dotted here and there on the mountain's-side, each tiny dot a home, were lonely wooden cottages, so dwarfed by the towering heights that they appeared too small for toys... . In the quiet air, there was a sound of distant singing – shepherd voices; but, as one bright evening cloud floated midway along the mountain's-side, I could almost have believed it came from there, and was not earthly music. All at once, in this serenity, great Nature spoke to me.

Dickens also sent the Dorrit family to Switzerland, on their journey to Italy, via the Great St Bernard Pass, one of the highest roads in the country:

> In the autumn of the year, Darkness and Night were creeping up to the highest ridges of the Alps. It was vintage time in the valleys on the Swiss side of the Pass of the Great Saint Bernard, and along the banks of the Lake of Geneva. The air there was charged with the scent of gathered grapes... . The air had been warm and transparent through the whole of the bright day. Shining metal spires and church-roofs, distant and rarely seen, had sparkled in the view; and the snowy mountain-tops had been so clear that unaccustomed eyes, cancelling the intervening country, and slighting their rugged heights for something fabulous, would have measured them as within a few hours easy reach. Mountain-peaks of great celebrity in the valleys ... were yet distinctly defined in their loneliness above the mists and shadows.
>
> Seen from these solitudes, and from the Pass of the Great Saint Bernard ... the ascending Night came up the mountain like a rising water. When it at last rose to the walls of the convent of the Great Saint Bernard, it was as if that weather-beaten structure were another Ark, and floated on the shadowy waves.
>
> Darkness, outstripping some visitors on mules, had risen thus to the rough convent walls, when those travellers were yet climbing the mountain. As the heat of the glowing day when they had stopped to drink at the streams of melted ice

and snow, was changed to the searching cold of the frosty rarefied night air at a great height, so the fresh beauty of the lower journey had yielded to barrenness and desolation. A craggy track, up which the mules in single file scrambled and turned from block to block, as though they were ascending the broken staircase of a gigantic ruin, was their way now. No trees were to be seen ... . Blackened skeleton arms of wood by the wayside pointed upward to the convent as if the ghosts of former travellers overwhelmed by the snow haunted the scene of their distress. Icicle-hung caves and cellars built for refuges from sudden storms, were like so many whispers of the perils of the place...

At length, a light on the summit of the rocky staircase gleamed through the snow and mist. The guides called to the mules, the mules pricked up their drooping heads, the travellers' tongues were loosened, and in a sudden burst of slipping, climbing, jingling, clinking, and talking, they arrived at the convent door.

The Great St Bernard Pass is also the starting point for Dickens's ghostly short story *To Be Read At Dusk* (1852):

Five couriers, sitting on a bench outside the convent on the summit of the Great St. Bernard in Switzerland, looking at the remote heights, stained by the setting sun as if a mighty quantity of red wine had been broached upon the mountain top, and had not yet had time to sink into the snow.

In this story the narrator talks of a place that had fascinated Dickens, the hut in which where the bodies of deceased travellers were kept.

Dickens had written to Forster in 1846, when he first visited the pass and stayed at the monastery (which he calls a convent) at its summit:

the ascent, lying through a place called the valley of desolation, is very awful and tremendous, and the road is rendered toilsome by scattered rocks and melting snow... . I wish to God you could see that place. A great hollow on the top of a range of dreadful mountains, fenced in by riven rocks of every shape and colour: and in the midst, a black lake, with phantom clouds perpetually stalking over it. Peaks, and points, and plains of eternal ice and snow, bounding the view, and shutting out the world on every side: the lake reflecting nothing: and no human figure in the scene... . Beside the convent, in a little outhouse with a grated iron door which you may unbolt for yourself, are the bodies of people found in the snow who have never been claimed and are withering away – not laid down, or stretched out, but standing up, in corners and against walls; some erect and horribly human, with distinct expressions on the faces; some sunk down on their knees; some dropping over on one side; some tumbled down altogether, and presenting a heap of skulls and fibrous dust. There is no other decay in that atmosphere; and there they remain during the short days and the long nights, the only human company out of doors, withering away by grains, and holding ghastly possession of the mountain where they died.

In *Little Dorrit*, the Dorrit family are newly wealthy and only recently released from debtors' prison. Fanny Dorrit, determined to be viewed as one born into money, has a conversation with a rather patronising 'insinuating traveller', who wants to assume the role of the seasoned rover whilst assuming everyone else a mere tourist in need of his advice. When he asks how Fanny and her younger sister are coping with the rigours of travelling, Fanny responds haughtily that she is merely 'incommoded' by the necessity of journeying so far by mule. She talks of how inconvenient it is 'to leave the carriages ... and the impossibility of bringing anything that one wants to this inaccessible place, and the necessity of leaving every comfort behind, is not convenient.'

Many Victorian travellers would have empathised with Fanny's comments. Having to negotiate mountains long before the invention of railway tunnels or aeroplanes was not an easy feat. When Dickens mentions in the text the story of a family of travellers who froze to death, and whose bodies remained forever preserved by the cold of the mountain, he was echoing a very prevalent fear, one that all travellers of this time feared – of winter arriving earlier than expected and of snow closing off all passages back to safety.

Dickens and Travel: The Start of Modern Travel Writing

Switzerland also appeared in the Christmas story of 1867, which was written jointly by Wilkie Collins and Dickens. In the suitably melodramatic *No Thoroughfare*, the Swiss Alps provide an essential plot point. On 23 August, Dickens wrote to Collins:

> Let us arrange to culminate in a wintry flight and pursuit across the Alps ... say the Simplon Pass – under lonely circumstances, and against warnings. Let us get into the horrors and dangers of such an adventure under the most terrific circumstances... . There we can get Ghostly interest, picturesque interest, breathless interest of time and circumstance, and force the design up to any powerful climax we please.

By specifying the Simplon Pass, Dickens was making sure that the title *No Thoroughfare* was echoed in people's knowledge of how dangerous the journey was. Only the most intrepid of travellers to Europe would attempt the Simplon Pass.

In *No Thoroughfare*, a woman gives up her child to the Foundling Hospital in London (a place that had also inspired Dickens when writing *Oliver Twist*). Many years later, having discovered that her baby was given the name of Walter Wilding, she is able to claim him. What neither she nor the child she adopts is aware of is that her baby had already been adopted, and the Walter Wilding whom she claimed was a boy who had been given the same name. The truth is discovered after the woman's death. When the man who believed he was her son and has inherited her fortune discovers what has happened, he tries to discover what had happened to her real son. A former nurse from the Foundling Hospital tells him that the baby was very ill, but this adoptive mother had assured the nurse not to be alarmed because 'He will be brought up in a better climate that this – I am going to take him to Switzerland.' Coincidentally, another of the novel's characters is a Swiss man named M. Jules Obenreizer He lives in an area of London, where most of his compatriots also live:

> A curious colony of mountaineers has long been enclosed within that small flat London district of Soho. Swiss watchmakers, Swiss silver-chasers, Swiss jewellers, Swiss

> importers of Swiss musical boxes and Swiss toys of various kinds, draw close together there. Swiss professors of music, painting, and languages; Swiss artificers in steady work; Swiss couriers, and other Swiss servants chronically out of place; industrious Swiss laundresses and clear-starchers; mysteriously existing Swiss of both sexes; Swiss creditable and Swiss discreditable; Swiss to be trusted by all means, and Swiss to be trusted by no means; these diverse Swiss particles are attracted to a centre in the district of Soho. Shabby Swiss eating-houses, coffee-houses, and lodging-houses, Swiss drinks and dishes, Swiss service for Sundays, and Swiss schools for week-days, are all to be found there. Even the native-born English taverns drive a sort of broken-English trade; announcing in their windows Swiss whets and drams, and sheltering in their bars Swiss skirmishes of love and animosity on most nights in the year.

Over the years, Dickens's imagination turned Switzerland into a tranquil paradise he often longed to return to, even though, in reality, he had found it a very difficult place in which to work. In 1851, he wrote to Forster from the Strood Valley in England, saying the scenery reminded him of Lausanne and

> I very nearly packed up a portmanteau and went away, the day before yesterday, into the mountains of Switzerland, alone! Still the victim of an intolerable restlessness, I shouldn't be at all surprised if I wrote to you one of these mornings from under Mont Blanc. I sit down between whiles to think of a new story, and, as it begins to grow, such a torment of a desire to be anywhere but where I am; and to be going I don't know where, I don't know why; takes hold of me, that it is like being driven away. If I had had a passport, I sincerely believe I should have gone to Switzerland the night before last.

Yet when Dickens returned to Lausanne, briefly, in 1853, on his holiday with Wilkie Collins and Augustus Egg, he wrote to Catherine in bewilderment at how poorly his memory of their time in Lausanne had served him: 'I have forgotten my way about this place. I ... was quite at a loss in the town itself – and have at this moment no remembrance whatever of where the banker's is!'

In around 1860, Dickens met the French actor Charles Fechter, whom Dickens saw perform *Hamlet* in Paris and London. The two men became friends, and when Dickens and Collins were working on the stage version of *No Thoroughfare* Fechter was the person they had in mind for one of the major roles. Just before Christmas 1864, Dickens received word from Higham Railway Station, the local train station to his home, Gad's Hill Place in Kent, that a large number of enormous packing cases had arrived, addressed to him. The men from the Dickens's Christmas house party all travelled to the station to help take the large present home. It was a gift from Fechter and inside the packing cases were all the components of a Swiss chalet, ready to be assembled. Dickens had it built in the grounds of Gad's Hill Place and it became his favoured writing place on warm days. He wrote to Fechter that he had 'never worked better anywhere' and he called it his 'most delightful summer atelier'. It became a little piece of his Swiss idyll in south-east England.

Dickens the Francophile

'Paris is just what you know it – as bright, and as wicked, and as wanton, as ever.'
Letter from Charles Dickens to
William Haldimand, 27 November 1846

The very first time that Charles Dickens travelled to the 'Continent' (as mainland Europe was known by people from the British Isles), was in 1837. That June, when Charles and Catherine's first child, Charley, was a few months old, the new parents left their baby at home and travelled to France and Belgium, in the company of Hablot Knight Browne, aka the illustrator Phiz. This was the beginning of Dickens's love affair with overseas travel, despite suffering through a rough Channel crossing. Dickens wrote to John Forster from Calais:

> We arrived here in great state this morning – I very sick, and Missis very well… . We have arranged for a post coach to take us to Ghent, Brussels, Antwerp, and a hundred other places that I cannot recollect now and couldn't spell if I did. We went this afternoon in a barouche to some gardens where the people dance, and where they were footing it most heartily – especially the women who in their short petticoats and light caps look uncommonly agreeable. A gentleman in a blue surtout and silken Berlins accompanied us from the Hotel, and acted as Curator. He even waltzed with a very smart lady (just to show us, condescendingly, how it ought to be done) and waltzed elegantly too. We rang for slippers after we came back, and it turned out that this gentleman was the 'Boots'. Isn't this French?

Dickens and Travel: The Start of Modern Travel Writing

Dickens was not the only member of his family to fall in love with France. In May 1841, he sent an exasperatingly amused letter to John Forster: 'I have a letter from my father ... informing me that it will not be possible for him to stay more than another year in Devonshire, as he must then proceed to Paris to consolidate Augustus's French.'

In June 1850, Dickens was a passenger on an exciting new route: the South Eastern Railway's overnight train from London to Paris. The Double Special Express left London Bridge Station on the evening of 22 June and reached Paris at 8.45am on 23 June. Dickens wrote to Forster, 'The twelve hours' journey here is astounding – marvellously done, except in the means of refreshment, which are absolutely none.'

The following year, the railway was advertising an even faster service: 'London to Paris in 11 hours by Special Express Train and Steam Ship.' Passengers could either go by train to Folkestone and boat to Boulogne, or a train to Dover and boat to Calais. From Boulogne or Calais, they travelled by train to Paris. Dickens took the new service in February 1851, and wrote an article for *Household Words*, 'A Flight' (published on 30 August 1851). He began the article with a prediction that one day someone would invent a flying machine for

> a flight to Paris ... [but] At present, my reliance is on the South Eastern Railway Company, in whose Express Train here I sit, at eight of the clock on a very hot morning, under the very hot roof of the Terminus at London Bridge, in danger of being 'forced' like a cucumber or melon.... And a Flight to Paris in eleven hours! ... I can fly with the South Eastern, more lazily, at all events, than in the upper air. I have but to sit here thinking as idly as I please, and be whisked away.

As the train starts to move, Dickens's narrator comments on how pleasant it is to feel the fresh air as they whizz past 'Bermondsey where the tanners live. Flash! The distant shipping in the Thames is gone. Whirr! ... The hop-gardens turn gracefully towards me ... then whirl away. So do the pools and rushes, haystacks, sheep, clover in full bloom ... corn-sheaves, cherry-orchards, apple-orchards ... cottages, gardens, now and then a church.'

The narrator's fellow passengers are assigned nicknames. An attractive and elegant young Frenchwoman is referred to as the Compact Temptress and her female companion is designated Mystery; a stressed Englishman is called the Demented Traveller and a sleek Englishman, whom Dickens assumes works in the Stock Exchange, is named Monied Interest. As the travellers change from the train to the boat at Folkestone, Dickens writes, 'And now I find that all the French people on board begin to grow, and all the English people to shrink. The French are nearing home, and shaking off a disadvantage, whereas we are shaking it on.'

Arriving in Boulogne, the narrator comments,

> Now, I tread upon French ground, and am greeted by the three charming words, Liberty, Equality, Fraternity, painted up (in letters a little too thin for their height) on the Custom House wall – also by the sight of large cocked hats, without which demonstrative head-gear nothing of a public nature can be done on this soil.

The lunch at Boulogne railway station is described as 'Large hall, long counter, long strips of dining-table, bottles of wine, plates of meat, roast chickens, little loaves of bread, basins of soup, little caraffes of brandy, cakes and fruit'.

The French land through which the train journeys is another world. Gone are the dust heaps of London and the hop gardens of Kent. It flies past 'Fields, windmills, low grounds, pollard-trees, windmills, fields, fortifications, Abbeville, soldiering and drumming'. Dickens describes the train journey as one of dreamlike indolence, on which passengers are freed 'from all responsibility, except the preservation of a voucher ruled into three divisions, of which the first was snipped off at Folkestone, the second aboard the boat, and the third taken at my journey's end.' He ends the article with fulsome praise: 'So, I pass to my hotel, enchanted; sup, enchanted; go to bed, enchanted … blessing the South Eastern Company for realising the Arabian Nights in these prose days, murmuring, as I wing my idle flight into the land of dreams.'

Dickens wrote about travelling in France again in his 1863 article 'The Calais Night Mail', part of *The Uncommercial Traveller* series:

Calais up and doing at the railway station, and Calais down and dreaming in its bed; Calais with something of 'an ancient and fish-like smell' about it, and Calais blown and sea-washed pure; Calais represented at the Buffet by savoury roast fowls, hot coffee, cognac, and Bordeaux; and Calais represented everywhere by flitting persons with a monomania for changing money.

In the same year, he published a story in the special Christmas issue of *All The Year Round,* entitled 'Mrs Lirriper's Lodgings'. This was followed by a sequel for the special Christmas issue of 1864, entitled 'Mrs Lirriper's Legacy'. In the latter, Mrs Lirriper travels to France and narrates the experience:

But my dear the blueness and the lightness and the coloured look of everything... . And as to lunch why bless you if I kept a man-cook and two kitchen-maids I couldn't got it done for twice the money ... of Paris I can tell you no more my dear than that it's town and country both in one, and carved stone and long streets of high houses and gardens and fountains and statues and trees and gold ... and clean table-cloths spread everywhere for dinner and people sitting out of doors smoking and sipping all day long and little plays being acted in the open air for little people and every shop a complete and elegant room... . And as to the sparkling lights my dear after dark ... and the crowd of theatres and the crowd of people and the crowd of all sorts, it's pure enchantment.

Another place Dickens visited multiple times was Marseilles. He was fascinated by its multiculturalism, a place teeming with travellers and workers from all over the globe. It was a place where anything might, conceivably, happen. *Little Dorrit* opens with a long description of Marseilles:

Thirty years ago, Marseilles lay burning in the sun... . Everything in Marseilles, and about Marseilles, had stared at the fervid sky, and been stared at in return, until a staring habit had become universal there. Strangers were stared out of countenance by staring white houses, staring white walls, staring white streets, staring tracts of arid road, staring hills from which verdure was burnt away. The only things to be seen not fixedly staring and glaring were the vines drooping under their load of grapes... . There was no wind to make a ripple on the foul water within the harbour, or on the beautiful sea without... . Boats without awnings were too hot to touch; ships blistered at their moorings; the stones of the quays had not cooled, night or day, for months. Hindoos, Russians, Chinese, Spaniards, Portuguese, Englishmen, Frenchmen, Genoese, Neapolitans, Venetians, Greeks, Turks, descendants from all the builders of Babel, come to trade at Marseilles, sought the shade alike...

So, with people lounging and lying wherever shade was, with but little hum of tongues or barking of dogs, with occasional jangling of discordant church bells and rattling of vicious drums, Marseilles, a fact to be strongly smelt and tasted, lay broiling in the sun one day.

Paris – 'Bright ... Wicked ... and Wanton'

'There is no such place for material in my way, as Paris.'
Letter from Charles Dickens to
Thomas Mitton, 12 August 1844

Of all the places Dickens fell in love with in France, Paris always held a special place in his heart. He travelled there with his family, with friends and alone, and it seems to have been somewhere he felt he could be his true self – or perhaps the man he aspired to be, but didn't manage to achieve elsewhere.

In August 1844, Dickens wrote to his friend Count D'Orsay, about visiting Paris en route to Italy:

> I cannot tell you what an immense impression Paris made upon me. It is the most extraordinary place in the World. I was not prepared for, and really could not have believed in, its perfectly distinct and separate character. My eyes ached and my head grew giddy, as novelty, novelty, novelty; nothing but strange and striking things; came swarming before me. I cannot conceive any place so perfectly and wonderfully expressive of its own character; its secret character no less than that which is on its surface; as Paris is. I walked about the streets – in and out, up and down, backwards and forwards – during the two days we were there; and almost every house, and every person I passed, seemed to be another leaf in the enormous book that stands wide open. I was perpetually turning over, and never coming any nearer the end. There never was such a place for a description.

Paris – 'Bright ... Wicked ... and Wanton'

When the Dickens family left Lausanne, in the autumn of 1846, they travelled to Paris, so Dickens could write. John Forster wrote, 'That same Saturday night [Dickens] took a colossal walk about the city, of which the brilliancy and brightness almost frightened him' after the quietness of Lausanne. Initially, they stayed at the Hotel Brighton on the Rue de Rivoli, but Charles and Catherine were eager to find a house to rent and after four days house hunting took on the lease for what Dickens described as 'the most preposterous house in the world' in a letter to his friend Lavinia Watson.

> The bedrooms are like opera boxes. The dressing-rooms, staircases, and passages, quite inexplicable. The dining room is a sort of cavern, painted (ceiling and all) to represent a Grove, with unaccountable bits of looking-glass sticking in among the branches of the trees. There is a gleam of reason in the drawing room. But it is approached, through a series of small chambers, like the joints in a telescope, which are hung with inscrutable drapery. The maddest man in Bedlam, having the materials given him, would be likely to devise such a suite, supposing his case to be hopeless and quite incurable.

Their new home was 48 Rue de Courcelles, Faubourg St Honore. It was a very cold and snowy winter, and Dickens declared to Forster that not only did the windows and doors refuse to close but 'there's not a door or window in all Paris that shuts; not a chink in all the billions of trillions of chinks in the city that can be stopped to keep the wind out. And the cold!' Paris was also very expensive, as he explained to Forster, 'Everything is enormously dear. Fuel, stupendously so. In airing the house, we burnt five pounds' worth of firewood in one week!! We mix it with coal now, as we used to do in Italy, and find the fires much warmer.'

One thing Dickens wanted to do in Paris was to sell the travelling carriage that he had commissioned before their trip in Italy. It had travelled with them throughout much of Europe, but it was time to get back the money he had spent commissioning it – and innovations in transport were being made all the time and perhaps Dickens wanted something more up to date.

In early December, he wrote again of how very cold the weather was and of how dangerous the city could be. He and Georgina had been out walking one evening when they saw an attempted mugging: 'we saw a man fall upon another, close before us, and try to tear the cloak off his back.... . After a short struggle, the thief fled (there were thousands of people walking about), and was captured just on the other side of the road.'

A few days later, Dickens left Paris temporarily, once again needing to travel to London to promote his latest Christmas book, *The Battle of Life*. It had also been dramatised, produced by Dickens's friend and theatrical manager Albert Smith, at the Lyceum Theatre in Covent Garden. Dickens was disappointed by the rehearsals, writing despondently to Catherine of substandard acting and a confusing script. He was cheered, however, by the audience response on the opening night, writing home about 'immense enthusiasm ... great uproar and shouting' in the theatre.

He arrived back in Paris in time for a family Christmas, and they were joined a few days later by John Forster. On 27 January, Dickens wrote to Lady Blessington about their friend's fervent tourism, which Dickens was tolerating with amusement:

> Forster has been cramming into the space of a fortnight, every description of impossible and inconsistent occupation in the way of sight-seeing. He has been now at Versailles, now in the Prisons, now at the Opera, now at the Hospital, now at the Conservatoire, and now at the Morgue, with a dreadful insatiability. As I have been at all these places too, ... [I] have been whirled out of one into another with breathless speed.

The family spent their time in Paris in a whirl of social life, going to theatres and restaurants and watching a 'new shew-piece called the French Revolution, in which there is ... a series of battles (fought by some five hundred people who look like fifty thousand) that are wonderful in their extraordinary vigor and truth.' In his letter to Lady Blessington, Dickens also mentioned, with a casualness masking his excitement, meeting Victor Hugo. Dickens was suitably awed by the grandeur with which Hugo was surrounded, although he made light of it:

> We were at his house last Sunday week. A most extraordinary place, looking like an old curiosity shop, or the Property

Room of some gloomy vast old Theatre. I was much struck by Hugo himself, who looks like a Genius, as he certainly is very interesting from head to foot. His wife is a handsome woman with flashing black eyes, who looks as if she might poison his breakfast any morning when the humor seized her. There is also a ditto daughter of fifteen or sixteen, with ditto eyes, and hardly any drapery above the waist, whom I should suspect of carrying a sharp poignard in her stays but for her not appearing to wear any. Sitting among old armour, and old tapestry, and old coffers, and grim old chairs and tables, and old Canopies of state from old places, and old golden lions going to play at skittles with ponderous old golden balls, they made a most romantic show, and looked like a chapter out of one of his own books.

In his *Life of Charles Dickens*, Forster wrote:

> we supped with Dumas himself, and Eugène Sue, and met Théophile Gautier and Alphonse Karr. We saw Lamartine also, and had much friendly intercourse with Scribe, and with the kind good-natured Amedée Pichot. One day we visited in the Rue du Bac the sick and ailing Chateaubriand...; found ourselves ... in the sculpture-room of David d'Angers; and closed that day at the house of Victor Hugo, by whom Dickens was received with infinite courtesy and grace.... Rather under the middle size, of compact close-buttoned-up figure, with ample dark hair falling loosely over his close-shaven face, I never saw upon any features so keenly intellectual such a soft and sweet gentility, and certainly never heard the French language spoken with the picturesque distinctness given to it by Victor Hugo. He talked of his childhood in Spain, and of his father having been Governor of the Tagus in Napoleon's wars; spoke warmly of the English people and their literature; declared his preference for melody and simplicity over the music then fashionable at the Conservatoire; referred kindly to Ponsard, laughed at the actors who had murdered his tragedy at the Odéon, and sympathized with the dramatic venture of Dumas. To Dickens he addressed very charming

flattery, in the best taste; and my friend long remembered the enjoyment of that evening.

This Parisian adventure, flavoured as it was with the wonder of having visited Victor Hugo, dined with Alexandre Dumas, and where the family had shopped at the most fashionable clothing establishments, came to a very abrupt end. Charles and Catherine (who was heavily pregnant with her seventh child) received the news that Charley, at boarding school in England, had contracted scarlet fever and was extremely ill. His parents rushed home, escorted by Louis Roche, leaving the other children and Georgina in Paris. Roche then returned to take the rest of the family safely back to London. They arrived to the news that Charley was recovering.

Dickens returned to Paris in the summer of 1850 with Daniel Maclise. Dickens had thought about writing an article on Parisian theatre, but reported to his editor W. H. Wills 'There is nothing doing at the Theatres'.

A letter to Catherine was addressed 'In a Café, Paris':

> Being out with Regnier[16] (and frightfully bored by sights I don't care for) I plunge into a café to save the Post. The Hotel Brighton was full – ditto Meurice's – Paris being crammed (strange to say) with foreigners. But Regnier had taken us a very nice apartment at the Hotel Windsor.... It is in the Rue de Rivoli, close to the Brighton.... It is much hotter than in Genoa in July. I can do nothing but drink, and go to sleep in the daytime.

From Paris, they travelled to Rouen and Dieppe, from where they took a boat back to England. The record of how much such a trip cost in the 1850s is recorded in a letter from Dickens to Maclise: 'The Sum Total of our expenses, from home back again, is £20..12..6 each.'

The allure of Paris continued and, the following year, Dickens wrote to Angela Burdett-Coutts, 'I am running off to Paris, for a *Household Words* purpose, by the Mail Train tonight.' The trip was initially just with his illustrator John Leech, until Dickens wrote to Leech, 'I never was more astounded than I have been by a proposal from [the Hon] Spencer Lyttelton, to go with us to Paris! As he is the jolliest of the jolly I have

---

16. Their friend, the actor François Regnier.

Paris – 'Bright ... Wicked ... and Wanton'

said Yes – hoping you will like the addition of a man with high spirits, who is up to anything.' Their friend Count D'Orsay was also in the city, and Dickens wrote to Catherine about their social life:

> I received your letter this morning (on returning from an expedition to a market 13 miles away, which involved the necessity of getting up at 5).... . We had D'Orsay to dinner yesterday, and I am hurried to dress now, in order to pay a promised visit to his 'atelier'. ... Lord and Lady Castlereagh live downstairs here, and we went to them in the evening, and afterwards brought him upstairs to smoke. Tonight we are going to see Lemaitre in the renowned Belphegor piece. Tomorrow at noon, we leave Paris for Calais (the Boulogne boat does not serve our turn)... . It continues to be delightful weather here – frosty, but very clear and fine... . Spencer Lyttelton is a capital companion on a trip, and a great addition to the party. We have got on famously, and been very facetious.

At the start of 1855, Dickens was feeling restless and miserable; his cure was to plan a holiday to Paris with Wilkie Collins. On 3 February, he wrote to Collins:

> On looking to Bradshaw[17], I find that if we go by Boulogne, Sunday the 11th will suit us admirably. We shall leave London Bridge at a quarter to 11 in the forenoon – cross at a quarter to 3 – and get to Boulogne about 5. We can then have my two small sons to dinner at the Hotel des Bains, and go on to Paris at 1/2 past 12 on Monday. This seems easy I think?

Shortly after their arrival, on 14 February Wilkie Collins wrote a long letter to his mother, Harriet Collins, giving a tantalising glimpse of travel in the 1850s:

> The sea-passage was, for the time of year, an easy one... . Compared with French frost, our national frost seems to be

---

17. Bradshaw's Guides were a series of travel guides containing railway timetables.

always wrapped up in more or less of soft fog. We should have felt this difference unpleasantly enough on the railway from Boulogne to Paris – but for the excellent metal cases of boiling water placed in each carriage, and renewed several times in the course of the journey. These kept our feet and legs warm, and made the air like the air of a room.... . We are settled here in a delightful apartment, looking out on the Tuileries, gorgeously-furnished drawing room – bedrooms with Turkey carpets – reception room – hall – cupboard – passages – all to ourselves. Paris is snowed up. The Boulevard pavement is inches thick with snow and ice – the Cafés are filled with shivering Frenchmen who congregate round the stoves. It is the height of the gay season here, in spite of the weather. The great masked ball at the Opera takes place this week. The two Theatres we have been to, up to this time, proved to be well filled. In short Paris amuses itself as gaily as ever.

In the letter, Collins writes that the Crimean War[18] is barely spoken of in Paris, but the upcoming Exposition Universelle was being greatly anticipated. The city was expecting an influx of English-speaking tourists for the exhibition, and everywhere they went, people were learning English: 'Shopkeepers, cabmen & waiters, if they only know two words of our language, let off these two words ... in the most vehemently persevering way.'

All of these brief trips whetted Dickens's desire to get to know the city properly. He wanted to become a Parisian. After his holiday with Collins, he began planning another overseas adventure and in the autumn of 1855, the Dickens family moved to Paris. By this time the Exposition Universelle had opened. It was a spectacle worth seeing, with hall after hall filled with artistic, engineering and scientific wonders from all over the globe. The exhibition, however, seemed to engender more gloom in Dickens, who mused in a letter to his publishers, Bradbury & Evans, 'England has become a mere second-rate power ... [the] result of toadyism and mismanagement.'

---

18. The Crimean War took place from 1854 to 1856.

Paris – 'Bright ... Wicked ... and Wanton'

The Dickens family took up residence at 49 Avenue des Champs Elysées, which the author described in a letter to W. H. Wills as 'the smallest place you ever saw, but ... exquisitely cheerful and vivacious ... and with a moving panorama always outside.' By this time, Mamie and Katey were 17 and 16 years old, and living in Paris was a wonderful way of 'finishing' their education. They took lessons, toured the city and visited art galleries with Anny and Minny Thackeray[19], whose grandparents lived in Paris and who were also staying in the city for several months. Dickens was, perhaps, thinking of his daughters' experiences some years later when, in *Great Expectations*, Miss Havisham sends Estella to France as part of her education.

Dickens loved Parisian nightlife, frequently attending theatres, private dinners and parties. He loved going out to dinner, and one of his favourite restaurants in Paris was Les Trois Frères Provençaux, which was inside the Palais Royale. The restaurant, which had been founded in the eighteenth century, closed down in 1872, two years after Dickens's death. It had been so popular with British tourists that the *Pall Mall Gazette* wrote an obituary for it: 'The Trois Frères has grown from small beginnings into an international institution.... . It has fallen draped decorously in its mantle, and we fear its fall is ominous of the general struggle for existence in luxurious Paris.'

By 1855, Charley Dickens was already working and the other Dickens boys (except Edward, the youngest) were at boarding school, but they were all in Paris for the Christmas holidays. Their father wrote a witty letter to his friend Edmund Yates (who had just become a father) about celebrating a family Christmas with all nine of his children in a dining room the size of a bathtub.

Many years later, a decade and a half after Charles Dickens's death, Charley published a guidebook entitled *Dickens's Dictionary of Paris, An Unconventional Handbook* (1885). He wrote of his family's old neighbourhood:

> Every afternoon, almost from New Year's Day until the end
> of the summer, the Champs Elysées are now thronged with

---

19. Anny and Minny were the daughters of William Makepeace Thackeray and his estranged wife Isabella. Anny became a famous novelist and remained lifelong friends with Katey Dickens.

carriages driving up and down the avenue, and with people who go there to walk, or to sit down upon the chairs in the fine weather, much in the same way that in London people crowd into Hyde Park during the same months of the year.

Charles Dickens engendered in all his children a love of travelling. Charley's book is written with the assurance of a seasoned traveller, one who, from his early childhood, had become accustomed to travelling great distances and adapting to new customs and languages. In his book Charley showed that he also inherited his parents' love of good food:

> Suppers are perhaps less frequent in Paris than formerly, perhaps because the dinner hours has come to be later, but all the houses just mentioned remain open at night, and suppers for large or small parties may be served in private rooms. These private rooms in the Paris restaurants are everywhere called 'cabinets particuliers'. … when all is told, one's dinner bill will not come to more money than at a good restaurant in London. Also, if the truth be spoken, the dinner in Paris will be both better and pleasanter.

Despite Charles Dickens's love of Paris, he was less than enamoured of the city's weather. To family friend Mary Boyle, he wrote in January 1856:

> It is clear to me that climates are gradually assimilating over a great part of the world, and that in the most miserable time of our year there is very little to choose between London and Paris – except that London is not so muddy. I have never seen dirtier or worse weather than we have had here, ever since I returned. In desperation I went outside the Barriers last Sunday on a headlong walk, and came back with top-boots of mud on, and my very eyebrows smeared with mud. Georgina is usually invisible during the walking time of the day. A turned-up nose may be seen in the midst of a heap of splashes – but nothing more.

To outside observers, Charles Dickens and his family were having a wonderful time in their Parisian life, visiting galleries and museums in the day and theatres in the evenings, dining at fine restaurants and being introduced to the most exciting people in Parisian society. It was, however, during their months in Paris, that the problems in the marriage really became apparent. In a city famed for its lovers, Charles made it clear that Catherine irritated him in almost everything she did; this made Catherine nervous, which increased her husband's irritation. The problems between them had been exacerbated a few months earlier, when Charles had received a letter from a Mrs Winter. This was the married name of Maria Beadnell, who had broken Dickens's heart before he met Catherine. They began a passionate correspondence. Dickens's letter on 3 April 1855 explained to Maria how he saw travel as a cure for dark moods and for 'the restlessness and waywardness of an author's mind':

> I am going off; I don't know where or how far, to ponder about I don't know what. Sometimes I am half in the mood to set off for France, sometimes I think I will go and walk about on the seashore for three or four months, sometimes I look towards the Pyrenees, sometimes Switzerland. I made a compact with a great Spanish authority last week, and vowed I would go to Spain. Two days afterwards Layard and I agreed to go to Constantinople ... To-morrow I shall probably discuss with somebody else the idea of going to Greenland or the North Pole.

Throughout their time in Paris, Catherine grew increasingly unhappy, while Dickens was lionised. The marriage was fated to come to an end, only a couple of years after their time living in Paris. Desperate not to lose her husband, Catherine attempted to take as full a part as possible in his life of celebrity, but even this seemed to irritate him. He wrote a particularly unpleasant letter to Wilkie Collins about all the women in his family irritating him during a dinner at Les Trois Frères Provençaux, complaining that Catherine ate too much while his daughters and sister-in-law picked at their food: 'Mrs. Dickens nearly killed herself, but the others hardly did that justice to the dinner that I had expected.' As Lillian Nayder points out in her biography of Catherine, Dickens didn't elaborate to Collins about his own eating patterns at the dinner.[20]

---

20. *The Other Dickens: A Life of Catherine Hogarth* by Lillian Nayder (2012).

At a party given by the singer Pauline Viardot, Charles and Catherine were introduced to the author George Sand.[21] She lived next door to one of the most fashionable portrait studios in Paris, run by two Dutch-born brothers, Ary and Henri (or Hendrik) Scheffer. Together, the illustrious neighbours hosted one of the city's most exclusive salons.

Dickens was painted by both Scheffer brothers and was unhappy with both portraits (as he was with almost every portrait of himself). In the November, the Scheffers invited the Dickens family and the Thackeray girls to a party, where Dickens was prevailed upon to give a special reading of *The Cricket on the Hearth* – allegedly he had no idea he was expected to be a performer as well as a guest.

The apartment on the Avenue des Champs Elysées was, as always, filled with visiting friends, including Wilkie Collins, William Charles Macready and one of Charles's younger brothers, the visionary engineer Alfred Dickens. Alfred was currently basking in the fame – and notoriety – of having carried out a thorough investigation into problems caused by appalling sanitary conditions in one of London's poorest areas. Alfred's detailed report led to furious questions being asked in Parliament and would later lead to sanitary reform across the British Isles.

Dickens loved to absorb himself in the life of wherever he was living and, for a time, Paris became the pinnacle of everything good. When he had to return to London for a few days for business, he wrote to Catherine that it was not only ugly in comparison with Paris, but that he was finding it 'hideous to behold'.

They remained in Paris until the summer of 1856, while Dickens was writing *Little Dorrit*. On 10 May 1856, while the family was preparing for a summer in Boulogne, Dickens published an article in *Household Words* entitled 'Railway Dreaming'. It begins with the narrator musing about train travel: 'In what autumn and spring was it that those Champs Elysées trees were yellow and scant of leaf when I first looked at them out of my balcony, and were a bright and tender green when I last looked at them on a beautiful May morning?' but continues with the idea that, when on a train, the idea of place becomes confused and that Paris and the Moon could be as one. The article continues with the idea of Parisians as 'Mooninians' and includes a telling phrase about Dickens's state of mind in Paris:

---

21. George Sand was the pseudonym of Amantine-Lucile-Aurore Dudevant.

> I am not a lonely man, though I was once a lonely boy; but that was a long time ago. The Moonininan capital, however, is the place for lonely men to dwell in... . I sometimes like to pretend to be childless and companionless and to wonder whether, if I were really so, I should be glad to find somebody to ask me out to dinner, instead of living under a constant terror of weakly making engagements that I don't want to make...

In 1862, Dickens was back in Paris, but his life had changed astoundingly in the few years since living there. By this time, he was legally separated from his wife, his reputation had been through some difficult setbacks and he had undergone more episodes of depression. From his rented accommodation at Rue du Faubourg St Honoré, 27, he wrote to Angela Burdett-Coutts' companion, Mrs Brown:

> It is amazing to behold the changes in this place, and the vast works doing and done. But I notice (having been much in the country-parts of France this summer), that as Paris swells, the provincial towns of the second and third degree collapse. 'Maison a vendre' – 'Maison a vendre' – everywhere – Towns falling to pieces – grass growing over the public buildings – population Heaven knows where.

Georgina and Mamie came to join him in Paris, accompanied by Mamie's pet dog Mrs Bouncer, a much-loved Pomeranian. Dickens wrote to his sister Letitia, 'We have a pretty apartment here, but house rent is awful to mention... . Mrs. Bouncer (muzzled by the Parisian Police) is also here, and is a wonderful spectacle to behold in the streets, restrained like a raging Lion.' Dickens enjoyed the sensation of living in Paris again. He went back to England for a family Christmas but soon returned to Paris. That winter, he gave a series of fundraising readings from his Christmas stories, at the British Embassy, in aid of the British Charitable Fund.

Boulogne: The Best Wine and Delicious Views

'There is a charming walk, arched and shaded by trees, on the old walls that form the four sides of this High Town, whence you get glimpses of the streets below ... and of the hills and the sea.'
'Our French Watering Place',
(1854)

In the autumn of 1852 (some years before the marriage came to an end), following a family summer in Dover, Charles, Catherine and Georgina travelled to Boulogne. They spent a fortnight in the Hotel des Bains. As usual, Dickens attempted to entice his friends to join them, writing to Thomas Beard, 'The tidal train from Folkestone (see list for hour, which varies each day) will only lengthen your journey two hours in all. It is not a bad place by any means, and I hope you will like the novelty.'

In Boulogne, Dickens worked on *Bleak House* and thought about how much he would like to spend a whole summer in France. He wrote of this longing to Forster:

> It is as quaint, picturesque, good a place as I know; the boatmen and fishing-people quite a race apart, and some of their villages as good as the fishing-villages on the Mediterranean. The Haute Ville, with a walk all round it on the ramparts, charming. The country walks, delightful. It is the best mixture of town and country (with sea air into the bargain) I ever saw; everything cheap, everything good; and please God I shall be writing on those said ramparts next July.

Boulogne: The Best Wine and Delicious Views

This desire began a new chapter in the Dickens family's life, and the pleasures of long summers in English seaside towns were swapped for the more exotic appeal of the coastline of northern France. Dickens planned their next adventure with his usual energy. He, Catherine and Georgina arrived in Boulogne in early June 1853 to sort out their accommodation. On 13 June 1853, Dickens wrote to W. H. Wills:

> I have signed, sealed, and delivered a contract for a house (once occupied for two years by a man I knew in Switzerland) which is not a large one, but stands in the midst of a great garden, with what the landlord calls a 'forest' at the back; and is now surrounded by flowers, vegetables, and all manner of growth. A queer, odd, French place – but extremely well supplied with all table and other conveniences, and strongly recommended. The address is
> Chateau des Molineaux
> Rue Beaurepaire
> Boulogne
>
> There is a coach-house, stabling for half a dozen horses, and I don't know what. We take possession this afternoon, and are now laying in a good stock of creature-comforts. So no more at present...

Once their accommodation had been arranged, the children arrived to join their parents and aunt, and the family stayed in Boulogne until October. Dickens was being grandiose in giving the address of the house as a chateau – it seems the locals knew it as the Villa des Molineaux (sometimes spelt as Moulineaux). Dickens wrote to Wills again a few days later:

> we should be delighted to see you at any time. If you suppose this place to be in a street, you are hugely mistaken. It is in the country, though not more than ten minutes walk from the Post office, and is the best doll's house of many rooms in the prettiest French grounds and the most charming situation I have ever seen – the best place I have ever lived in, abroad, except at Genoa. You can scarcely imagine the beauty of the

air on this richly wooded hill side. As to comforts in the house, there are all sorts of things, beginning with no end of the coldest water and running through the most beautiful flowers down to English footbaths and a Parisian Liqueur-stand.

One of the things that enchanted Dickens most about Boulogne was his landlord. As John Forster related in his biography of Dickens, the author sent him a glowing account of M. Ferdinand Beaucourt-Mutuel, although Dickens was seemingly bemused by why men in France chose to combine their surnames with those of their wives:

> the landlord – M. Beaucourt – is wonderful. Everybody here has two surnames (I cannot conceive why), and M. Beaucourt, as he is always called, is by rights M. Beaucourt-Mutuel. He is a portly jolly fellow with a fine open face; lives on the hill behind, just outside the top of the garden.... . He is extraordinarily popular in Boulogne (the people in the shops invariably brightening up at the mention of his name, and congratulating us on being his tenants), and really seems to deserve it. He is such a liberal fellow that I can't bear to ask him for anything, since he instantly supplies it whatever it is.

On 23 June, he wrote to his friend and illustrator Frank Stone about what would greet him if he travelled to Boulogne:

> I may mention for your guidance ... that you have nothing on earth to do with your luggage when it is once in the boat, until after you have walked ashore. That you will be filtered, with the rest of the passengers, through a hideous, whitewashed, Quarantine-looking Custom House, where a stern man of a military aspect will demand your passport. That you will have nothing of the sort, but will produce your card with this addition – 'Restant à Boulogne, Chez M. Charles Dickens, Chateau des Molineaux'. That you will then be passed out at a little door, like one of the ill-starred prisoners on the bloody September night, into a yelling and shrieking crowd, cleaving the air with the names of the different hotels – exactly seven thousand, six hundred, and

fiftyfour, in number. And that your heart will be on the point of sinking with dread, when you will find yourself in the arms of the Sparkler of Albion.[22]

Dickens also tempted Stone with the promise of 'by far the best wine at tenpence a bottle that I have ever drunk anywhere. I really desire no better.' To Wilkie Collins, Dickens promised, 'You shall have a Pavilion room in the garden, with a delicious view, where you may write... . Coming by South Eastern Tidal Train ... you come in five hours. No passport wanted.'

In the months before they had arrived in Boulogne, Catherine and many of Charles's friends had been growing increasingly concerned about the author's health. He had been working so hard that he had been physically ill and his emotional strain was also apparent. His family and friends feared he was about to have a breakdown, so a change of pace from London to the pretty French coastal town was deemed necessary medicine. By the time the children arrived, their father was starting to look and feel better. He wrote to Mark Lemon, 'I think you may like to know under my own hand that I am Myself again, and in a highly vigorous condition; working, walking, eating, and drinking – my bottle of wine a day – at tenpence.' It is sad, however, to see the number of letters Dickens wrote from Boulogne asking friends to stay, suggesting that he was desperate to escape from family life.

In a letter to Forster, Dickens described their new home, and complained about the weather:

> O the rain here yesterday! A great sea-fog rolling in, a strong wind blowing, and the rain coming down in torrents all day long... . This house is on a great hill-side, backed up by woods of young trees. It faces the Haute Ville with the ramparts and the unfinished cathedral – which capital object is exactly opposite the windows. On the slope in front, going steep down to the right, all Boulogne is piled and jumbled about in a very picturesque manner. The view is charming – closed in at last by the tops of swelling hills; and the door is within ten minutes of the post office, and

---

22. The Sparkler of Albion was a nickname used for Dickens by himself and his friends.

within quarter of an hour of the sea. The garden is made in terraces up the hillside, like an Italian garden; the top walks being in the before-mentioned woods.... There are at present thousands of roses all about the house, and no end of other flowers. There are five great summer-houses, and (I think) fifteen fountains – not one of which (according to the invariable French custom) ever plays.

The weather was cold and wet for much of the summer, and at those times Charles felt his gloom return, writing to Angela Burdett-Coutts in July that no unexpected weather condition would now surprise him, even snow in the middle of summer. On the days when they could enjoy sunshine, however, the Dickens family revelled in their surroundings. They went to the beaches and swam in the sea, visited the annual August fair and the weekly Sunday fête, walked along the pier and listened to travelling musicians, went to the theatre and enjoyed the many attractions offered by a town at the height of tourist season – at a time when tourism was booming. By the early 1850s, Boulogne was welcoming increasing numbers of overseas visitors every year.

In her research into Charles Dickens's long summers in Boulogne, historian Janine Watrin wrote of Dickens following a 'strict routine' of writing in the morning and spending the afternoons on 'long exploratory walks'. Dickens considered himself a Francophile, or, as he wrote to Forster, 'a naturalised Frenchman'. In his 1854 article 'Our French Watering Place', Dickens writes that archetypal British tourists insist Italy is better than France, but Dickens disagrees. He feels that the government of Italy has changed the country he once called home. Now, his heart belongs to France.

He was also very impressed by French social care, writing to Dr William Brown:

> I took a trip to Amiens the other day, where there is a great deal done for the health and comfort of the working people which we might copy to advantage. The more I look about me the more convinced I become, that if we would only condescend to amuse our people a little more, they would drink and do worse a good deal less.

Dickens began making ambitious plans for his younger sons. He was so taken with Boulogne – despite the rain – that he determined to find a school there, so his sons could benefit from a French education. Over the next few years, four of the Dickens boys, Frank and Alfred from 1853, Sydney from 1855 and Henry from 1858, were educated at a small boarding school on the Rue de l'Oratoire, run by a Mr Gibson, who had formerly taught at Eton, and the Reverend W. Bewsher. In 1855, Wilkie Collins wrote about seeing Sydney leaving for his first term in Boulogne:

> The boys went back to school yesterday, with their elder brother for escort. We saw them off [from Folkestone] and little Sydney (going to school for the first time) accepted his fate like a hero. His pluck was undiminished when I last saw him, very small ... a threatening sea before him, and the horrid perspective of the schoolmaster awaiting him on the opposite shore.

Despite Wilkie's fears, the boys all seem to have been very happy. In 1856, Dickens replied to a friend who was considering the school for his own children:

> They take none but English boys, but French is the ordinary language of the boys' lives.... I pay for each of my boys £40 a year. This includes their French and Classical education (the latter as at Eton) and the usual branches of knowledge. Dancing, Fencing, German, Music, &c. are extra... . Two months vacation in the summer; none at Christmas unless the parents wish. I have three boys there, and they are very happy, and I have found nothing to object to. One of them was ill there, and was thoroughly comfortable. Their manners are well looked after, and their clothes ... particularly well kept. Mrs. Bewsher represents the domesticity of the establishment (Mr. Gibson is a widower) and there are an English lady housekeeper and an ancient French Griffin housekeeper. All these authorities I know, and their behaviour to the boys, and the behaviour of the boys to them is just what it should be.

In 1854, the family returned for a second summer in Boulogne. Once again they rented a home from M. Beaucourt-Mutuel, the Villa du Camp de Droite. It was as pleasant as the Villa des Molineaux, but with the advantage of larger rooms. Great excitement was caused by the nearby presence of an encampment of soldiers. As Dickens watched the camp being set up, the sight of tents and horses made him think of the Arabian Nights stories, which had fed his childhood imagination. M. Beaucourt-Mutuel had been a soldier when young, and Dickens watched with admiration as his landlord drank and swapped stories with the militia.

For some time, Dickens had been thinking about writing a companion article to 'Our English Watering Place' and in 1854, he published 'Our French Watering Place', in which M. Beaucourt-Mutuel appears as M. Loyal Devasseur, an admiring description that spans several pages:

> It is never going to rain, according to M. Loyal. When it is impossible to deny that it is now raining in torrents, he says it will be fine – charming – magnificent to-morrow. It is never hot on the Property, he contends. Likewise it is never cold. The flowers, he says, come out, delighting to grow there; it is like Paradise this morning; it is like the Garden of Eden... . Good M. Loyal! Under blouse or waistcoat, he carries one of the gentlest hearts that beat in a nation teeming with gentle people. He has had losses, and has been at his best under them.

Dickens continued, with admiration, to relate the story of a bereaved mother and her children, unable to pay the rent, whom his landlord had allowed to live rent-free in one of his villas for a year. When Dickens asked if he had ever received the rent, the landlord said expansively that 'le bon Dieu' would repay him. Beaucourt-Mutuel was a character whom Dickens would have rejoiced in creating for one of his novels. Because the landlord already existed, Dickens delighted in making him a focal point of his article. Almost a decade later, in 1862, an older version of the landlord, this time under his own name, made an appearance in the Christmas story, *Somebody's Luggage*:

> The morning walk of Monsieur Mutuel was in the brightest patch that the sun made in the Grande Place of a dull old

fortified French town. The manner of his morning walk was with his hands crossed behind him; an umbrella, in figure the express image of himself, always in one hand; a snuffbox in the other. Thus, with the shuffling gait of the Elephant (who really does deal with the very worst trousers-maker employed by the Zoological world, and who appeared to have recommended him to Monsieur Mutuel), the old gentleman sunned himself daily when sun was to be had – of course, at the same time sunning a red ribbon at his button-hole; for was he not an ancient Frenchman?

In 'Our French Watering Place', Dickens also wrote about his growing appreciation for Boulogne, a place which, until he spent time there, had previously been considered a mere inconvenient stop during an uncomfortable journey between London and Paris. The author enumerates, wittily, the town's bad points – smelly drains and rubbish left to decay in the streets – before rhapsodising about Boulogne's charms, including being 'an uncommonly good town to eat and drink in':

> It is more picturesque and quaint than half the innocent places which tourists, following their leader like sheep, have made imposters of. To say nothing of its houses with grave courtyards, its queer by-corners, and its many-windowed streets white and quiet in the sunlight, there is an ancient belfry.... There is a charming walk, arched and shaded by trees, on the old walls that form the four sides of this High Town, whence you get glimpses of the streets below ... and of the hills and the sea.

In spite of his proud assertion that tourism hasn't yet reached his French Watering Place, his article reveals that the town is filled with English residents and visitors. Dickens writes of how many English children he sees, accompanied by 'governesses reading novels' and 'nursemaids exchanging gossip', in contrast to the quaintly dressed French children. On his walks he notes aged men dressed in clothes of fading gentility, market traders peddling an array of goods, peasant women with their 'jolliest' of donkeys, 'girl-porters waiting to be hired with baskets at their backs', brightly dressed fishing people bringing their catch to be sold, and a drinks seller, described as a 'weazen little old man in a cocked hat, wearing a cuirass of drinking-glasses'.

Travelling with the Dickens family in that second summer in Boulogne, were Betty and Lally Lemon, the daughters of family friends. As Mamie and Katey always felt outnumbered living with seven brothers, they loved having two other girls with them. Unseasoned travellers themselves, the Lemon parents packed in their daughters' luggage twenty-four pairs of brand-new stockings, still in their packaging. As a result, these were seized with glee by the customs officers who demanded import tax. Dickens recorded drolly in one of his letters, 'Duty on said stockings, 8 francs'.

Blissfully unaware of the expenses of customs and excise, the four girls spent a glorious summer, often in the company of Anny and Minny Thackeray, who were spending the summer in France with their grandparents. Their father, at Dickens's recommendation, rented a villa close to their own. While his parents and children were installed there for several months, Thackeray was able to travel to and from London throughout the summer.

It was an exciting summer to be in Boulogne. Emperor Napoleon III was in town, together with Prince Albert. The sight of the British Royal Yacht in the harbour caused great excitement to locals and tourists. It was also, however, a rather frightening summer. The theatre burned down, despite the best efforts with buckets of water to put out the fire, and there was an outbreak of cholera – known then as 'the English cholera'. Mamie Dickens contracted the disease. After a very worrying couple of days, she recovered, although many others were less fortunate.

Two years later, the family returned to Boulogne. Edward Dickens, known as 'Plorn', was four years old and Mamie wrote about her memories of her father watching his youngest child grow up during those elongated family holidays, just before the end of the marriage:

> the Plorn would be carried about in his father's arms to admire the flowers, or as he got older trot along by his side. The remembrance of these two, hand in hand, the boy in his white frock and blue sash, walking down the avenue, always in deep conversation, is a memory inseparable from those summers at Boulogne.

Boulogne: The Best Wine and Delicious Views

What was to be their final family summer in France was blighted by sadness. The family had taken their pets to Boulogne (where Mamie's pet canary, Dick, was in constant peril from the local cats). The much-adored Timber, the dog whom Charles and Catherine had been given in America fourteen years earlier, died in Boulogne, surrounded by the family who loved him and the scent of the 'millions of roses' about which Charles had written in letters to friends.

Although cholera was still a worry, the biggest fear that summer was diphtheria. It ravaged the poorer areas of Boulogne, with new deaths – often of children – being reported every day. Then, at the end of August, they heard that two of their friends, the playwright Gilbert à Beckett and his little son, had died of diphtheria. The Dickens family left Boulogne as quickly as they could, for the safety of London.

Some years later, in 1862, Dickens was back in France, living between Boulogne and Paris. That autumn, Mamie and Georgina travelled to meet him, but their boat was caught up in such a strong gale that it was re-routed from Boulogne to Calais. Dickens wrote about it to his friend Mrs Brown; it is a letter that shows how much his travels influenced his novels:

> They were out in the great gale ... and were carried ... into Calais at last... . I stood five hours on the end of the pier at Boulogne in the height and fury of the storm, and it was a wonderful sight. To my great consolation I only saw one thing missed in the Copperfield storm. But it was a very picturesque thing. After it became dark, the surf ran out so far (two or three miles perhaps), and so high, that when a greater wave than usual broke, what was seen of its white top was so like light, as to induce the Boatmen over and over again to cry out, 'There's the steamer! I saw her fire as she rolled!'

In his *Recollections* (published in 1934, a year after he died), my great great grandfather, Henry Fielding Dickens, wrote about those Boulogne summers, during which he had been a teenager:

> Of the Villa Moulineaux at Boulogne ... I have a general remembrance of lovely gardens straggling up the hillside

with a blaze of bright colours, and of a picturesque chalet called 'Tom Pouce', which was reserved for Wilkie Collins when he was there; but otherwise there are only two incidents which I can recall. One was of a great fire in the town, in the theatre, which was totally destroyed. I remember watching it from our house on the hill. It was a great blaze on account of the absence of water supply, which had to be passed from hand to hand in buckets. The other was our journey home in 1856. We travelled in those days in steamers of the General Steam Navigation from Boulogne direct to London Bridge, or rather to Gravesend, which was about four miles from Gad's Hill. The boats were very small their accommodation far from comfortable. We crossed in a very violent gale, and when I was put to bed I was given a chocolate cigar to keep me quiet, which I clutched in my hand all through that stormy night.

Condette: La Maison Dickens

> *'I shall never forget that talk ... [my father] wished, he said, that he had been "a better father, a better man" ... he was not a good man, but he was not a fast man, but he was wonderful! He fell in love with this girl, I did not blame her – it is never one person's fault.'*
> Kate Perugini, née Dickens, interviewed
> in the 1920s by Gladys Storey for
> *Dickens and Daughter* (1939)

In 1857 Charles Dickens fell in love with the actress Ellen Ternan. He was 45 and Ellen was 18, the same age as Charles and Catherine's younger daughter, Katey. Although few of Dickens's readers or contemporaries were aware of the truth, it was this love affair that led to the end of the Dickens marriage. Although they did not divorce, Charles applied for a legal separation, leaving Catherine humiliated and heartbroken. Catherine left the family home in 1858, after twenty-two years of marriage.

Dickens was adept at PR and he was popular, two things that helped to prevent the scandal of his marital breakdown from swamping his reputation. Even though his family and friends knew about Ellen, the wider public did not; the majority seemed to believe his version of the separation, which blamed Catherine for the breakdown of the marriage. Victorian Britain was a very misogynistic place, a country in which men were permitted – legally – to behave in almost any way they liked towards women. Catherine Dickens suffered greatly, not only from the unhappiness of the end of her marriage, but at the very public spectacle that her own private misery had become. To add insult to injury, her sister Georgina chose to remain living with Catherine's husband, continuing the role of 'second mother' to Catherine's children. The rest of the Hogarth family sided with Catherine against Georgina, and the Hogarth/Dickens family became painfully fractured and estranged. Amid all this chaos, Dickens was determined to keep Ellen's name and their relationship away from the public lens. Instead, whenever he needed to explain her presence, he would describe her as a family friend, or his goddaughter.

As is detailed in Claire Tomalin's biography of Ellen, *The Invisible Woman*, Dickens employed a great deal of subterfuge in trying to keep his relationship a secret. Using false names, he was able to visit her regularly, but they were constantly fearful of their secret being revealed to the public. One place they were able to live together easily was France. It seems that when Dickens wanted a place to hide away with his lover, he spoke to his friendly former landlord M. Beaucourt-Mutuel, who owned a little farmhouse in the hamlet of Condette, a short distance from Boulogne. Throughout the early 1860s, Dickens and Ellen often escaped across the English Channel to be alone in Condette. Although Dickens believed that he was doing so incognito, it seems that the locals were all fully aware that the secretive inhabitants of the farmhouse were the famous English author and his young girlfriend, and it became known locally as 'la Maison Dickens'. Today, there is a plaque to the author on the surrounding wall.

Towards the end of her life, Katey Dickens – by now a famous artist and known by her married name of Kate Perugini – was interviewed by a friend named Gladys Storey, who was writing a book. Katey revealed that Ellen and her father had 'a baby boy who died'. It seems that the baby was born in France, possibly in Condette.

A Study in Idleness

'They had no intention of going anywhere in particular; they wanted to see nothing, they wanted to know nothing, they wanted to learn nothing, they wanted to do nothing. They wanted only to be idle.'
From 'The Lazy Tour of Two Idle
Apprentices' by Charles Dickens
and Wilkie Collins (1857)

On 29 August 1857, a despondent Charles Dickens wrote to Wilkie Collins. He was desperate for excitement, for an escape from his marital home and to be with someone with whom he could talk about his desperate infatuation with Ellen Ternan. In the letter, he wrote:

> Partly in the grim despair and restlessness of this subsidence from excitement, and partly for the sake of *Household Words*, I want to cast about whether you and I can go anywhere – take any tour – see any thing – whereon we could write something together. Have you any idea, tending to any place in the world?

This was the beginning of what would become known as 'The Lazy Tour of Two Idle Apprentices'. 'The Lazy Tour' begins with the words,

> In the autumn month of September, eighteen hundred and fifty-seven ... two idle apprentices, exhausted by the long, hot summer, and the long, hot work it had brought with it, ran away from their employer. They were bound to a highly meritorious lady (named Literature)... . The misguided young men who thus shirked their duty to the mistress from whom they had received many favours, were actuated by the low idea of making a perfectly idle trip, in any direction.

Their fictional names of Thomas Idle (Wilkie Collins) and Francis Goodchild (Charles Dickens) were an homage to the eighteenth-century artist William Hogarth, taken from the names of characters in his 1747 series *Industry and Idleness*. At the start of the story, their shared idleness scuppers their initial plans of walking to their destination:

> These two had sent their personal baggage on by train: only retaining each a knapsack. Idle now applied himself to constantly regretting the train, to tracking it through the intricacies of Bradshaw's Guide, and finding out where it is now – and where now – and where now – and to asking what was the use of walking, when you could ride at such a pace as that.

After a half-hearted attempt, they decided that the farthest they should walk would be to Euston Station. From there they took the train north 'and carried their knapsacks in the luggage-van'. From their description, we get a multi-sensory idea of what it was like to travel by train in the nineteenth century. The express train caused 'a smell like a large washing day'[23] and 'a sharp issue of steam as from a huge brazen tea urn'. It shrieked 'in hysterics of such intensity', and the refreshment rooms were 'uncomfortable' with rude staff and inedible food. The passengers whiled away the journey by watching animals in fields beside the train tracks, and noticed how, the further north they travelled, the landscape changed, ravaged by the Industrial Revolution:

> The pastoral country darkened, became coaly, became smoky, became infernal, got better, got worse, improved again, grew rugged, turned romantic; was a wood, a stream, a chain of hills, a gorge, a moor, a cathedral town, a fortified place, a waste. Now, miserable black dwellings, a black canal, and sick black towers of chimneys; now, a trim garden, where the flowers were bright and fair... . The temperature changed, the dialect changed, the people changed ... yet all so quickly, that the spruce guard in the London uniform and silver

---

23. Dickens had used a similar phrase in *A Christmas Carol* (1843), about the smell of the boiling of the Christmas pudding.

lace, had not yet rumpled his shirt-collar, delivered half the dispatches in his shiny little pouch, or read his newspaper.

In reality, Dickens and Collins left London by train on 7 September 1857 and took a train to Carlisle in Cumbria (then known as Cumberland). There, both southern authors seemed surprised to see so many men and women wearing clogs. They were gently scathing of Carlisle, writing: 'Something in the way of public amusement had happened last month, and something else was going to happen before Christmas; and, in the meantime there was a lecture on India for those who liked it – which Idle and Goodchild did not', although its nearby villages and countryside were praised for being 'picturesque and pleasant'.

From Carlisle they rode for fourteen miles to the village of Hesket Newmarket (in what is now known as the Lake District National Park), because Dickens wanted to climb Carrock Fell. In much of Dickens's travel writing, pub landlords seem to be the strangers he likes best. The landlord of the Queen's Head in Hesket Newmarket was so obliging that he took them by dogcart[24] to the foot of the fell, promising to guide them to the top.

Unfortunately, the genial landlord had one major flaw: having not climbed Carrock Fell for about twenty years, he got them lost and, after reaching the top, admitted he had no idea of how to get back down. They reached the summit just after midday, but there was a thick mist, which Dickens described to Forster as 'dead darkness as of night'. Dickens proposed that their only hope of finding the way back was to follow the river and its rocky, unpredictable course; eventually his two companions agreed. After two hours spent in 'leaps, splashes and tumbles', Collins fell and sprained his ankle badly. Dickens and the pub landlord had to carry him for the remainder of the journey.

The idle apprentices' next stop was a detour to Wigtown, where Collins was seen by a doctor, from where they moved on to Allonby. Forster wrote in his biography of Dickens:

> Allonby his letters presented as a small untidy outlandish place; rough stone houses in half mourning, a few coarse

---

24. The term 'dogcart', found in much Victorian writing, refers to a small carriage once pulled by large dogs, before this practice was outlawed in Britain, in the mid-nineteenth century. By the time of the Two Idle Apprentices tour, a dogcart was a small carriage pulled by horses, but still retaining its earlier name.

yellow-stone lodging houses with black roofs (bills in all the windows), five bathing-machines, five girls in straw hats, five men in straw hats (wishing they had not come); very much what Broadstairs would have been if it had been born Irish, and had not inherited a cliff.

Dickens and Collins stayed for two nights at the Ship Inn in Allonby, where the pub's records show that they ordered beer, wine, lemonade, tea, porter and brandy. In 'The Lazy Tour', Allonby was described:

There were fine sunsets at Allonby when the low flat beach, with its pools of water and its dry patches, changed into long bars of silver and gold in various states of burnishing, and there were fine views – on fine days – of the Scottish coast. But, when it rained at Allonby, Allonby thrown back upon its ragged self...

From Allonby they travelled to Lancaster, where they stayed at the King's Arms pub. Dickens wrote home that his bedroom was huge and contained two enormous four-poster beds, 'each as big as Charley's room at Gad's Hill'.[25] Dickens also wrote about the dinner he and Collins enjoyed on the day of their arrival: 'two little salmon trout; a sirloin steak; a brace of partridges; seven dishes of sweets; five dishes of dessert, led off by a bowl of peaches; and in the centre an enormous bride-cake'. The hotel was renowned for serving wedding cake every day, irrespective of whether there had been a wedding or not.

In Lancaster, Dickens was impressed by the pub landlord, Mr Sly, and fascinated by an itinerant salesmen he saw in the town. Eight years later, in 1865, both characters would appear in his Christmas story, *Dr Marigold's Prescriptions*. Dr Marigold – a 'cheapjack', or pedlar – comments, 'We were down at Lancaster, and I had done two nights more than fair average business ... in the open square there, near the end of the street where Mr. Sly's King's Arms and Royal Hotel stands.'

From Lancaster the two friends journeyed to Doncaster, where Dickens had booked rooms at the Angel Hotel. Allegedly, they were there to experience the town's famous Race Week, but in reality Doncaster had been Dickens's goal when planning the trip. The entire Lazy Tour

---

25. Gad's Hill Place was his home in Kent.

had grown out of his desire to see Ellen Ternan, who was acting at the Doncaster Theatre Royal. They had met a few weeks earlier when Ellen, together with her mother and sister, had been engaged to perform alongside Dickens and Collins in a touring production of *The Frozen Deep*, a play Dickens had co-written with Wilkie Collins. This fateful trip to Doncaster led to the ending of the marriage between Charles and Catherine Dickens. 'The Lazy Tour' seems to have been conceived entirely from Dickens's desire to escape his home and pursue the woman with whom he had become infatuated. Although he and Collins talked about the possibility of a sequel, the suggested second tour didn't happen.

Travel was obviously firmly in Dickens's mind throughout that last year of his marriage. In addition to writing 'The Lazy Tour', he and Collins collaborated on a pirate story, which was set in an exotic location. Although Dickens had never ventured into South America, in *The Perils of Certain English Prisoners*, the narrator is a Royal Marine on a ship 'in the South American waters off the Mosquito shore'. The ship is headed, we learn, for a small island near Honduras and the scene is described by the narrator:

> The night came on, soon after .... . All the wonderful bright colors went out of the sea and sky, in a few minutes, and all the stars in the Heavens seemed to shine out together, and to look down at themselves in the sea, over one another's shoulders, millions deep. Next morning, we cast anchor off the Island. There was a snug harbor within a little reef; there was a sandy beach; there were cocoa-nut trees with high straight stems, quite bare, and foliage at the top like plumes of magnificent green feathers…

The story was published in the Christmas issue of *Household Words* and proved very popular in a year in which many of its readers were feeling furiously patriotic about what was then known in Britain as 'The Indian Mutiny'. Although the setting was South America, we know that Dickens was inspired by India, because he wrote in a letter: 'I wish to avoid India itself; but I want to shadow out in what I do, the bravery of our ladies in India.' He felt connected to what was happening in India because his fourth child, Walter, had set sail for India on 20 July 1857. Walter left England just one month before Dickens acted on stage with Ellen Ternan and became inspired to begin 'The Lazy Tour of Two Idle Apprentices'.

The Uncommercial Traveller

'I was over the river, and past the Old Kent-road, and out on Blackheath, and even ascending Shooter's Hill, before I had had time to look about me in the carriage, like a collected traveller.'
Charles Dickens from 'Travelling Abroad'
(7 April 1860)

In 1860, Dickens published another series of travel articles, *The Uncommercial Traveller*. Many of the articles were inspired by Dickens's walks around London, and are semi-autobiographical, evoking memories of his childhood and early career, alongside his imagination and storytelling. The most famous is 'Night Walks' (published on 21 July 1860), which relates how an insomniac Dickens walked around London at night and discovered the true extent of 'houselessness'.

In *The Uncommercial Traveller*, Dickens wrote about familiar scenes looked at through new eyes, as if he were a tourist seeing places he knew so well for the first time, as well as about being a traveller. The article 'Travelling Abroad' begins:

> I got into the travelling chariot, pulled up the steps after me, shut myself in with a smart bang of the door, and gave the word 'Go on!' ... I had two ample Imperials on the roof, other fitted storage for luggage in front, and other up behind; I had a net for books overhead, great pockets to all the windows, a leathern pouch or two hung up for odds and ends, and a reading-lamp fixed in the back of the chariot, in case I should be benighted. I was amply provided in all respects, and had no idea where I was going (which was delightful), except that I was going abroad.

'Travelling Abroad' is heavily nostalgic, drawing on Dickens's years of travelling and melding his memories into one evocative journey. It gives a fascinating insight into the practicalities of how Victorians travelled from England to France:

> Over the road where the old Romans used to march, over the road where the old Canterbury pilgrims used to go, over the road where the travelling trains of the old imperious priests and princes used to jingle on horseback between the continent and this Island through the mud and water, over the road where Shakespeare hummed to himself, 'Blow, blow, thou winter wind,' as he sat in the saddle at the gate of the inn yard noticing the carriers; all among the cherry orchards, apple orchards, corn-fields, and hop-gardens; so went I, by Canterbury to Dover... . Early in the morning I was on the deck of the steam-packet, and we were aiming at the bar in the usual intolerable manner, and the bar was aiming at us in the usual intolerable manner, and the bar got by far the best of it, and we got by far the worst – all in the usual intolerable manner.
>
> But, when I was clear of the Custom House on the other side, and when I began to make the dust fly on the thirsty French roads ... I began to recover my travelling spirits... . I felt that now, indeed, I was in the dear old France of my affections. I should have known it, without the well-remembered bottle of rough ordinary wine, the cold roast fowl, the loaf, and the pinch of salt, on which I lunched with unspeakable satisfaction, from one of the stuffed pockets of the chariot.

It is apparent this is a journey the narrator has made many times. He looks with fondness on remembered landmarks: 'posting houses ... dirty stable-yards, and clean post-masters' wives ... cathedrals that I got out to see ... little towns that appeared to have no reason for being towns... . I lay a night upon the road and enjoyed delectable cookery of potatoes.' Finally he arrives in Paris, where he takes an 'upper apartment ... in one of the hotels of the Rue de Rivoli', with a view of the Tuileries Garden.

In Paris, he is 'dragged by invisible force into the Morgue' (then a macabre tourist attraction, and one at which Dickens often found a gothic inspiration for his plots). Just as Dickens was haunted all around Rome, by imagined scenes of horror within the Colosseum, in Paris this narrator is haunted by the sights he witnesses at the morgue, with one corpse in particular seeming to follow him all around Paris.

The narrator goes to a wine shop, drinks brandy and decides to visit 'the great floating bath on the river'. The description of this visit evokes the colour and life of Paris of the 1860s as vividly as a contemporary painting:

> The bath was crowded in the usual airy manner, by a male population in striped drawers of various gay colours, who walked up and down arm in arm, drank coffee, smoked cigars, sat at little tables, conversed politely with the damsels who dispensed the towels, and every now and then pitched themselves into the river head foremost, and came out again to repeat this social routine.

After bathing, the narrator returns to his hotel, goes out for dinner and then takes in a public display of 'small-sword exercise, broad-sword exercise, wrestling, and other such feats'. Then he leaves Paris for Strasbourg, then travels on to Switzerland. In the mountains,

> a yoke of oxen were sometimes hooked on [to the carriage] before the post-horses.... Of a sudden, mist and rain would clear away, and I would come down into picturesque little towns with gleaming spires and odd towers; and would stroll afoot into market-places in steep winding streets, where a hundred women in bodices, sold eggs and honey, butter and fruit, and suckled their children as they sat by their clean baskets.

In the mountains, he left the carriage and rode a mule on which he went

> up a thousand rugged ways, and looked down at a thousand woods of fir and pine.... [The mule] brought me safely, in his own wise way, among the passes of the Alps, and here

I enjoyed a dozen climates a day ... now ... in the region of wind, now in the region of fire, and now in the region of unmelting snow and ice, beneath which the cataract was roaring; and here was received under arches of icicles, of unspeakable beauty.

When the narrator finally reaches the Lausanne shore of Lake Geneva, he rhapsodizes, 'I stood looking at the bright blue water, the flushed white mountains opposite, and the boats at my feet with their furled Mediterranean sails, showing like enormous magnifications of this goose-quill pen that is now in my hand.'

At the very end of the article, after several pages of travelling, Dickens admits that he had, in fact, 'merely shut myself, for half a minute, in a German travelling chariot that stood for sale in the Carriage Department of the London Pantechnicon ... [it] brought all these hints of travelling remembrance before me.'

Dickens returned to *The Uncommercial Traveller* in 1863. 'The Calais Night Mail' is about the port city British travellers both loathed, for its bureaucracy, and loved, as the gateway to the Continent. Dickens began the article with this dichotomy in mind:

> It is an unsettled question with me whether I shall leave Calais something handsome in my will, or whether I shall leave it my malediction. I hate it so much, and yet I am always so very-glad to see it, that I am in a state of constant indecision on this subject.

In the article, Dickens berates Dover for looking so cosy and welcoming with its clean, comfortable bedrooms, when he is about to leave it on a pitching and rolling boat to suffer seasickness throughout the hours of darkness:

> As I wait here on board the night packet, for the South Eastern Train to come down with the Mail, Dover appears to me to be illuminated for some intensely aggravating festivity in my personal dishonour... . A screech, a bell, and two red eyes come gliding down the Admiralty Pier with a smoothness of motion rendered more smooth by the

> heaving of the boat. The sea makes noises against the pier, as if several hippopotami were lapping at it.... We, the boat, become violently agitated.

Dickens, with the air of a supercilious seasoned traveller, asks of his readers why so many 'sea-going amateurs' put up an umbrella while travelling by boat, 'and hold it up with a grim and fierce tenacity'. This has a visual echo in a famous contemporary painting, Ford Madox Brown's *The Last of England* (1855). The painting shows a determined-looking couple on an emigrant ship hopelessly trying to shelter from the sea with an umbrella.

As the ship rolls, Dickens describes his journey:

> (I am sitting on the hardest of wet seats, in the most uncomfortable of wet attitudes, but I don't mind it,) and notice that I am a whirling shuttlecock between a fiery battledore of a lighthouse on the French coast and a fiery battledore of a lighthouse on the English coast; but I don't notice it particularly, except to feel envenomed in my hatred of Calais.

Some time later, as the ship approaches Calais, the excited traveller comes to the fore:

> I see the light of Cape Grinez ... and the light of Calais Harbour ... ahead and shining. Sentiments of forgiveness of Calais, not to say of attachment to Calais, begin to expand my bosom. I have weak notions that I will stay there a day or two on my way back.... And now, in the sudden relief and wiping of faces, everybody on board seems to have had a prodigious double-tooth out, and to be this very instant free of the Dentist's hands. And now we all know for the first time how wet and cold we are, and how salt we are; and now I love Calais with my heart of hearts!

Having cleared customs he heads for the train, recording the many different places one can travel to from Calais and observing the other passengers:

The train is light tonight, and I share my compartment with but two fellow-travellers; one, a compatriot in an obsolete cravat, who thinks it a quite unaccountable thing that they don't keep 'London time' on a French railway, and who is made angry by my modestly suggesting the possibility of Paris time being more in their way.

As the train speeds through the night, Dickens stares out of the window at the 'queer old stone farm-houses approached by drawbridges, and the windmills that you get at by boats ... the long monotonous miles of canal, with the great Dutch-built barges garishly painted' before settling down to sleep en route to Paris.

In *The Uncommercial Traveller*, which he returned to again in 1865, Dickens was also able to return to the travel writing that he had enjoyed on his North America and Italy trips, bringing his articles to life with witty observations, at times empathetic, at times excoriating, but always evoking in the reader a realisation that, no matter how much society and its rules changes, the quirks of travellers remain constant throughout the centuries.

Ruminating on the Railways

'There were railway patterns in its drapers' shops, and railway journals in the windows of its newsmen. There were railway hotels, office-houses, lodging-houses, boarding-houses; railway plans, maps, views, wrappers, bottles, sandwich-boxes, and timetables; railway hackney-coach and cabstands; railway omni-buses, railway streets and buildings, railway hangers-on and parasites, and flatterers out of all calculation. There was even railway time observed in clocks, as if the sun itself had given in.'

From *Dombey and Son*
(serialised 1846–1848)

Like many residents of the nineteenth century, a young Dickens had eyed the coming of the railways with a mixture of trepidation and excitement. The very first train journey in Britain took place in 1825, the year Charles Dickens turned 13, with the opening of the Stockton and Darlington line. Five years later, the year in which Charles Dickens had his eighteenth birthday and began his career in journalism, the *Rocket* made its first journey, on the Liverpool and Manchester Railway.

Dickens and his family witnessed the extraordinarily rapid changes to the landscape of London, as the city was carved up to create the railways. In *Dombey and Son* (1846–1848), Dickens described what many fellow Victorians were feeling, a sadness at the way the building of train lines was destroying homes, communities and scenery. When three of the novel's characters try to visit a neighbourhood they once knew, they discover 'There was no such place as Stagg's Gardens. It has vanished from the earth... .'

Despite the destruction caused by the creation of the railway, Dickens was also thrilled by this exciting new mode of transport, something that helped to feed his love of travelling and innovation. In 1842, after his first experiences of American trains, Dickens wrote to John Forster:

> I have often asked Americans in London which were the better railroads, – ours or theirs? They have taken time for reflection, and generally replied on mature consideration that they rather thought we excelled; in respect of the punctuality with which we arrived at our stations, and the smoothness.... I wish you could see what an American railroad is.... It is never inclosed, or warded off. You walk down the main street of a large town; and, slap-dash, headlong, pell-mell, down the middle of the street, with pigs burrowing, and boys flying kites and playing marbles, and men smoking, and women talking, and children crawling, close to the very rails, there comes tearing along a mad locomotive with its train of cars, scattering a red-hot shower of sparks (from its wood fire) in all directions; screeching, hissing, yelling, and panting; and nobody one atom more concerned than if it were a hundred miles away. You cross a turnpike-road; and there is no gate, no policeman, no signal – nothing to keep the wayfarer or quiet traveler out of the way, but a wooden arch on which is written, in great letters, 'Look out for the locomotive'.

The railways appear regularly in Dickens's magazines *Household Words* and *All The Year Round*, in articles such as 'A Flight' (1851), and accounts of accidents and hazards faced by railway workers. In 'Railway Dreaming' (1856), Dickens wrote:

> I am never sure of time or place upon a Railroad. I can't read, I can't think, I can't sleep – I can only dream. Rattling along in this railway carriage in a state of luxurious confusion, I take I for granted I am coming from somewhere, and going somewhere else. I seek to know no more.... I know nothing about myself – for anything I know, I may be coming from the Moon.

His passion for railways changed, however, on 9 June 1865, when he was travelling back from France with Ellen Ternan and her mother. After disembarking at Folkestone, they boarded a train for London. According to each day's weather and tide conditions, the train's timetable had to be very variable. On that day, there was work being done on the railway tracks – perhaps the workers thought that the boat train had already passed that section of the line. For whatever reason, the train driver received no signal that there was a gap in the train tracks, at a crucial high point, on a bridge over the River Beult. When the train crashed at the gap in the rails, several of the carriages were precipitated off the bridge. There were 110 people on board, of whom ten were killed and fourteen seriously injured. Many others received less serious injuries and all were severely traumatised. Dickens would suffer the psychological effects of the crash for the rest of his life.

He and his companions were in the carriage that remained on the bridge, although its front half stuck out into the abyss, still attached to those that had hurtled into the gap. All three were lucky to survive. Dickens joined a group of people helping to pull dying, injured and terrified people out of the mangled carriages, as well as carrying out the dead. When all who could be freed had been brought to safety, Dickens went back inside his carriage – to retrieve his manuscript for the latest instalment of *Our Mutual Friend*. In the postscript for the book, Dickens wrote:

> On Friday the Ninth of June in the present year, Mr. and Mrs. Boffin (in their manuscript dress of receiving Mr. and Mrs. Lammle at breakfast) were on the South Eastern Railway with me, in a terribly destructive accident. When I had done what I could to help others, I climbed back into my carriage – nearly turned over a viaduct, and caught aslant upon the turn – to extricate the worthy couple. They were much soiled, but otherwise unhurt. The same happy result attended Miss Bella Wilfer on her wedding day, and Mr. Riderhood inspecting Bradley Headstone's red neckerchief as he lay asleep. I remember with devout thankfulness that I can never be much nearer parting company with my readers for ever, than I was then, until there shall be written against my life, the two words with which I have this day closed this book:– THE END.

Dickens became understandably anxious about travelling by train, but was unable to avoid doing so. In 1866, the year after the Staplehurst crash, George Dolby, Dickens's manager, recalled a less serious incident on another train journey:

> When we were nearing Preston, Mr. Dickens was entertaining me with a song and dance (the drinking song from *Der Freischutz*), with glass in hand, when the concussion of air, caused by the passing of an express train from the opposite direction, whisked a sealskin cap off his head, and away it flew into the darkness out of the opposite window.

Dolby assured a sceptical Dickens that he would get the cap retrieved and returned to him – and against the odds, he managed to do so. When they stopped at Preston, Dolby told the station master of the loss and offered a reward to any railway worker who found and returned it. A few days later, when Dickens was due to read at Liverpool, he received a parcel containing his cap.

Despite Dolby's jovial recollection, Dickens could not overcome his new fear of travelling by train, something that inspired his ghostly short story *The Signalman* (1866):

> The cutting was extremely deep, and unusually precipitate. It was made through a clammy stone that became oozier and wetter as I went down. For these reasons, I found the way long enough to give me time to recall a singular air of reluctance or compulsion with which he had pointed out the path.
>
> When I came down low enough upon the zig-zag descent, to see him again, I saw that he was standing between the rails on the way by which the train had lately passed, in an attitude as if he were waiting for me to appear. He had his left hand at his chin, and that left elbow rested on his right hand crossed over his breast. His attitude was one of such expectation and watchfulness, that I stopped a moment, wondering at it.
>
> I resumed my downward way, and, stepping out upon the level of the railroad and drawing nearer to him, saw that he

was a dark sallow man, with a dark beard and rather heavy eyebrows. His post was in as solitary and dismal a place as ever I saw. On either side, a dripping-wet wall of jagged stone, excluding all view but a strip of sky; the perspective one way, only a crooked prolongation of this great dungeon; the shorter perspective in the other direction, terminating in a gloomy red light, and the gloomier entrance to a black tunnel, in whose massive architecture there was a barbarous, depressing, and forbidding air. So little sunlight ever found its way to this spot, that it had an earthy deadly smell; and so much cold wind rushed through it, that it struck chill to me, as if I had left the natural world.

The Signalman was part of a series of short stories entitled *Mugby Junction*, in the Christmas edition of *All The Year Round*. It was published the year after the Staplehurst railway disaster. In *The Signalman*, the ringing of a phantom bell always presages an accident. The psychological scars of the Staplehurst crash never left Dickens, and the deaths of those people he had been unable save plagued his imagination. The accident blighted much of his second visit to America. He had become terrified of trains, but in order to cover American distances, he had no choice but to use them.

When one reads Charles Dickens's travel writing which pre-dates 1865, his enthusiasm for train journeys is apparent. After 1865, however, the author was continually haunted by recollections of the crash, and this did not abate, despite the many train journeys he needed to take. Dickens's death, on 9 June 1870, occurred on the fifth anniversary of the Staplehurst crash.

Returning to America

> *'Our travelling life had become so much a matter of system with us, that the routine of it became almost monotonous. Day after day we were doing the same things at the same time – packing our portmanteaus, travelling to a fresh town, unpacking the portmanteaus, attending to preliminary matters in connection with the Readings, dining, and after a rest for an hour or two, making for the hall, where the public sat expectant.'*
> George Dolby from *Charles Dickens As I Knew Him* (1885)

By the time Dickens returned to the USA, quarter of a century had elapsed since he had first visited, and the country had undergone a civil war. At this time, two years after the Staplehurst crash, Dickens's health was causing a great deal of concern to his family and friends, many of whom tried to warn him against undertaking such an arduous trip. Although Dickens insisted he was perfectly well, his health problems – both physical and emotional – were to trouble him throughout the months he spent overseas.

His tour manager George Dolby took an advance trip to America to make the necessary arrangements. He left for Boston on 3 August 1867, on the Cunard steamship *Java*. Dickens travelled with him to Liverpool to see him off. The author was intrigued to see the ship and discover what changes had been made in transatlantic passenger ships since his previous journey. Dolby soon reported that the American people were longing for Dickens to return, or as he wrote in his memoirs, 'There was no anxiety whatever about public feeling in America, and the *American Notes* and *Martin Chuzzlewit*.'

As there was to be a presidential election in the autumn of 1868, Dolby and Dickens's US publisher, James T. Fields, wanted Dickens to travel as soon as possible, to avoid the election mayhem. In his memoirs, Dolby provides a fascinating memory of what it was like to travel on an American railway in 1867:

> This was the first railway journey I had taken in the States. I must confess that the travelling did not strike me as being very comfortable. In those days, there was but one class of fare, everybody paying at the same rate ... all classes travelled together in a long car, built to carry fifty-two passengers... . At each end of the car was a stove, kept almost at a red heat during the winter months; and on the opposite side to the stove was a tank of iced water, a great luxury in hot weather ... the restlessly peripatetic dealers in newspapers, books, pamphlets, ivory pincushions, 'pop corn' ... give the traveller really no peace of mind on his journey and make him long for its termination.

Dolby was much more enamoured of the steamboats which took him from Massachusetts to New York. He was amazed to be on a three-decker boat with 'hot and cold baths, barbers' shops, cigar and newspaper stands, book-stalls, and hosiery establishments ... saloons and retiring rooms – not forgetting the drinking bars, where everything from a bottle of champagne to a cocktail and "eye opener" could be obtained.'

After a successful trip, Dolby returned to Britain, where he and Dickens worked out the final details. Dolby returned to America in mid-October, to ensure everything would be ready for the author. On arrival he learnt that American newspapers were full of 'ridiculous paragraphs ... about Mr. Dickens's health'. Dolby then embarked on the stressful task of overseeing ticket sales for the upcoming readings. On the morning the first series of Boston reading tickets went on sale, priced at $2, Dolby recorded, 'By eight o'clock in the morning the queue was nearly half a mile long, and about that time the employers of the persons who had been standing in the streets all night long began to arrive and take their places ... the sale lasted over eleven hours... . The receipts amounted to $14,000.'

Returning to America

Dickens set sail on the *Cuba* on 9 November 1867. This was a very different Dickens from the exuberantly dashing young man, about to turn 30, who had first landed in America at the start of 1842. That Charles Dickens had travelled happily with his young wife; now he was a grizzled middle-aged man, looking much older than his 55 years, and known to be estranged from his wife.

He was still suffering from the fall out caused by the public knowledge of the end of his marriage, as well as his own ensuing depression, the repercussions caused by his angry and irrational behaviour about the separation, and the psychological trauma of the Staplehurst rail crash. His initial plan had been to make the journey with his lover, Ellen Ternan, insisting he would be able to pass her off as his goddaughter. His friends and manager persuaded him that it wouldn't work, that everyone would see through the subterfuge, and that his reputation – and Ellen's – would be ruined. Although reluctant to believe them, Dickens had been persuaded to start without Ellen, with the proviso that, once he arrived, he would be able to send for her if he still thought it a good idea.

Once in America, he quickly realised the advice had been correct: many American settlers were still in thrall to their Puritan ancestry and he could not risk anyone discovering the true nature of his relationship with the young actress. Dickens sent Ellen a coded telegram telling her not to join him. Ironically, an object now in the archives at New York Public Library shows their relationship could have been discovered while Dickens was in America. Dickens's diary was either lost in New York, or it was stolen, and somehow ended up being preserved in the library.

Dickens always kept an appointment diary, something in which he made simple, short notations, but his usual practice was to destroy it at the end of every year. His little 1867 diary is filled with comments and memoranda about 'N', short for Nelly, Dickens's name for Ellen. There are allusions to his hopes of her joining him in America, as well as appointments from earlier in the year of when they had been househunting together (for a home for Ellen, which Dickens could visit easily). He became very anxious over the loss of this diary, although whoever possessed the diary after Dickens had lost it seems not to have understood the importance of the entries about 'N'.

On arrival in Boston, Dickens stayed at a grand new hotel, the Parker House. It had opened in 1855, designed for the discerning wealthy traveller. The elite of Boston might have enjoyed looking down on Dickens in 1842, as a young upstart, but by the time he returned, he had become one of the most famous men in the world, a lion of literature, used to being treated with the same reverence as royalty.

The Parker House was suitably regal, a five-story building in 'the Italian style' with a carved marble exterior, a grand marble foyer, and hot- and cold-running water in the bathrooms. The hotel had become associated with the Boston literati. Every month the Saturday Club would arrive to hold their meetings – and enjoy a sumptuous dinner – at the hotel's restaurant. Amongst its members was Dickens's friend Henry Wadsworth Longfellow.

. Unusually for one normally so sociable, on 30 November Dickens wrote to his son Charley from the Parker House: 'My great desire is to avoid much travelling, and to try to get the people to come to me, instead of my going to them. If I can effect this to any moderate extent, I shall be saved a great deal of knocking about.' At this stage, Dickens was still hoping that he would be able to go back to Canada at the end of the trip. He also wrote to Charley:

> I [received] ... a call from my old secretary ... Mr. Putnam. It was quite affecting to see his delight.... And when I told him that Anne was married, and that I had (unacknowledged[26]) grandchildren, he laughed and cried together. I suppose you don't remember Longfellow, though he remembers you in a black velvet frock very well. He is now white-haired and white-bearded, but remarkably handsome.

Despite this chance to meet up with old friends, on this second trip to America, Dickens was often unhappy. Being so far from home, without his lover or his children, made him miserable. George Dolby, although extremely loyal in his memoirs, must have found it a very trying experience. In the preface to his book, *Charles Dickens As I Knew Him* (1885), he wrote:

---

26. The word 'unacknowledged' was a joke. Dickens adored having grandchildren, but said that their existence made him feel old, so instead of them calling him grandfather, he taught them to nickname him Venerables.

> Dickens was my great hero – my 'Chief'– in the pleasant bygone days when we were 'on the road' together – by day and by night, week after week, month after month, right through the English and American tours; and his memory is heroic now that he has gone. His death closed the brightest chapter in my life.

That adoration, however, did not make Dickens any easier to live with during his periods of depression, self-anger, and frustration with his increasingly poor health and his difficult personal life. Dolby was worried about Dickens's health throughout the tour, and feared he would be unable to stick to their rigorous schedule, but, as Dolby recalled, Dickens insisted no one had a right to break a public engagement as long as they were well enough to be out of bed.

Their time in New York was enlivened by Dolby bursting into Dickens's room at midnight to tell him their hotel, the Westminster Hotel on Irving Place, was on fire. Dickens told his servant to pack up everything he needed for his readings, while he pocketed his 'jewels and papers' and Dolby grabbed up the money they had made so far. After all the excitement, and the arrival of the firemen and police, the fire was defeated, and everyone returned to their beds. Dickens wrote about the fire to Georgina, and commented, 'Dolby continues to be the most unpopular man in America (mainly because he can't get four thousand people into a room that holds two thousand), and is reviled in print daily.' He was not, however, feeling at all well and on 30 December, when he was back in New York, he wrote to Mamie, 'I have not been well, been very low, and have been obliged to have a doctor.'

The public had no idea of Dickens's lowering spirits. He was seen as the embodiment of Christmas, a bonhomous picture of joviality ready to entertain all who met him, and his readings were almost unanimously lauded. There was, however, one member of the New York City audience who remained unimpressed. Samuel Langhorn Clemens, who would later become known by the pen-name Mark Twain, was particularly irritated by Dickens's English accent. In a review that has a definite whiff of sour grapes about it, he described:

> a tall, 'spry,' (if I may say it,) thin-legged old gentleman, gotten up regardless of expense, especially as to shirt-front

and diamonds, with a bright red flower in his button-hole, gray beard and moustache, bald head, and with side hair brushed fiercely and tempestuously forward, as if its owner were sweeping down before a gale of wind, the very Dickens came! ... He strode – in the most English way and exhibiting the most English general style and appearance – straight across the broad stage, heedless of everything, unconscious of everybody, turning neither to the right nor the left – but striding eagerly straight ahead, as if he had seen a girl he knew turn the next corner... . His pictures are hardly handsome, and he, like everybody else, is less handsome than his pictures. That fashion he has of brushing his hair and goatee so resolutely forward gives him a comical Scotch-terrier look about the face.... This was Dickens – Dickens. There was no question about that, and yet it was not right easy to realize it. Somehow this puissant god seemed to be only a man, after all.... He read *David Copperfield*. He is a bad reader, in one sense – because he does not enunciate his words sharply and distinctly – he does not cut the syllables cleanly... . I was a good deal disappointed ... I will go further and say, a great deal disappointed.... Mr Dickens' reading is rather monotonous, as a general thing; his voice is husky; his pathos is only the beautiful pathos of his language – there is no heart, no feeling in it – it is glittering frostwork...

On 15 January, Dickens wrote to Charley from New York:

I have finished here (except four farewell nights in April), and begin four nights at Brooklyn, on the opposite side of the river, to-night; and thus oscillate between Philadelphia, Baltimore, and Washington, and then cut into New England, and so work my way back to Boston for a fortnight, after which come Chicago, Cincinnati, Detroit and Cleveland, and Buffalo, and then Philadelphia, Boston, and New York farewells. I will not pass my original bound of eighty-four readings in all. My mind was made up as to that long ago. It will be quite enough. Chicago is some fifteen hundred miles from here. What with travelling, and getting ready for reading, and reading, the days are pretty fully occupied. Not the less so because I rest very indifferently at night.

When planning the itinerary for the tour, George Dolby had not taken into account the difficulties of travelling by train in an American winter, especially to somewhere as cold and snowy as Chicago. The weather made some journeys impossible, so the itinerary was hastily redrawn. Between November 1867 and April 1868, Dickens and Dolby visited Boston, New York (and Brooklyn), Philadelphia, Baltimore, Washington (DC), Hartford, Providence, Syracuse, Rochester, Buffalo, Niagara Falls, Utica, Albany, Springfield, Worcester, New Haven, New Bedford and Portland (Maine), before going back to Boston and New York.

Although many of his letters are filled with witticisms and funny observations, Dickens was finding his work gruelling. On 15 January he wrote to Charley from New York:

> The people are exceedingly kind and considerate, and desire to be most hospitable besides. But I cannot accept hospitality, and never go out, except at Boston, or I should not be fit for the labour. If Dolby holds out well to the last it will be a triumph, for he has to see everybody, drink with everybody, sell all the tickets, take all the blame, and go beforehand to all the places on the list.

From Baltimore on 11 February, he wrote to his son Henry, 'The weather is very severe here, and the work is very hard.'

Many of Dickens's letters reveal his poor health and depressed spirits, so his friends decided to hold a special event to cheer him up. George Dolby and James T. Fields organised The Great American Walking Match. This was a competition between Fields's employee James Osgood and George Dolby. Dickens was named their trainer and umpire; he also wrote up a witty set of rules for the competition. It took place just outside Boston on 29 February 1868. Dolby's secretary Henry Templeton wrote an essay entitled 'The Great International Walking Match', jokily commenting that Dolby's defeat was largely due to Annie Fields (James's wife) riding her carriage alongside Osgood 'plying him with bread soaked in brandy'. The story of the competition had made it into the newspapers, and a huge crowd turned out to watch. Dickens wrote to Mamie:

> The walking-match came off on Saturday, over tremendously difficult ground, against a biting wind, and through deep snow-wreaths. It was so cold, too, that our hair, beards, eyelashes, eyebrows, were frozen hard, and hung with icicles. The course was thirteen miles. They were close together at the turning-point, when Osgood went ahead at a splitting pace and with extraordinary endurance, and won by half a mile. Dolby did very well indeed .... The whole thing was a great success, and everybody was delighted.

From Baltimore, at the end of January Dickens wrote that 'it has been snowing hard for four-and-twenty hours' and he was concerned that Dolby, who was on a train to New York, would be snowed up. From Philadelphia, Dickens wrote that the great actress Fanny Kemble, who was also touring America, booked tickets to Dickens's reading. In Washington, Dickens received invitations to visit President Andrew Johnson[27], and the president booked 'a whole row for his family every night'. He was in Washington for his birthday, where 'The papers here having written about this being my birthday, the most exquisite flowers came pouring in at breakfast time from all sorts of people.' His readings were also attended on several nights by a persistent dog, who managed to gain entry into the hall and bark at him during his readings.

Dickens also wrote from Washington to the actor Charles Fechter,

> If I could send you a 'brandy cocktail' by post I would. It is a highly meritorious dram.... My New York landlord made me a 'Rocky Mountain sneezer,' which appeared to me to be compounded of all the spirits ever heard of in the world, with bitters, lemon, sugar, and snow. You can only make a true 'sneezer' when the snow is lying on the ground.

He also wrote to friends and family of his enormous audiences and of how they all refused to believe that this was his farewell tour, but

---

27. A short time after meeting Dickens, President Andrew Johnson was impeached.

Dickens's own comments make it apparent that he knew it was. He was exhausted and felt ill for almost his entire trip. From Boston he wrote wearily to Mamie on 2 March, 'the storm prevails over an immense extent of country.... We are getting sick of the sound of sleigh-bells.' The following week he wrote to Fechter:

> I am growing very home-sick, and very anxious for the 22nd of April; on which day, please God, I embark for home. I am beginning to be tired, and have been depressed all the time (except when reading), and have lost my appetite ... how sorely I miss a dear friend, and how sorely I miss all art, in these parts. No disparagement to the country, which has a great future in reserve, or to its people, who are very kind to me.

Returning to Niagara – 'that wonderful place' – cheered Dickens's spirits, not least because they enjoyed 'two brilliant sunny days'. To William Macready, Dickens wrote:

> Niagara is not at all spoiled by a very dizzy-looking suspension bridge. Is to have another still nearer to the Horse-shoe opened in July. My last sight of that scene (last Sunday) was thus: We went up to the rapids above the Horse-shoe—say two miles from it – and through the great cloud of spray. Everything in the magnificent valley – buildings, forest, high banks, air, water, everything – was made of rainbow. Turner's most imaginative drawing in his finest day has nothing in it so ethereal, so gorgeous in fancy, so celestial. We said to one another (Dolby and I), 'Let it for evermore remain so,' and shut our eyes and came away.

Longfellow, who had been born in Portland, Maine, was pleased when Dickens and Dolby amended the schedule and arranged performances there. When Dickens arrived, however, he was feeling unwell, with a persistent cough, and was depressed. He wrote to Mamie on 29 March:

> I have coughed from two or three in the morning until five or six, and have been absolutely sleepless. I have had no

appetite besides, and no taste. Last night here I took some laudanum, and it is the only thing that has done me good. But the life in this climate is so very hard.

He also explained that their original schedule could never have been viable, so they had needed to cut down on the amount of work and forget about returning to Canada.

By the time he reached Maine, Dickens was longing to go home. He left unfavourable impressions of Portland, complaining about poor accommodation, bad food and the cold climate, although he was impressed by how many people turned out to hear his reading. Portland had been devastated by fire only a couple of years earlier, and as Dickens did his usual long walk around the town and along the sea shore, he noted the stubs of burnt trees and how much rebuilding was taking place.

As he left Portland by train, depressed, homesick and heartsick, an 11-year-old girl came to sit beside him. Her name was Kate Douglas Wiggin. Having been disappointed in her hopes of attending his reading, she was thrilled to recognise him on the train. Dickens, who always loved the company of children, was friendly and chatty. He asked Kate about her life, and regaled her with stories all the way to Boston. They discovered a shared love of pets and Kate told him that *David Copperfield* was her favourite book. Many years later, in 1912, Kate published an essay entitled 'A Child's Journey with Dickens':

> It seems to me that no child nowadays has time to love an author as the children and young people of that generation loved Dickens; nor do I think that any living author of to-day provokes love in exactly the same fashion. From our yellow dog, Pip, to the cat, the canary, the lamb, the cow, down to all the hens and cocks, almost every living thing was named, sooner or later, after one of Dickens's characters; while my favorite sled, painted in brown, with the title in brilliant red letters, was 'The Artful Dodger'.

Kate's mother and cousin had attended Dickens's performance, but Kate had been left behind. So she had slipped out of her bed and walked through the streets to look at the hall where he was reading and at the Preble Hotel, where he was staying:

The next morning we started on our railroad journey.... When the train stopped ... at North Berwick, the people ... suddenly arose and looked eagerly out at some object of apparent interest ... my small nose was quickly flattened against one of the panes. There on the platform stood the Adored One! ... I knew him at once! – the smiling, genial, mobile face, rather highly colored, the brilliant eyes, the watch chain, the red carnation in the button-hole, and the expressive hands, much given to gesture. It was only a momentary view, for the train started, and Dickens vanished, to resume his place in the car next to ours, where he had been, had I known it, ever since we left Portland.... I planted myself timorously down, an unbidden guest ... Dickens was looking out of the window, but he turned in a moment, and said with justifiable surprise:–

'God bless my soul, where did you come from?'

'I came from Hollis, Maine,' I stammered, 'My mother and her cousin went to your reading last night.... There was a lady there who had never heard of Betsey Trotwood, and had only read two of your books!'

'Well, upon my word!' he said; 'you do not mean to say that you have read them!'

'Of course I have,' I replied; 'every one of them but the two that we are going to buy in Boston, and some of them six times.... Of course,' I explained conscientiously, 'I do skip some of the very dull parts once in a while; not the short dull parts, but the long ones.'

He laughed heartily, 'Now, that is something that I hear very little about,' he said, 'I distinctly want to learn more about those very dull parts,'

And whether to amuse himself, or to amuse me, I do not know, he took out a note-book and pencil from his pocket and proceeded to give me an exhausting and exhaustive examination on this subject; ... I continued dealing these infant blows, under the delusion that I was flinging him bouquets...

'Did you want to go to my reading very much?'...

I faltered, 'Yes; more than tongue, can tell.' I looked up a second later, when I was sure that the tears in my eyes were not going to fall, and to my astonishment saw that Dickens's eyes were in precisely the same state of moisture. That was a never-to-be-forgotten moment, although I was too young to appreciate the full significance of it... .

'You are not travelling alone?' he asked, as he arose to put on his overcoat.

'Oh, no,' I answered, coming down to earth for the first time since I had taken my seat beside him, – 'oh, no, I had a mother, but I forgot all about her.'...

Dickens took me back to the forgotten mother, and introduced himself, and I, still clinging to his hand, left the car and walked with him down the platform until he disappeared in the carriage with Mr. Osgood, leaving me with the feeling that I must continue my existence somehow in a dull and dreary world.

Despite the kindly impression Dickens made on his young travel companion, he was feeling increasingly unwell. From Boston, on 7 April, he sent an extraordinary letter about his new 'medicinal' diet to his daughter Mamie:

> I cannot eat (to anything like the ordinary extent), and have established this system: At seven in the morning, in bed, a tumbler of new cream and two tablespoonsful of rum. At twelve, a sherry cobbler and a biscuit. At three (dinner time), a pint of champagne. At five minutes to eight, an egg beaten up with a glass of sherry. Between the parts, the strongest beef tea that can be made, drunk hot. At a quarter-past ten, soup, and anything to drink that I can fancy. I don't eat more than half a pound of solid food in the whole four-and-twenty hours, if so much.

On Saturday, 18 April 1868, a farewell banquet was held in Dickens's honour at Delmonico's restaurant in New York City. By this stage of his tour, he was suffering from constant coughing and catarrh, and was continuing to struggle with his depression. He was also in a great deal of pain, with a recurring problem in his left foot. Dickens arrived at the banquet late – something highly unusual for him – because his foot was so swollen he had not been able to put on his shoe. Despite the pain, as always, he put on a great performance, just as he had throughout his reading tour, giving little indication to those present just how ill he was feeling. He gave a speech about the changes that had taken place in the country since his previous visit, in which he included the comments:

> I henceforth charge myself ... to express my high and grateful sense of my second reception in America, and to bear my honest testimony to the national generosity and magnanimity. Also, to declare how astounded I have been by the amazing changes I have seen around me on every side.... Nor am I, believe me, so arrogant as to suppose that in five-and-twenty years there have been no changes in me, and that I had nothing to learn and no extreme impressions to correct when I was here first ... what I have resolved upon (and this is the confidence I seek to place in you), is, on my return to England, in my own person, in my own Journal, to bear, for the behoof of my countrymen, such testimony to the gigantic changes in this country.

As an apology to the people he had offended with his depictions of America in *American Notes* and *Martin Chuzzlewit*, Dickens asked his publishers to include a copy of his speech in every subsequent edition of those two books. He also publicly refuted the rumours which claimed he was 'hammering away at, a new book on America'.

After his return to England, Dickens wrote his final essays for his series *The Uncommercial Traveller*. One was about the journey from America back to England:

> I was resting on a skylight on the hurricane-deck.... It was high noon on a most brilliant day in April, and the beautiful bay was glorious and glowing.... The ship was fragrant with flowers. Something of the old Mexican passion for flowers may have gradually passed into North America, where flowers are luxuriously grown and tastefully combined in

the richest profusion.... These delicious scents of the shore, mingling with the fresh airs of the sea, made the atmosphere a dreamy, an enchanting one.

('Aboard Ship', 5 December 1868)

In a letter to his friend Lavinia Watson, he described the journey: 'I had not been at sea three days on the passage home when I became myself again ... a "deputation" ... came to ask me to read to the passengers that evening in the saloon. I respectfully replied that sooner than do it, I would assault the captain, and be put in irons.'

'Revolving Restlessly, Australia in My Head'

'Here are some people David knows, going out to Australia shortly. If you decide to go, why shouldn't you go in the same ship? You may help each other.'
From *David Copperfield* (1850)

In 1850, in the very first volume of his new magazine *Household Words*, Dickens published an article entitled 'A Bundle of Emigrants' Letters'. The article had grown out of his association with a philanthropist entitled Mrs Chisholm (who unwittingly inspired Mrs Jellyby in *Bleak House*). She was hoping to establish a charity called A Family Colonisation Loan Society, arranging interest-free loans to enable people to join family members in 'the colonies'. One of Mrs Chisholm's chief concerns, as reiterated by Dickens in the article, was that 'it is melancholy to reflect that thousands of British subjects should wander about, more like spectres than beings of flesh and blood; and that hundreds should die from starvation, while our vast colonies could provide abundantly for them.'

Dickens sometimes poked gentle fun at the letter writers, but he was intrigued by the letters and their minutiae about Australian life. One man living in Melbourne wrote to his wife in England in an effort to persuade her to join him:

> do keep up your spirits and come as soon as you can ... the best flour is only 20 shilling the sack and such quality that you cannot buy in England the bread is the best bread I ever eat in my life and the meat very fine and no price at all ... every body has what is called a lamp over here which

costs about 7 or 8 shilling and you can bake your bread or your dinners at your own fireplace.... . I am still living in the little cottage and I have worked very hard lattely... . I never had the slightest cough since I came here ... I have not the slightest wish to see England again...

One rather poignant letter, from 'a poor woman' reunited with her children, perhaps illustrates what Dickens hoped his characters in *David Copperfield* would find when they landed in this new country of promised possibility:

[my children] safely arrived by the Castle Eden all in good health. They however left their box of clothes behind at Plymouth and I have not as yet been able to get any account of it. It appears to be lost, but as *they* arrived safe I do not care to trouble any one to enquire for this. The oldest girl got married about five months since to a respectable young man a tradesman, a pretty good match the next boy is apprenticed six months ago to the wheelwright business and the next boy is four months apprenticed to a boot and shoemaker – the other little one I have myself. My own health is pretty good, and although times are rather dull just now yet I hope that I shall find enough to do to keep along with. Many ships have arrived here with emigrants and this for a time causes rather more to be looking for situations than there are situations to be filled, but most of them go into the country...

Dickens also included an unintentionally amusing letter from a clergyman living in Sydney, bemoaning the type of people emigrating to Australia:

Sydney is at present crowded with respectable young men, – Bankers and merchant's clerks, artists and such kind of people are not wanted at all, so that many of them having small means are quite in despair. They are almost useless to the settlers and people in the Bush and can find no occupation in town and are therefore liable to every temptation.

'Revolving Restlessly, Australia in My Head'

In much of his fiction, Dickens concentrated on criminals, criminality and the deep injustices that happen often because of the rigid Victorian class system. In *Great Expectations* we learn that Abel Magwitch fell into a life of crime because he was desperate for food:

> In jail and out of jail, in jail and out of jail, in jail and out of jail. There, you've got it. That's my life pretty much, down to such times as I got shipped off ... I've been done everything to, pretty well – except hanged.... . They always went on agen me about the Devil. But what the Devil was I to do? I must put something into my stomach, mustn't I?

Much of the novel's plot leads back to Magwitch and the repercussions of his actions – even though he is absent for much of the book, having been transported to Australia. When *Great Expectations* was published, the majority of British people knew little about Australia, other than its reputation as a place to which convicts had been sent. Dickens himself was fascinated to know more about the country. At the end of *David Copperfield*, the Micawber family emigrates to Australia, to join forces with Daniel Peggotty, Martha and Emily, all of whom are hoping to find a better life in the antipodes. David narrates seeing the Micawbers when they had decided to emigrate:

> Shall I ever forget how, in a moment, he was the most sanguine of men, looking on to fortune; or how Mrs. Micawber presently discoursed about the habits of the kangaroo! Shall I ever recall that street of Canterbury on a market-day, without recalling him, as he walked back with us; expressing, in the hardy roving manner he assumed, the unsettled habits of a temporary sojourner in the land; and looking at the bullocks, as they came by, with the eye of an Australian farmer!

The Dickens family was to become intimately connected with Australia, through two of Dickens's children. Alfred D'Orsay Tennyson Dickens set sail for Australia on 5 June 1865, on the ship *London*. It took him just under two months to travel across the world, arriving in Melbourne in 4 August. Three years later, his youngest sibling, Edward Bulwer Lytton

Dickens was sent to join him. Alfred had left England at the age of 19; Edward was only 16 years old when he set sail for an unknown continent.

Although the Dickens children were well-travelled compared to most of their peers, their only knowledge of the world was of Europe. Alfred arrived in this extraordinary new country, armed only with letters of introduction and the fame of his surname. It must have been a wondrous thing to have his young brother arrive, at last a family member with whom Alfred could share the responsibility of this new life. Edward, although young, arrived with vital skills, having spent two years studying at Cirencester Agricultural College.

A few years after the Dickens boys moved to Australia, the author Anthony Trollope travelled to visit his son who was also living there. Of Sydney, he wrote:

> [it] is one of those places which, when a man leaves it knowing that he will never return, he cannot leave it without a pang and a tear. Such is its loveliness ... it has none of those worst signs of novelty which make the cities of the New World unpicturesque and distasteful.... . The Australian cities have had the advantage of our deficiencies.

Of the city, where Alfred and Edward lived, Trollope noted:

> There is perhaps no town in the world in which an ordinary working man can do better for himself and for his family with his work then he can at Melbourne... . I would say to any young man whose courage is high and whose intelligence is not below par, that he should not be satisfied to remain at home; but should come out, – to Melbourne ... and try to win a higher lot and a better fortune than the old country can afford to give him.

In 1924, an article appeared in the Perth *Sunday Times*, written by Trevellyan Jones, a friend of Alfred and Edward Dickens in Melbourne. He wrote of how the arrival of two of Charles Dickens's sons in Australia created a renewed interest in reading Dickens, and led to the gathering of 'bohemians' to create Dickens clubs. Most reports show Alfred as the hardworking, well-respected businessman who became a pillar of Melbourne society, and Edward as the irresponsible brother, who was frequently in debt and died in poverty. Jones, however, although kindly describing Alfred as 'a conspicuous figure ... quite the "lion of the hour," and a welcome guest at all functions' praised Edward more highly. Edward – who moved to New South Wales, where he became both an MP and a bankrupt – is described as a man trusted by the people, seen as someone who truly worked on making things better and lauded as 'the settlers' friend'.

In June 1861, Dickens wrote to Forster that 'A man from Australia is in London ready to pay £10,000 for eight months there.' In 1862 he wrote again to Forster saying, 'I think all the probabilities for such a country as Australia are immense ... [but] I dread the thought more than I can possibly express', mostly it seemed because it would be such a long journey away from his family. He wrote to his sister Letitia in November 1862:

> Moreover – this is a secret – I am again deliberating whether I will or will not go away for a whole year, and read in Australia; and there are so many reasons for and against, and I am so very unwilling to go, that it causes me great uneasiness of mind in trying to do right and to decide for the best.

To W. H. Wills, he wrote, 'I am again revolving restlessly, Australia in my head!'

He deliberated for several years, planning the tour carefully, then firmly deciding against it, only to return to the idea again and start re-planning it. The offer must have been repeated, because he wrote to Alfred, who didn't arrive in Australia until 1865, that he had decided against an Australian tour. According to Trevellyan Jones's article, Dickens's letter said, 'I should like to come to Australia. It is a very tempting offer, but that vast expanse of sea and the many months the journey would occupy combine in impelling me to forgo the great pleasure of seeing you, and to decline the very generous offer.'

Despite this, he continued to ponder it, just as he had done his second tour of the USA. In 1866, Dickens had written definitively to his American publisher and friend James T. Fields:

> I really do not know that any sum of money that could be laid down would induce me to cross the Atlantic to read.... .

> It is a delightful sensation to move a new people; but I have but to go to Paris, and I find the brightest people in the world quite ready for me. I say thus much in a sort of desperate endeavor to explain myself to you. I can put no price upon fifty readings in America, because I do not know that any possible price could pay me for them. And I really cannot say to any one disposed towards the enterprise, 'Tempt me', because I have too strong a misgiving that he cannot in the nature of things do it.

A year later, however, in June 1867, Dickens wrote to Fields, 'I have this morning resolved to send out to Boston in the first week of August, Mr. Dolby, the secretary and manager of my Readings.' Dolby would also bring with him Dickens's latest manuscript, a collection of four short stories for children, written specifically for the American market and entitled *Holiday Romance*. There had been much speculation about Dickens's plans, and he advised Fields, 'We mean to keep this all STRICTLY SECRET, as I beg of you to do, until I finally decide for or against.'

Dickens's change of heart about his American tour makes it possible that he might have had a similar change of heart about the Australian tour, which had been proposed and rejected several times already. Perhaps one day he might have decided to travel to the other side of the world, where two of his sons had made their home, had he not died so suddenly.

Although he didn't ever travel to New Zealand, the country gets a mention in several dispatches in *Household Words* and *All The Year Round*. It also gets a witty mention in Dickens' and Wilkie Collins's Christmas story *No Thoroughfare*. When Walter Wilding is attempting to find out what happened to a church minister who gave a reference to a woman who adopted a baby from the Foundling Hospital, he is handed a book very solemnly. The title page of the book relates: 'The matyrdom of the Reverend John Harker in New Zealand. Related by a former member of his flock.' The suggestion is that Dickens and Collins thought it a savage country.

Alfred and Edward were not the only Dickens children to travel the world. Of the seven Dickens boys, five lived overseas. Walter went to India at the age of 16, as a cadet in the East India Company. He died there at the age of 22 and was buried in Calcutta.[28] Frank also moved to India, tragically arriving to hear the news that his brother had died while he was on his journey out there. He arrived in 1864, with a commission to join the Bengal Mounted Police and remained in India for six years, only returning to England after his father's death in 1870. A couple of years later, he moved to Canada where he became a Mountie – an officer in the North West Mounted Police. He is buried in Moline, Illinois, which he was visiting during a lecture tour of America.

Perhaps the Dickens boy who saw the most of the world was Sydney, who joined the Navy as a teenager and seldom returned to England. He began his career in Canada and spent much of his life in the South Pacific. When he died in 1872, he had not seen his family for several years. His burial at sea took place from HMS *Topaze* in the Indian Ocean.

Although Charley, the eldest son, settled in England, in his early career he travelled overseas. He worked in the tea industry, so was sent to Asia 'to learn the business'. In 1888, he also travelled to America on a speaking tour, on which he was accompanied by his daughter Sydney (named after her uncle).

It is unknown why Dickens sent so many of his sons overseas, although it was common practice for many families in the mid-nineteenth century. Because Dickens died young, at the age of 58, he never saw any of his emigrant sons again after they had left England. Today, there are Dickens descendants and relatives living in most continents of the world.

---

28. Present day Kolkatta. The location of Walter's grave is unknown, but his headstone survives and can be seen at South Park Street Cemetery in Kolkatta. Walter was reportedly buried in the Military Cemetery, now known as Bhowanipore Cemetery, but when I visited I discovered that, although there was a request for Walter to be buried there, and it was where his gravestone was found, there are no official records of the burial having taken place. In 1911, his gravestone was described as 'near the entrance to the cemetery'. By the 1980s, his damaged gravestone was one of many that had been left piled up, possibly waiting to be destroyed. Thanks to the Indian Dickens Fellowship and students from Jadavpur University, Walter's gravestone was rescued and moved to the city's other cemetery, where it rests against another grave.

Travelling with Dickens

'I had been travelling, for some days; resting very little in the night, and never in the day. The rapid and unbroken succession of novelties that had passed before me, came back like half-formed dreams; and a crowd of objects wandered in the greatest confusion through my mind, as I travelled on...'
Charles Dickens, *Pictures from Italy* (1846)

Almost everywhere I have travelled, I have discovered a connection with my great great great grandfather. It has been amazing to me to discover not only how much Dickens was inspired by the world, but how much the world has remained inspired by him. In India, a 12-year-old girl came eagerly to talk to me about *Great Expectations*, her 'favourite book'; she had read it multiple times. On the same trip, I met an elderly woman who told me that when she had been to London she hadn't needed a map, as her knowledge of Dickens had helped her navigate her way around the city. When walking through a market in Havana, Cuba, I was approached by a bookseller, who wanted to sell me a copy of *Martin Chuzzlewit*. When I checked into my hotel in Ljubljana, the man on reception looked at my passport – which includes the name Dickens – and asked if I were related to Charles Dickens. He told me that that 'every school child in Slovenia reads Charles Dickens'.

I've been taken to a bar named Oliver Twist in Zagreb and to one called Pickwick's in Vienna. There's a Charles Dickens Tavern in Melbourne, Australia, a Dickens Inn in Whangerei, New Zealand, and countless others all over the world, named either after Dickens himself, one of his books, or one of his many characters. Branches of the Dickens Fellowship, Dickens Societies and Pickwick Clubs span several continents and embrace many languages, and in 2012 countless countries held Dickens Bicentenary events. Annual Dickens festivals are celebrated in places which the author never managed to visit, yet they still celebrate his life and work as happily as if he had been a part of their community.

In *Little Dorrit*, Mr Meagles says, 'One always begins to forgive a place as soon as it's left behind.' This perspicacious comment applies to much of Dickens's travelling. Even places he disliked fired his imagination and inspired his writing. I wish that Dickens had lived long enough to visit his sons in Australia and India, maybe even to travel to the South Pacific and visit Sydney on his ship, and to have left us a record of these journeys.

When Charles Dickens died so unexpectedly in 1870, he left many books unwritten, many travelogues yet to be planned and much of the world unvisited, yet his travel writing, letters home and travel sections in his novels have provided us with an intimate insight into what it was like to be a nineteenth-century traveller.

Dickens and Travel Bibliography

Baker, William and Clarke, William M. (eds.), *The Letters of Wilkie Collins, Vol. 1 1838–1865*, Macmillan, 1999

Collins, Philip, (ed.), *Dickens Interviews and Recollections*, Macmillan, 1981

Collins, Philip, (ed.), *Sikes and Nancy*, Oxford, 1983

Cooke, Jim, *Charles Dickens's Ireland*, The Woodfield Press, 1999

Dana, Henry Wadsworth Longfellow, 'Longfellow and Dickens, The Story of a Transatlantic Friendship', a speech given 2 June 1942. (Accessed via the Maine Historical Society) https://www.hwlongfellow.org/pdf/danamanuscript.pdf

Dickens, Charles Jnr, *Dickens's Dictionary of Paris, An Unconventional Handbook*, Macmillan, 1885

Dolby, George, *Charles Dickens As I Knew Him*, Haskell House, 1885

Downey, Arthur T., *The Creole Affair: The Slave Rebellion that Led the U.S. and Great Britain to the Brink of War*, Rowman & Littlefield, 2014

Fitzgerald, Percy Hetherington, *The History of Pickwick; an Account of its Characters, Localities, Allusions and Illustrations*, Chapman and Hall, 1891

Forster, John, *The Life of Charles Dickens*, in two volumes, Chapman and Hall, 1872–1874

Forsyth, Neil, 'The Need for Streets: Dickens in Switzerland', in Leroy, Maxime (ed.), *Dickens and Europe,* Cambridge, 2013

Heineman, Helen K., *Three Victorians in the New World*, Peter Lang, 1992

Hollington, Michael (ed.), *The Reception of Charles Dickens in Europe*, Bloomsbury, 2013

Kaplan, Fred, *Dickens and Mesmerism: The Hidden Springs of Fiction*, Princeton University Press, 1975

Kaplan, Fred, *Dickens: A Biography*, Avon Books, 1990

Kitton, Frederic G. *Charles Dickens: His Life, Writings and Personality*, Caxton, 1901

Eds, Lang, Cecil Y., and Shannon Jr, Edgar F., *The Letters of Alfred Lord Tennyson: 1821–1850*, Harvard University Press, 1981

Munson, James and Mullen, Richard, *The Smell of the Continent: The British Discover Europe*, Pan, 2010

Nayder, Lillian, *The Other Dickens: A Life of Catherine Hogarth*, Cornell University Press, 2011

Orestano, Francesca, 'Back to Italy: Dickens's Stereoscopic Views', in Leroy, Maxime (ed.), *Dickens and Europe,* Cambridge, 2013

Payne, Edward F., *Dickens Days in Boston: A Record of Daily Events*, Houghton Mifflin, 1927

Schlicke, Paul, 'Boz in the North', *Scottish Review of Books*, 2 March 2012

Slater, Michael, *Charles Dickens*, Yale, 2009

Tomalin, Claire, *Charles Dickens: A Life*, Penguin, 2011

Van Dam, Frederik, *Anthony Trollope's Late Style: Victorian Liberalism and Literary Form*, Edinburgh University Press, 2016

Zboray, Ronald J., and Zboray, Mary Saracino, *Literary Dollars and Social Sense: A People's History of the Mass Market Book*, Routledge, 2013

Index

A

Adams, John Quincy 76, 77
Albaro – see 'Genoa'
Alexander, Francis 44, 45
All The Year Round 3, 32, 196, 235, 238, 258
Allonby 225-226
American Notes 41-42, 52, 56-57, 58-59, 61, 64, 65, 66, 68, 71, 78, 81-82, 85-86, 87, 93, 96, 98, 99, 101, 102, 166, 239, 251
Arabian Nights viii, 62, 131, 195, 216
Atlantic Ocean 42-43, 51
Austin, Letitia (née Dickens) 209, 257
Australia x, 30, 32, 37, 65-66, 172, 253-258, 260
Avignon 107, 120

B

Baltimore (USA) 61, 75, 80, 244-246
Barham, Dr Charles 16-17
Barnaby Rudge 46, 70, 149
Barnard Castle 13-14
Barnum, P.T. 132-133
Barrett Browning, Elizabeth 182
Barrow, Thomas 2
Bath 4, 5, 105
The Battle of Life 183, 184, 186, 200
Beard, Thomas 126, 160, 210
Beaucourt-Mutuel, Ferdinand 212, 216-217, 222

Belfast 35, 38-39
Belgium 163, 193
Bleak House 169, 210, 253
Blessington, Countess of 126, 159, 200
Birmingham (UK) 85, 105, 167
Bologna 128-130
Boston (USA) 40, 42, 43-45, 47-50, 52, 53-54, 55, 57, 58, 61, 62, 66, 71, 98
Boulogne 106, 169, 194, 195, 203, 204, 208, 210-220, 222, 241, 244-247
Bradbury and Evans 104, 137, 204
Bremer, Frederick 8
Brighton 21-22
British Museum 2, 88
Broadstairs – see 'Kent'
Brown, Anne 42, 80, 84-85, 91-92, 99, 102, 103, 242
Browne, Hablot Knight – see 'Phiz'
Buffalo 96, 97, 244, 245
Burdett-Coutts, Angela 160, 169, 170, 171, 183, 202, 209, 214
Burnett, Frances (née Dickens) 43
Burnett, Henry 180
Byron, Lord George Gordon 114, 129, 141

C

Cairo (Illinois, USA) 90, 91, 93
Calais 176, 193, 194, 195-196, 203, 219, 231, 232-233

Index

Cameron, Julia Margaret 18
Canada 43, 54, 80, 97, 98-102, 242, 248, 259
Carondelet (USA) 93
Carrock Fell 225
Carrara 142-144, 167
carriages – see 'travelling by coach'
Chapman and Hall 6, 104
Charleston (Virginia, USA) 77
Chicago 244, 245
The Chimes iv, 109, 137
A Christmas Carol 19, 24-25, 62, 104, 137, 165
Christmas ix, 19, 25, 31, 104, 109, 136, 137, 138, 139, 140, 165, 175, 184, 186, 190, 192, 196, 200, 205, 209, 215, 216, 224, 225, 226, 227, 238, 243, 258
Cincinnati 85, 86-87, 93, 244
Cinque Terre 141-142
Civita Vecchia 107, 123, 140, 173
Cleveland 96, 244
coaches – see 'travelling by coach'
Collins, Wilkie 169, 170, 171, 173, 174, 175, 176, 190, 191, 192, 203-204, 207, 208, 213, 215, 220
Condette 221-222
Cornwall 16-17, 146
The Cricket on the Hearth 208
Cunard 41-44, 67, 239

D

Dana, Henry 44, 50
Dana, Richard Henry 47-48, 50
David Copperfield 3, 16, 165, 186, 219, 244, 248, 253, 254, 255
De Cerjat, William 175-176
de la Rue, Augusta 113, 127
de la Rue, Emile 113, 118, 127, 162
death penalty 37, 154, 155, 156, 162

depression viii, x, 115, 116, 135, 171, 178, 185, 209, 214, 223, 241, 243, 245, 247, 248, 250
Dexter, Henry 45
Dickens, Alfred D'Orsay Tennyson 65-66, 183, 185, 215, 255-257, 258
Dickens, Alfred Lamert 208
Dickens, Augustus 194
Dickens, Catherine (née Hogarth) 8, 9, 13, 14, 15, 18, 19, 21, 24, 28, 33, 41-43, 44, 45, 48, 50, 51, 53, 54-56, 58-59, 61, 62, 65, 66, 67, 68, 69, 73, 75, 77-78, 80, 83-84, 85, 86, 93, 91-92, 96, 98, 100, 101-102, 103, 104, 105, 106, 111, 113, 124, 126, 127, 135, 137, 143, 145, 146, 150, 152-153, 155, 156-157, 158-161, 168, 177, 191-192, 199, 200, 203, 209, 210, 211, 213, 219, 221-222, 241
Dickens, Charley 15, 32, 51, 106, 111, 175, 176, 183, 184, 193, 202, 205, 206, 226, 242, 244, 245, 259
Dickens, Dora 102, 103
Dickens, Edward ('Plorn'), 205, 255-257, 258
Dickens, Elizabeth (née Barrow) 1, 2, 17
Dickens, Frank 105, 106, 111, 205, 215, 259
Dickens, Fred 41, 123-124, 125, 178, 184
Dickens, Henry Fielding 24, 205, 215, 219-220, 245
Dickens, John 1, 2, 15, 17, 194
Dickens, Katey – see 'Perugini, Kate'
Dickens, Mamie (Mary) 29, 33, 34, 36, 51, 86, 106, 111, 183, 184, 205, 209, 218, 219, 243, 246, 247, 250
Dickens, Sydney 205, 215, 259, 261

Dickens and Travel: The Start of Modern Travel Writing

Dickens, Walter 51, 106, 111, 205, 227, 258-259
Dickens Fellowship 48, 66, 143, 259, 260
D'Orsay, Count 107, 114, 121-122, 125, 140, 168, 198, 203
Doctor Marigold's Prescriptions 29, 226
dogs 35, 60, 62, 84, 106, 128, 132, 157, 197, 209, 219, 225, 246, 248
Dolby, George 29, 35, 36, 38, 237, 239, 240, 242-243, 245-246, 247-248, 258
Dombey and Son 21, 34, 35, 183, 184, 185, 234
Doncaster 226-227
Dublin 34, 35-36, 38, 39
Dumas, Alexandre 201, 202

E
Edinburgh 23-25, 28, 29
Egg, Augustus 169, 173, 174-175, 191
emigration 65, 87, 100, 113, 169, 232, 253-254, 255, 259
Evening Chronicle 6
Everett, Edward 45
Everett Hale, Sarah Preston 45, 46
Exeter 4, 17

F
Fechter, Charles 192, 246, 247
Felton, Cornelius 15, 17, 46, 59, 62, 98-99, 101
Ferrara 129-130
Fields, Annie 44, 245
Fields, James T. 44, 240, 245, 257-258
Fitzgerald, Percy 8
Fletcher, Angus 25, 26, 27, 28, 113, 115, 125, 143
Florence 111, 129, 160, 161

Fonblanque, Albany 76
Forster, John, ix, 1, 2, 8, 17, 21, 23, 25, 26-29, 43, 46, 53, 54, 56, 58, 61, 67, 72, 74, 76-77, 79-80, 95, 98, 99, 100, 104-105, 109, 111, 115-116, 117, 118, 120, 122, 123, 124, 126, 131, 143, 146, 157, 162, 163, 165, 169, 177, 178, 180, 181, 182, 183, 184, 185, 188, 191, 193, 194, 199, 200, 201, 210, 212, 213, 214, 225, 235, 257
France ix, 4, 104, 106, 107, 108-109, 110, 118, 120, 137, 166, 168, 185, 193-222, 229, 236

G
Gad's Hill Place 35, 192, 220, 226
Geneva ix, 167, 178, 182, 184, 185
Genoa iv, ix, 106-107, 113-127, 130, 137, 138, 139, 140, 141, 153, 157, 159, 162, 168, 169, 171, 172, 173, 174, 177, 178, 202, 211
Glasgow 23, 28, 29
Great Expectations 205, 255, 260
Greta Bridge 13
Grip (raven) 70

H
Halifax (Canada) 43, 98
Harrisburg 80-82
Hartford (USA), 55, 56, 57-58, 103
Harvard 46, 51
Herculaneum 157, 158, 159, 167
Hogarth, George 15, 57
Hogarth, Georgina 19, 29, 33, 34, 35, 41, 106, 111, 135, 140, 157, 158-159, 171, 172, 173, 174, 184, 199, 202, 206, 207, 209, 210, 211, 219, 221-222, 243
Hogarth, William 224
Horne, Richard Henry 19

Index

Household Words 8, 19, 175, 194, 202, 208, 223, 227, 235, 253, 258
Hughes, Reverend Stephen 30
Hugo, Victor 200-201, 202

I
India 227, 258-259, 260, 261
Industrial Revolution viii, 224
international copyright 40, 57-58
Ireland, 32, 33-39, 100
Irving, Washington 40-41, 62, 76, 102
Isle of Wight 18, 19, 127
Italy ix, 103, 104, 105, 106, 107, 108, 110, 111, 112, 113-135, 137, 139, 140-164, 165, 166, 167, 168-169, 170-175, 176, 177, 183, 186, 187, 198, 199, 214, 233

J
Jerrold, Douglas 120, 134, 137-138, 163, 181
Jousiffe, Captain 108, 140

K
Kemble, Fanny 246
Kent 10, 15, 16, 18, 19-20, 35, 40, 87, 94, 102, 103, 106, 137, 163, 166, 176, 192, 194, 195, 210, 215, 226, 229, 231, 236
Kolkatta 259

L
Lake Erie 95-96
Latimer, Elizabeth Wormeley 48-49, 55
Lausanne 170, 175, 178, 180, 183, 184, 185-186, 191-192, 199, 231
The Lazy Tour... 223-227
Leghorn – see 'Livorno'
Leech, John (& family) 18-19, 21-22, 127, 202

Lemon, Mark (& family) 213, 218
Leyland, Joseph 26
Lincoln, Abraham 75
Little Dorrit 104, 107, 165, 166-168, 173, 187, 189, 196, 208, 261
Liverpool ix, 30, 34, 41, 98, 101, 105, 234, 237, 239
Livorno 107, 123, 144, 161, 172-173
London, viii, ix, 1, 2, 3, 4, 5, 6, 8, 9, 10, 15, 17, 19, 23, 34, 35, 37, 38, 43, 45, 47, 51, 54, 59, 61, 63, 64, 76, 85, 100, 103, 106, 109, 110, 121, 124, 126, 137, 138, 148, 149, 152, 157, 161, 163, 165, 166, 168, 175, 176, 178, 180, 181, 185, 190, 192, 194, 195, 200, 202, 203, 206, 208, 213, 217, 218, 219, 220, 224, 225, 228, 231, 233, 234, 235, 236, 257, 260
Longfellow, Henry Wadsworth 44, 46, 50, 51, 242, 247
Looking-Glass Prairie 91-92
Louisville 87, 89, 93
Lowell (USA) 52-53
Lyons 107

M
Mackay, Charles 6
Maclise, Daniel 17, 51, 62, 121, 161, 162, 163, 202
Macready, Catherine 41
Macready, William Charles 41, 102, 137, 138, 182, 208, 247
Manin, Daniele 169
Mantua 133-134
Marseilles 107, 111, 120, 123, 124, 138, 139, 166, 172, 196, 197
Martin Chuzzlewit 60, 70, 73, 91, 104, 106
Master Humphrey's Clock 33
Mazzini, Giuseppe 168

Melbourne 30, 65, 253, 255, 256, 260
mesmerism 19, 127
Milan ix, 105, 134-135, 163, 171
Mirror of Parliament 2
Mississippi river 88, 90, 91, 93, 95
Mitton, Thomas 109, 125, 153, 157, 159, 162, 175, 181, 183, 198
Modena 128, 129, 161
Monthly Magazine 5
Montreal 98, 99-101
Morning Chronicle 23

N

Naples 105, 107, 123, 140, 156-157, 159, 160, 163, 171, 172, 173-174, 175, 176
Native Americans 81-82, 86, 87-89, 95
New Haven (USA) 58
New York City 40, 48, 49, 51, 58, 59, 60-67, 68, 71, 73, 91, 101, 132, 240, 241, 243-245, 246, 250
New Zealand 258, 260
Niagara 95, 97, 98-99, 159, 245, 247
Nice 107, 124, 138
Nicholas Nickleby 9, 10, 12, 14, 46
No Thoroughfare 136, 190, 192, 258

O

O'Farrell, Henry 37
Old Curiosity Shop 40, 46
Oliver Twist 18, 46, 155, 190, 260
Our Mutual Friend viii, 178, 236
Ouvry, Fred 38

P

Paris ix, 67, 76, 106, 107, 124, 137, 138, 140, 160, 169, 175, 176, 179, 184, 185, 186, 192, 193, 194, 196, 198-209, 212, 217, 219, 229-230, 233, 258

Park, John 55-56
Parma 128
Pasquin, Antoine Claude – see 'Valery'
Payne, Edward F. 48
The Perils of Certain English Prisoners 227
Perugini, Kate 51, 86, 106, 111, 174, 183, 184, 205, 218, 221, 222
Philadelphia 40, 49, 68-73
Phiz 9, 10, 12, 13, 193
Piacenza 127
Pickwick, Eleazer 5
Pickwick, Moses 5
The Pickwick Papers 5, 6, 7, 8, 21, 23-24, 46
Pisa 144, 173
Pittsburgh 82, 84, 85
Plymouth 17
Poe, Edgar Allan 70
police 30, 36, 37, 38, 63-64, 79, 86, 174, 209, 235, 243, 259
Pompeii 157-159, 167, 173
Portland (Maine, USA) 245, 247, 248-249
poverty 34, 63-64, 66, 72, 77, 90, 100, 128, 134, 144, 157, 159, 163, 170, 172, 176, 184, 208, 216, 219, 224, 228, 254, 257
Prince Albert 16, 18, 37, 133, 218
Prince Alfred, 37
prisons & prisoners viii-ix, 1, 29, 37, 61, 64-65, 71-72, 73, 80, 81, 107, 131, 155, 161, 169, 189, 200, 212, 227
public readings 33, 34-35, 36, 37-39
Punch 19
Putnam, George Washington 44-45, 49-50, 55, 61, 69-70, 75, 77, 78, 83, 84, 91, 92, 93, 96, 102

Index

Q
Quebec City 99
Queen Victoria 16, 18, 37, 46, 47, 63, 133, 225

R
racism 37, 52, 61, 64, 72, 73-74, 75, 77, 78-80, 81-82, 86, 88, 92, 95, 102
railways 4, 8, 17, 19, 35, 37, 52, 53, 56, 58, 68-69, 75, 79, 80, 84, 95-96, 97, 102, 144, 176, 179, 180, 189, 194, 195-196, 202, 203, 204, 208, 210, 213, 224, 225, 229, 231, 232-233, 234–238, 240, 241, 245, 246, 248-249
Richmond (Virginia, USA) 77, 78-79, 80
Richmond (Surrey, UK) 184-185
Roche, Louis 107, 108-111
Rome ix, 104, 105, 140, 142, 145, 147-164, 167, 168, 173, 174, 175, 176, 230
Royal Charter (shipwreck) 30-31

S
Sand, George 208
Sandusky 93, 95, 96
Scheffer, Ary 208
Scheffer, Henri (Hendrik) 208
Scotland 23-29, 57, 113
Scott, Sir Walter 28, 57, 87
Scroggie, Ebenezer Lennox 24-25
Scrooge, Ebenezer 24-25
seasickness 32, 34, 42-43, 51, 98, 138, 173, 193, 231
servants 7, 10, 22, 40, 42, 61, 80, 84-85, 94, 99, 102, 103, 104, 106, 107, 108, 109, 110, 115, 117-118, 126, 143, 150, 161-162, 171, 174, 179, 191, 196, 209, 242, 243

Seymour, Robert 6-7
Shakespeare 1, 131, 132-133, 134, 192, 229
Shaw, William 11-12, 13
Shelley, Mary 141, 164
Shelley, Percy Bysshe 141, 161
Sicily 105, 140, 159, 175
The Signalman 237-238
Siena 145
Simplon Pass 135-136, 169, 170, 190
Sketches by Boz 5-6, 15, 40
slavery 61, 73-74, 75, 77, 78-80, 92
Smith, Adam 24
Smith, Albert 200
Smith, Arthur 33, 34, 35
Southwood Smith, Dr Thomas 16, 169
Sparks, Jared 46
St Louis 91-93
stagecoach – see 'travelling by coach'
Stanfield, Clarkson 17, 118, 125, 149
Stone, Frank 212-213
Storey, Gladys 221, 222
supernatural 23
Swinburne, Algernon Charles 18
Switzerland ix, 62, 103, 104, 107, 110, 137, 163, 166, 167, 170, 177-192, 207, 211, 230
Sydney 37, 254, 256

T
A Tale of Two Cities 4, 72, 106-107
Tennyson, Alfred, Lord 18, 182, 183
Ternan, Ellen 221, 222, 223, 227, 236, 241, 247
Thackeray, Anny 205, 208, 218
Thackeray, Minny 205, 208, 218
Thackeray, William Makepeace 19, 205, 218

269

theatre 1, 24, 28, 33, 46, 66, 98, 99, 100, 123, 126, 143, 152, 196, 200, 202, 204, 205, 207, 214, 218, 220, 227
Tiffany & Co 66
To Be Read At Dusk 127, 177, 188
Toronto 99
trains – see 'railways'
travelling by boat 19, 27, 32, 36, 37, 40, 41-44, 56-57, 58-59, 60, 68, 73, 79, 82-84, 85-86, 87-88, 89-90, 91, 93, 96-97, 99, 101, 106, 107, 123, 130, 138-139, 140, 170, 172-173, 179, 193, 194, 195, 202, 203, 212, 219, 220, 232, 240
travelling by coach 2, 4, 5, 7, 8, 10, 12, 13, 17, 18, 27, 28, 35, 36, 44, 62, 63, 80-81, 91-92, 93-95, 96-97, 98, 99, 106, 108, 110, 111, 113-114, 123, 129, 134, 135-137, 138, 145, 146, 147, 150-152, 156, 158, 159, 167, 170, 174, 175, 185, 189, 199, 206, 225, 229, 230, 231-232
travel writing ix, x, 3, 14, 30, 32, 41, 52, 56, 58-59, 61, 64, 65, 66, 68, 71, 78, 81-82, 85, 87-89, 93-94, 96-97, 98-99, 101, 106, 108-109, 110, 112, 113, 114, 116, 117, 118, 127, 130, 133, 134, 136, 140, 141, 144, 145, 147, 148, 149, 154, 158, 159, 161, 164, 166, 169, 195-196, 223-226, 228-233, 238, 251-252
Trollope, Anthony 256
Turin 105, 123, 171, 176
Tyler, John 76

U

The Uncommercial Traveller ix, 3, 30, 32, 110, 169, 195, 228-233, 251-252
United Vagabonds 101
USA ix, 33, 40-97, 98, 101, 157, 166, 235, 238, 239-252

V

Valence 107
Valery 105, 119, 123
Venice 104, 130-132, 148, 167, 174, 175
Verona 131-134
Vesuvius (Mount) 145, 156, 157-158, 159, 167, 176
Virginia 77-79, 80

W

Wales 30-32, 36, 37
Walpole, Horace 111, 112
Warren's Blacking factory viii, 1
Washington, DC 67, 74, 75-77, 79, 80, 88
Washington, George 51, 63
Wetmore Story, William 49
White, Reverend James 18
Wiggin, Kate Douglas 248-250
Wills, W.H. 202, 205, 211, 257
Winckworth, Simon 169
Winter, Maria (née Beadnell) 207
Wollstonecraft, Mary 164
Worcester (USA) 55-56

Y

Yorkshire 9-14, 15, 105
Yorkshire schools 9, 10-12, 13